BANANA SUNDAY

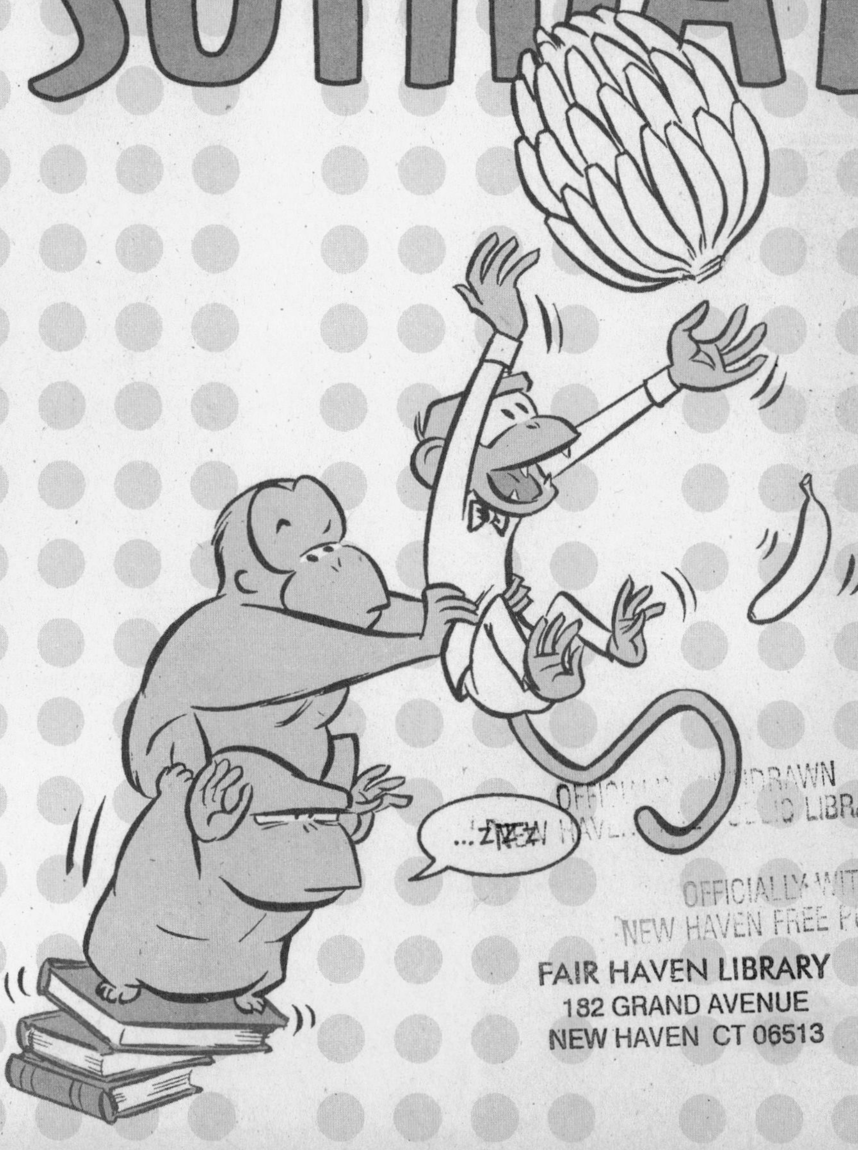

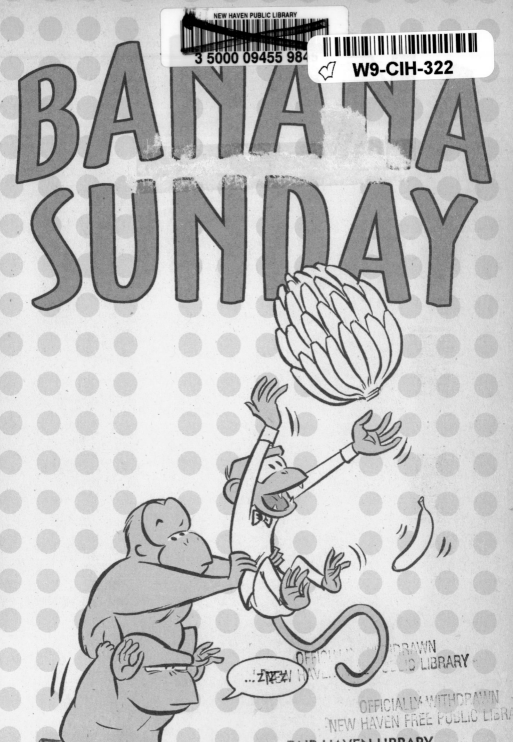

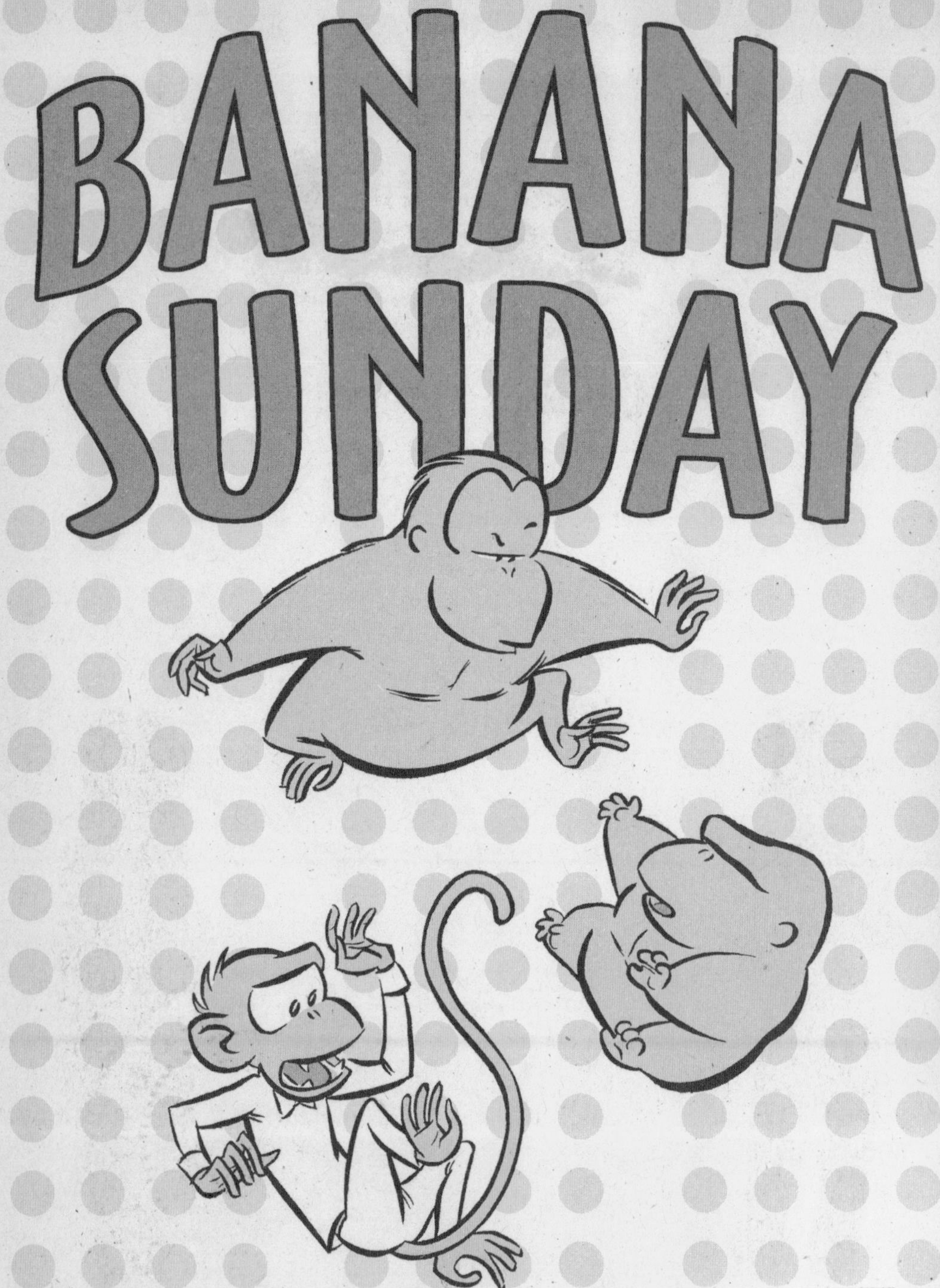
BANANA
SUNDAY

written by
Root Nibot

illustrated by
Colleen Coover

book design by
Keith Wood

edited by
James Lucas Jones

ōni
PRESS

Published by Oni Press, Inc.

Joe Nozemack, publisher

James Lucas Jones, editor in chief

Randal C. Jarrell, managing editor

Maryanne Snell, marketing & sales director

Douglas E. Sherwood, editorial intern

This volume collects

Banana Sunday

issues 1-4.

ONI PRESS, INC.
1305 SE Martin Luther King Jr. Blvd.
Suite A
Portland, OR 97214
USA

www.onipress.com

First edition: March 2006
ISBN 1-932664-37-8

1 3 5 7 9 10 8 6 4 2

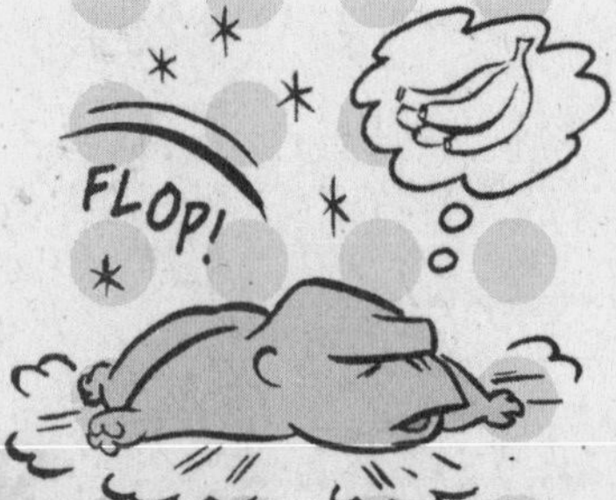
FLOP!

PRINTED IN CANADA.

BANANA SUNDAY

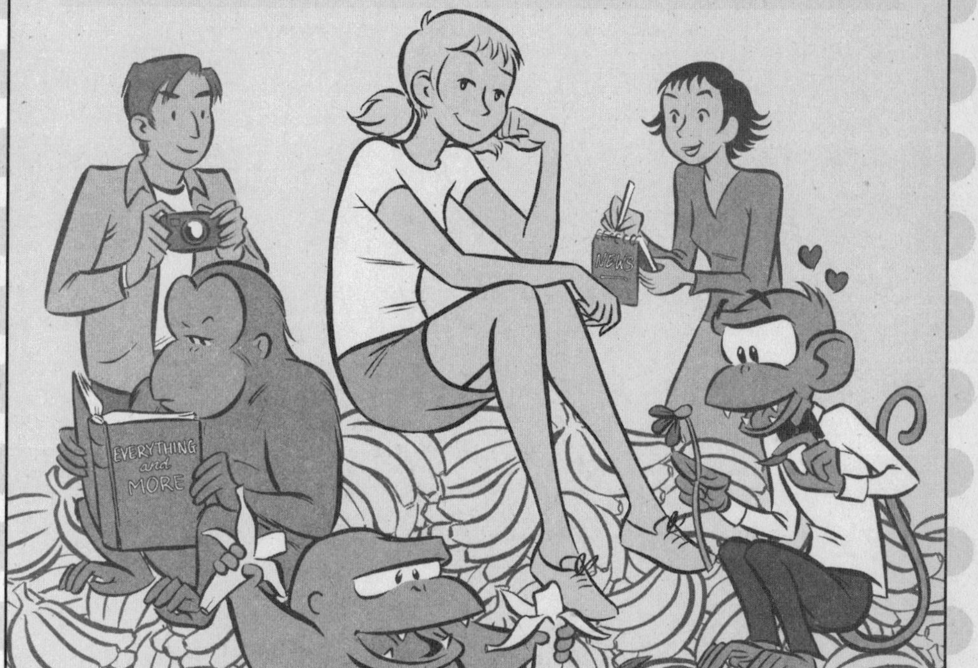

NEWS
EVERYTHING and MORE

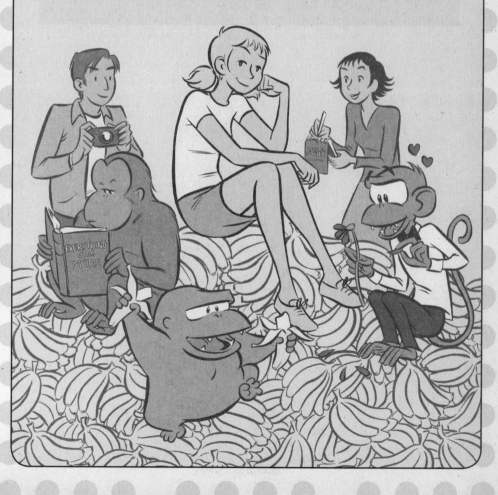

one

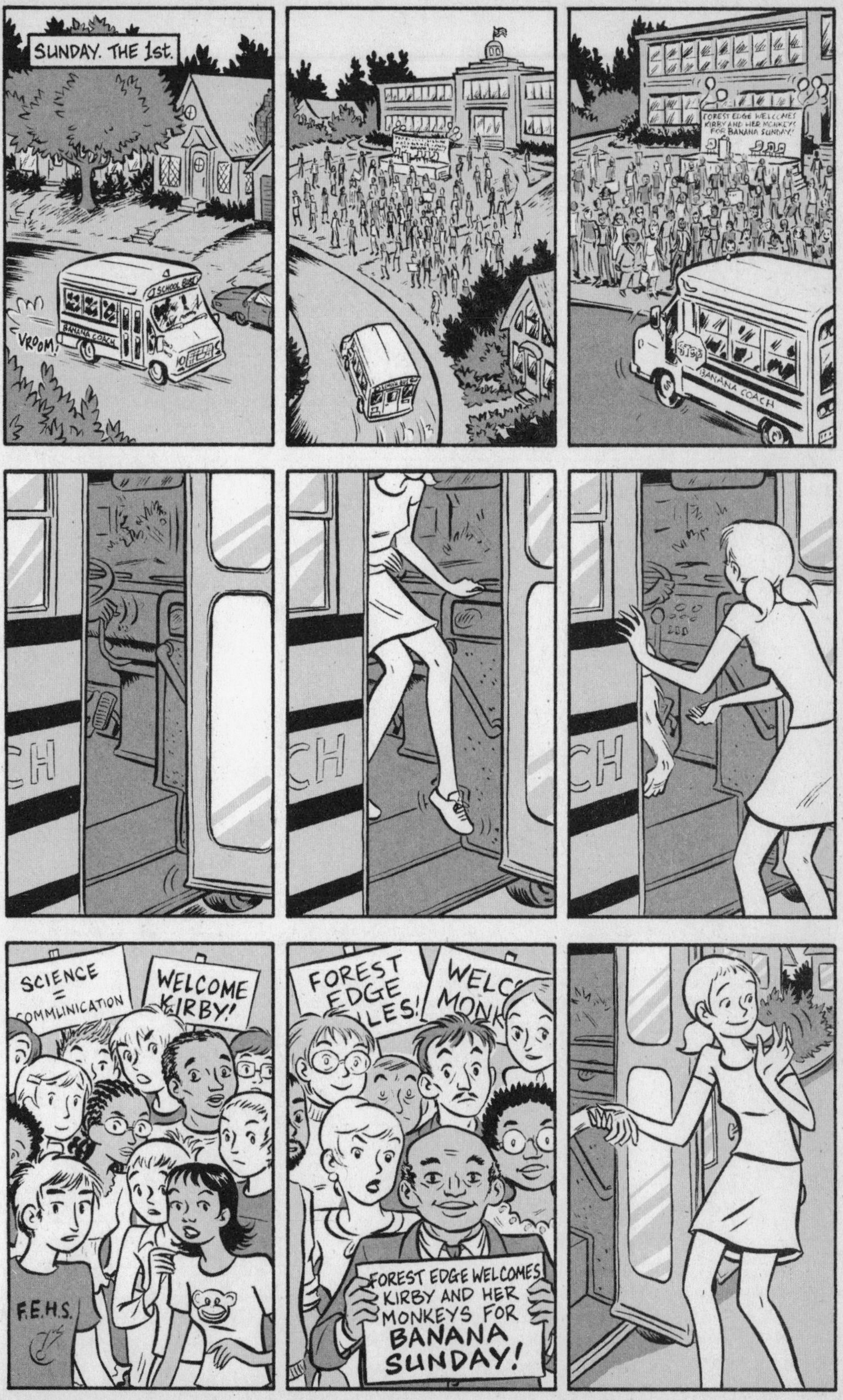
SUNDAY. THE 1st.
SCHOOL BUS
BANANA COACH
VROOM!
FOREST EDGE WELCOMES KIRBY AND HER MONKEYS FOR BANANA SUNDAY!
STOP
BANANA COACH
SCIENCE = COMMUNICATION
WELCOME KIRBY!
F.E.H.S.
FOREST EDGE
FOREST EDGE WELCOMES KIRBY AND HER MONKEYS FOR BANANA SUNDAY!

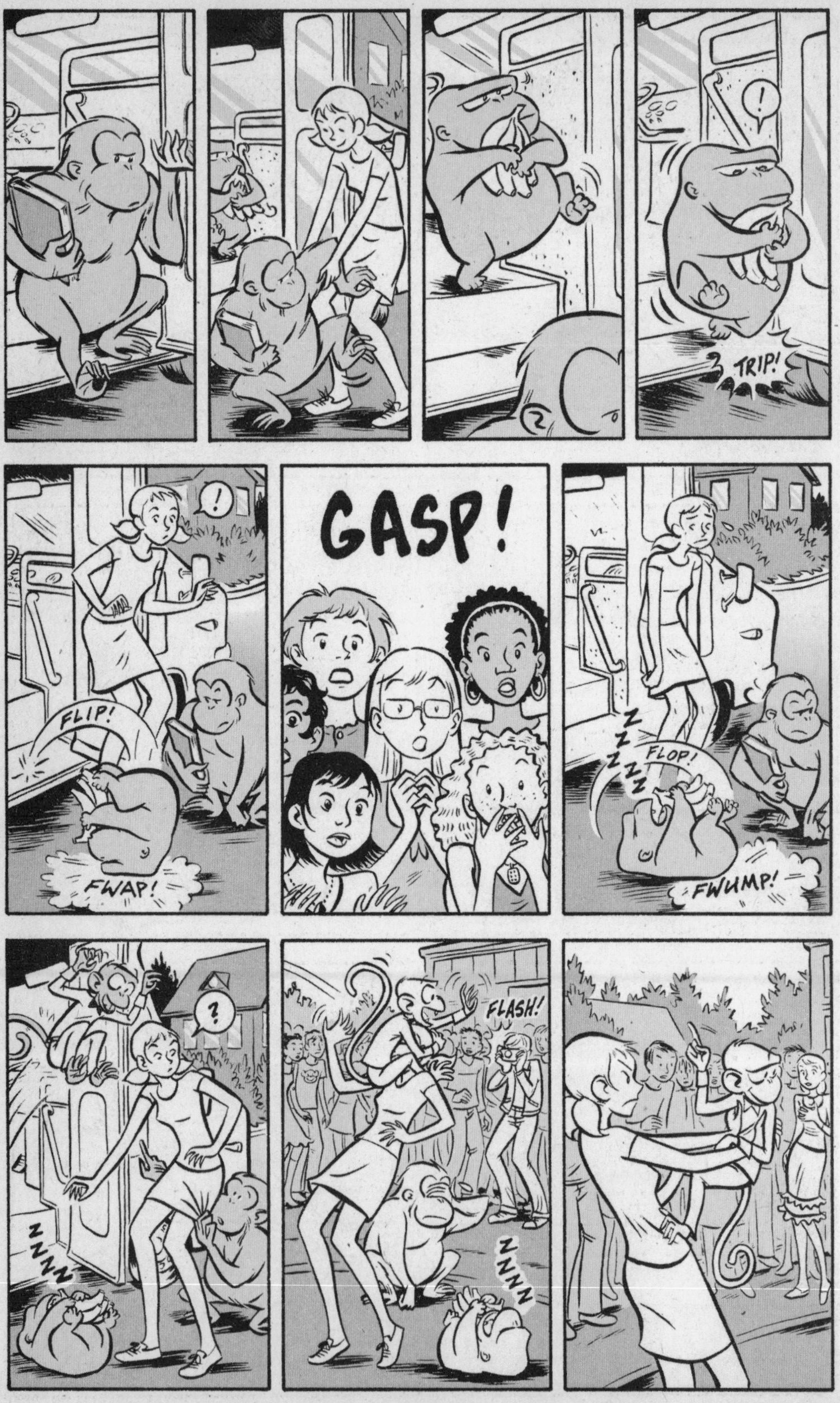
!
TRIP!
!
FLIP!
FWAP!
GASP!
FLOP!
FWUMP!
?
FLASH!

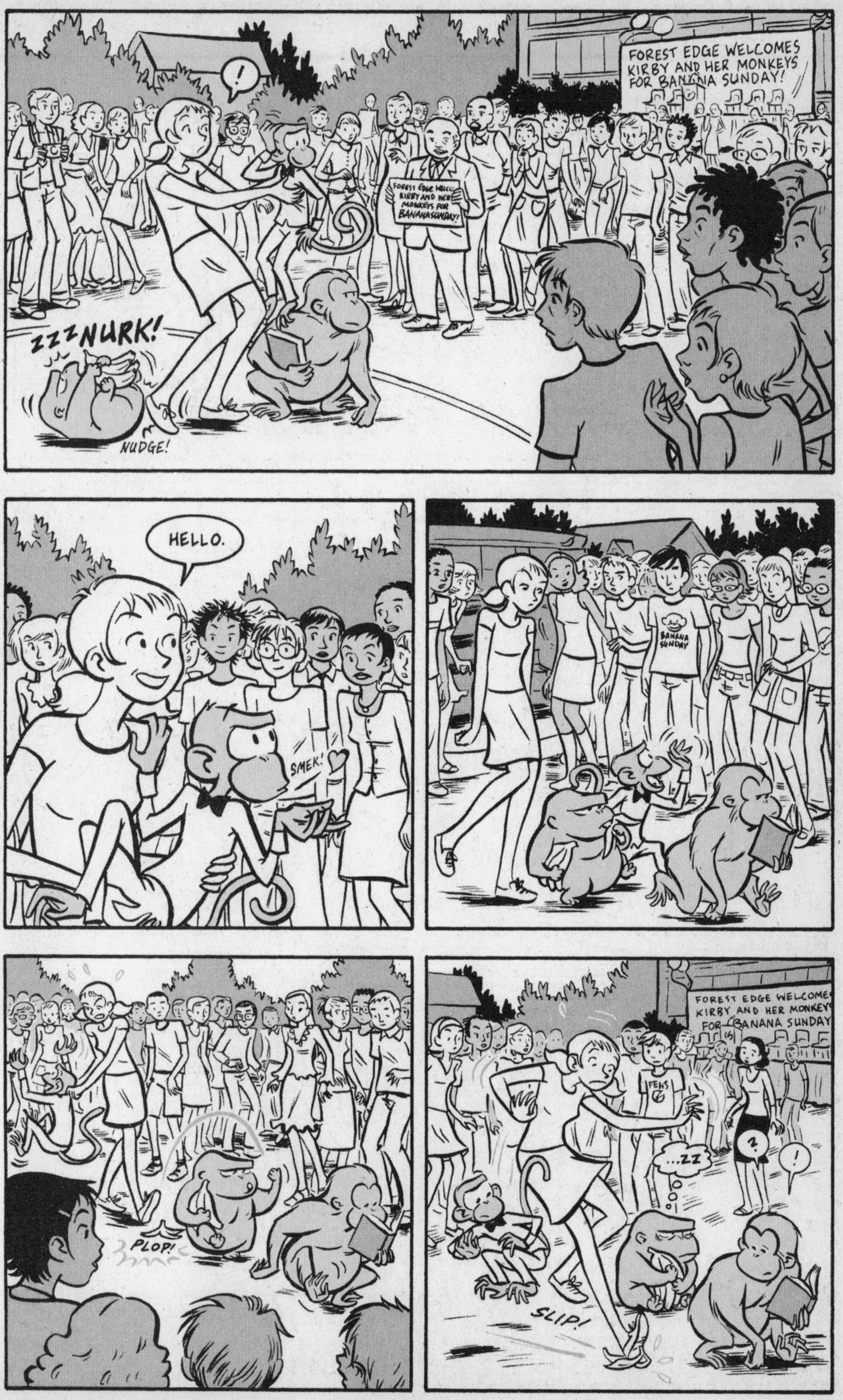

!
FOREST EDGE WELCOMES KIRBY AND HER MONKEYS FOR BANANA SUNDAY!
ZZZNURK!
NUDGE!
HELLO.
SMEK!
BANANA SUNDAY
PLOP!
FOREST EDGE WELCOME KIRBY AND HER MONKEY FOR BANANA SUNDAY
FENS
?
!
...ZZ
SLIP!

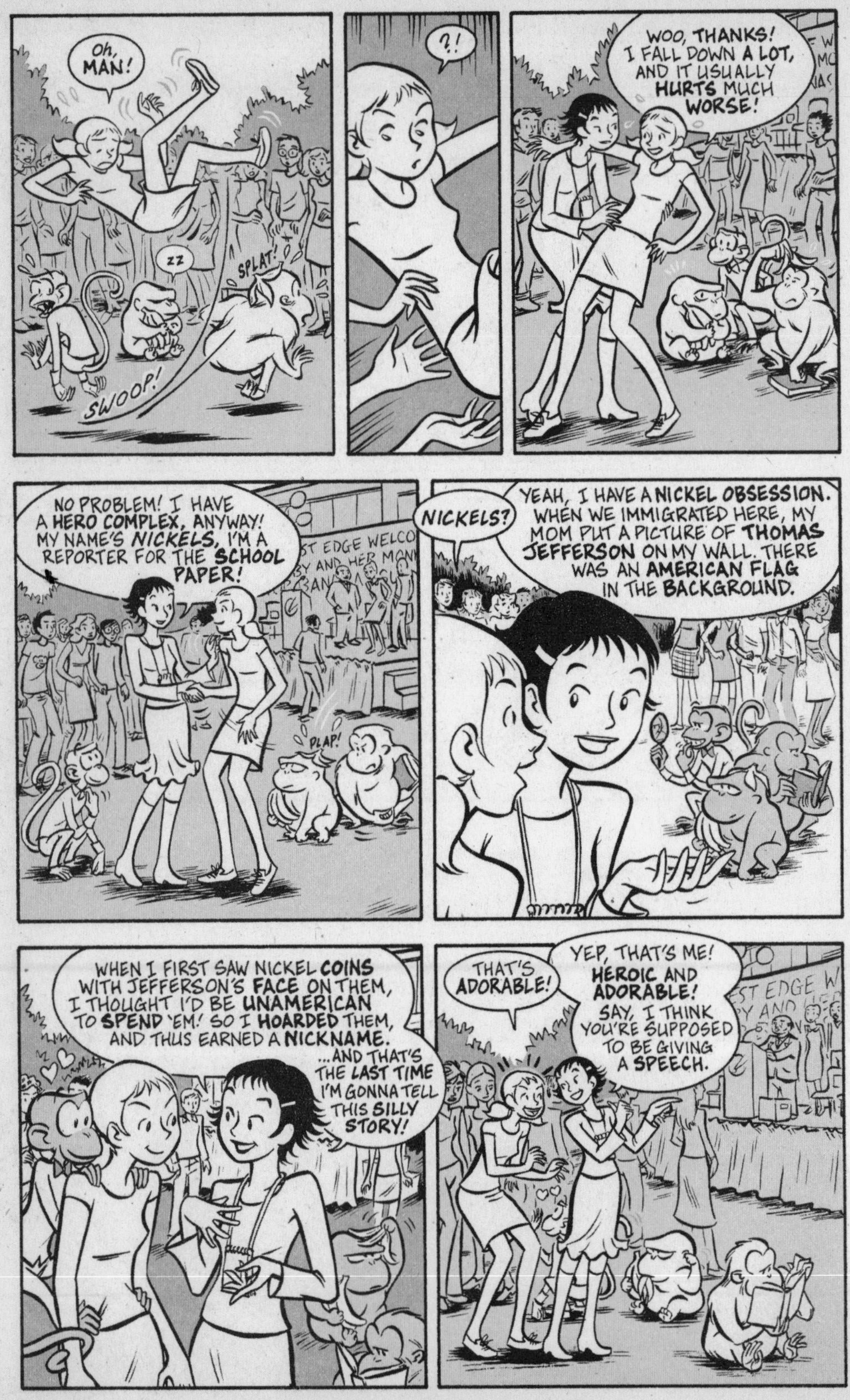
Oh, MAN!
ZZ
SPLAT!
SWOOP!
?!
WOO, THANKS! I FALL DOWN A LOT, AND IT USUALLY HURTS MUCH WORSE!
NO PROBLEM! I HAVE A HERO COMPLEX, ANYWAY! MY NAME'S NICKELS, I'M A REPORTER FOR THE SCHOOL PAPER!
PLAP!
NICKELS?
YEAH, I HAVE A NICKEL OBSESSION. WHEN WE IMMIGRATED HERE, MY MOM PUT A PICTURE OF THOMAS JEFFERSON ON MY WALL. THERE WAS AN AMERICAN FLAG IN THE BACKGROUND.
WHEN I FIRST SAW NICKEL COINS WITH JEFFERSON'S FACE ON THEM, I THOUGHT I'D BE UNAMERICAN TO SPEND 'EM! SO I HOARDED THEM, AND THUS EARNED A NICKNAME.
...AND THAT'S THE LAST TIME I'M GONNA TELL THIS SILLY STORY!
THAT'S ADORABLE!
YEP, THAT'S ME! HEROIC AND ADORABLE! SAY, I THINK YOU'RE SUPPOSED TO BE GIVING A SPEECH.

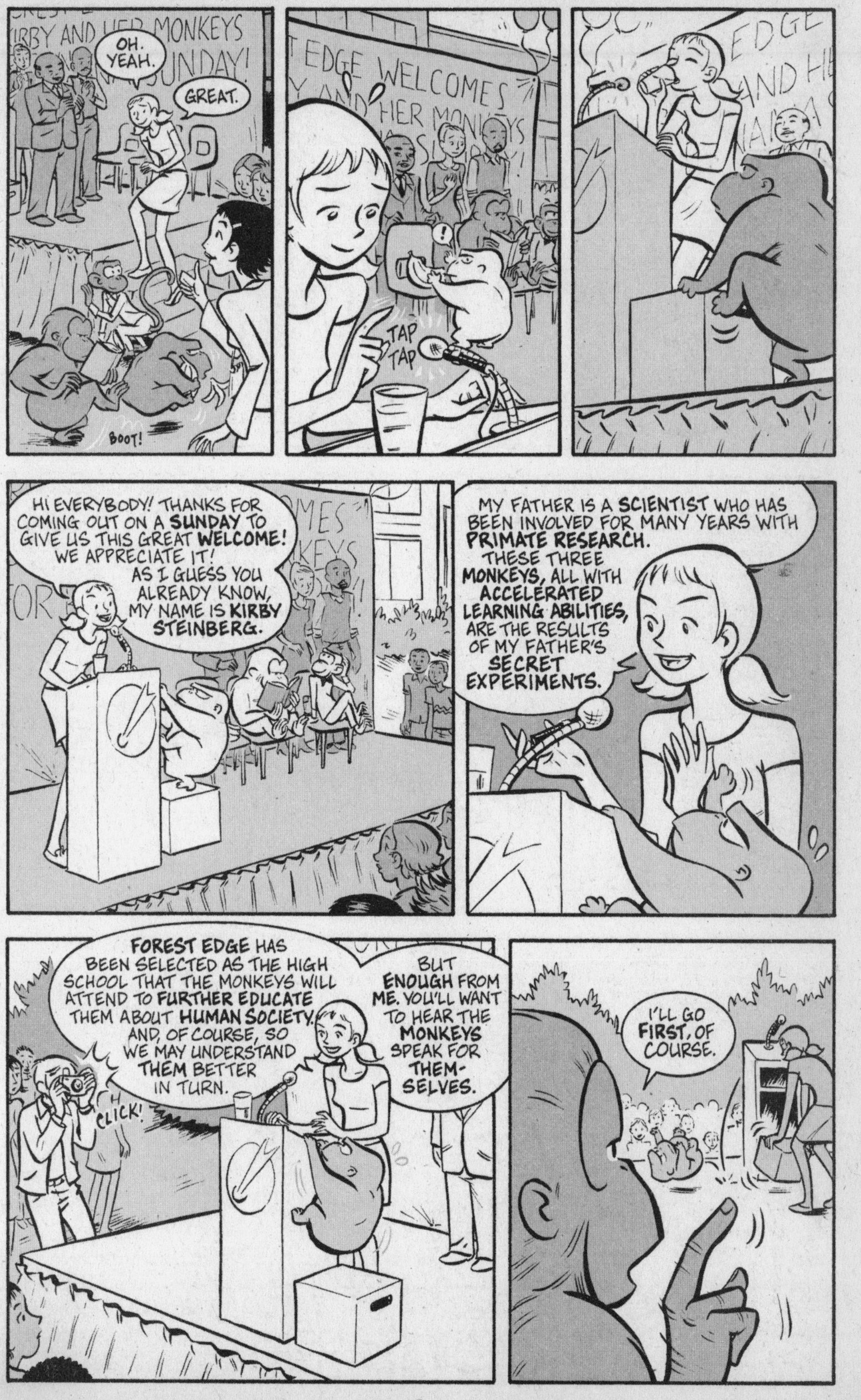
OH. YEAH.
GREAT.
BOOT!
TAP TAP
HI EVERYBODY! THANKS FOR COMING OUT ON A SUNDAY TO GIVE US THIS GREAT WELCOME! WE APPRECIATE IT!
AS I GUESS YOU ALREADY KNOW, MY NAME IS KIRBY STEINBERG.
MY FATHER IS A SCIENTIST WHO HAS BEEN INVOLVED FOR MANY YEARS WITH PRIMATE RESEARCH.
THESE THREE MONKEYS, ALL WITH ACCELERATED LEARNING ABILITIES, ARE THE RESULTS OF MY FATHER'S SECRET EXPERIMENTS.
FOREST EDGE HAS BEEN SELECTED AS THE HIGH SCHOOL THAT THE MONKEYS WILL ATTEND TO FURTHER EDUCATE THEM ABOUT HUMAN SOCIETY.
AND, OF COURSE, SO WE MAY UNDERSTAND THEM BETTER IN TURN.
BUT ENOUGH FROM ME. YOU'LL WANT TO HEAR THE MONKEYS SPEAK FOR THEMSELVES.
CLICK!
I'LL GO FIRST, OF COURSE.

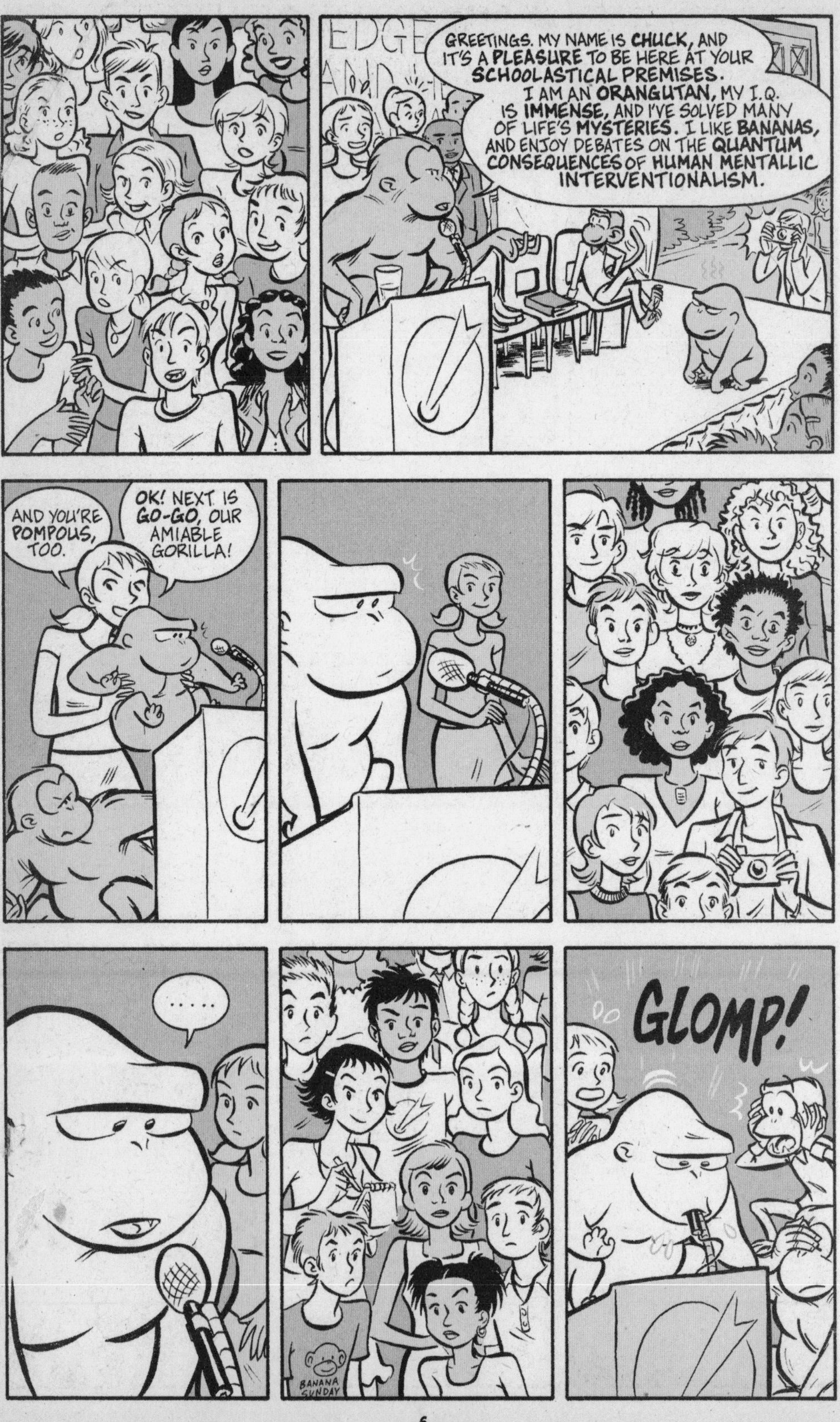
EDGE
GREETINGS. MY NAME IS CHUCK, AND IT'S A PLEASURE TO BE HERE AT YOUR SCHOOLASTICAL PREMISES.
I AM AN ORANGUTAN, MY I.Q. IS IMMENSE, AND I'VE SOLVED MANY OF LIFE'S MYSTERIES. I LIKE BANANAS, AND ENJOY DEBATES ON THE QUANTUM CONSEQUENCES OF HUMAN MENTALLIC INTERVENTIONALISM.
AND YOU'RE POMPOUS, TOO.
OK! NEXT IS GO-GO, OUR AMIABLE GORILLA!
. . . . .
BANANA SUNDAY
GLOMP!

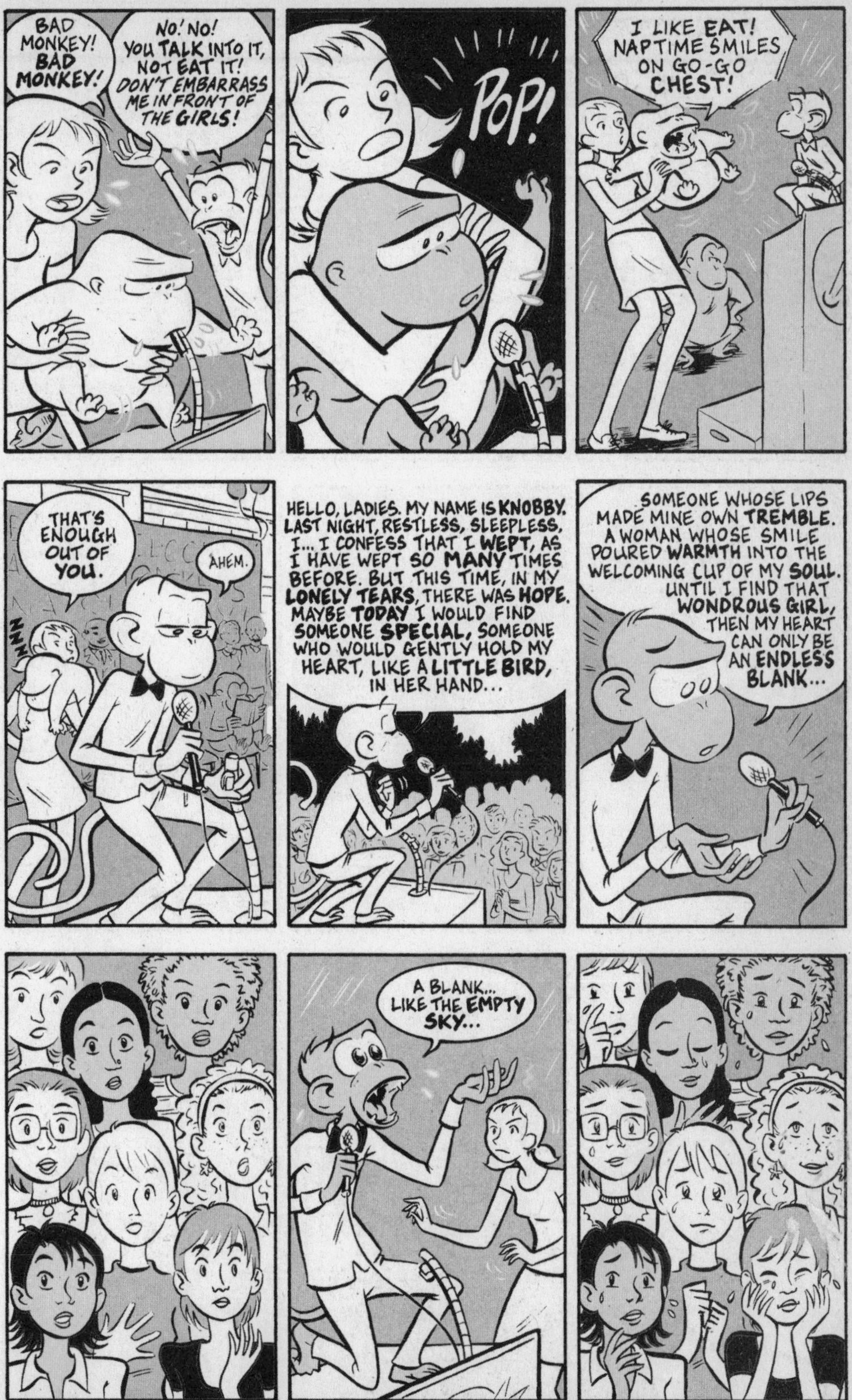

BAD MONKEY! BAD MONKEY!
NO! NO! YOU TALK INTO IT, NOT EAT IT! DON'T EMBARRASS ME IN FRONT OF THE GIRLS!
POP!
I LIKE EAT! NAPTIME SMILES ON GO-GO CHEST!
THAT'S ENOUGH OUT OF YOU.
AHEM.
HELLO, LADIES. MY NAME IS KNOBBY. LAST NIGHT, RESTLESS, SLEEPLESS, I... I CONFESS THAT I WEPT, AS I HAVE WEPT SO MANY TIMES BEFORE. BUT THIS TIME, IN MY LONELY TEARS, THERE WAS HOPE. MAYBE TODAY I WOULD FIND SOMEONE SPECIAL, SOMEONE WHO WOULD GENTLY HOLD MY HEART, LIKE A LITTLE BIRD, IN HER HAND...
SOMEONE WHOSE LIPS MADE MINE OWN TREMBLE. A WOMAN WHOSE SMILE POURED WARMTH INTO THE WELCOMING CUP OF MY SOUL. UNTIL I FIND THAT WONDROUS GIRL, THEN MY HEART CAN ONLY BE AN ENDLESS BLANK...
A BLANK... LIKE THE EMPTY SKY...

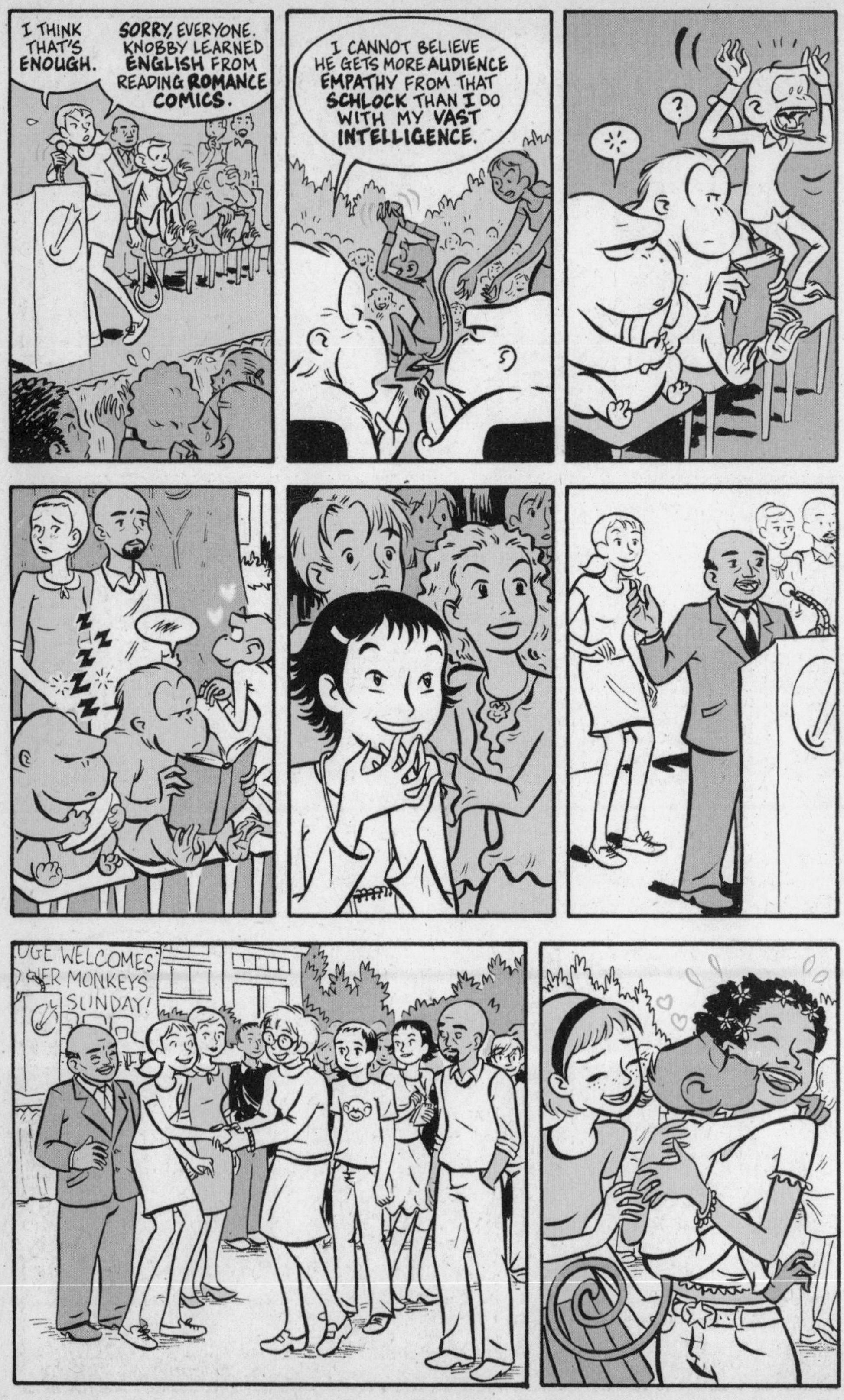
I THINK THAT'S ENOUGH.
SORRY, EVERYONE. KNOBBY LEARNED ENGLISH FROM READING ROMANCE COMICS.
I CANNOT BELIEVE HE GETS MORE AUDIENCE EMPATHY FROM THAT SCHLOCK THAN I DO WITH MY VAST INTELLIGENCE.
?
ZZZZZ
WELCOMES
MONKEYS
SUNDAY!

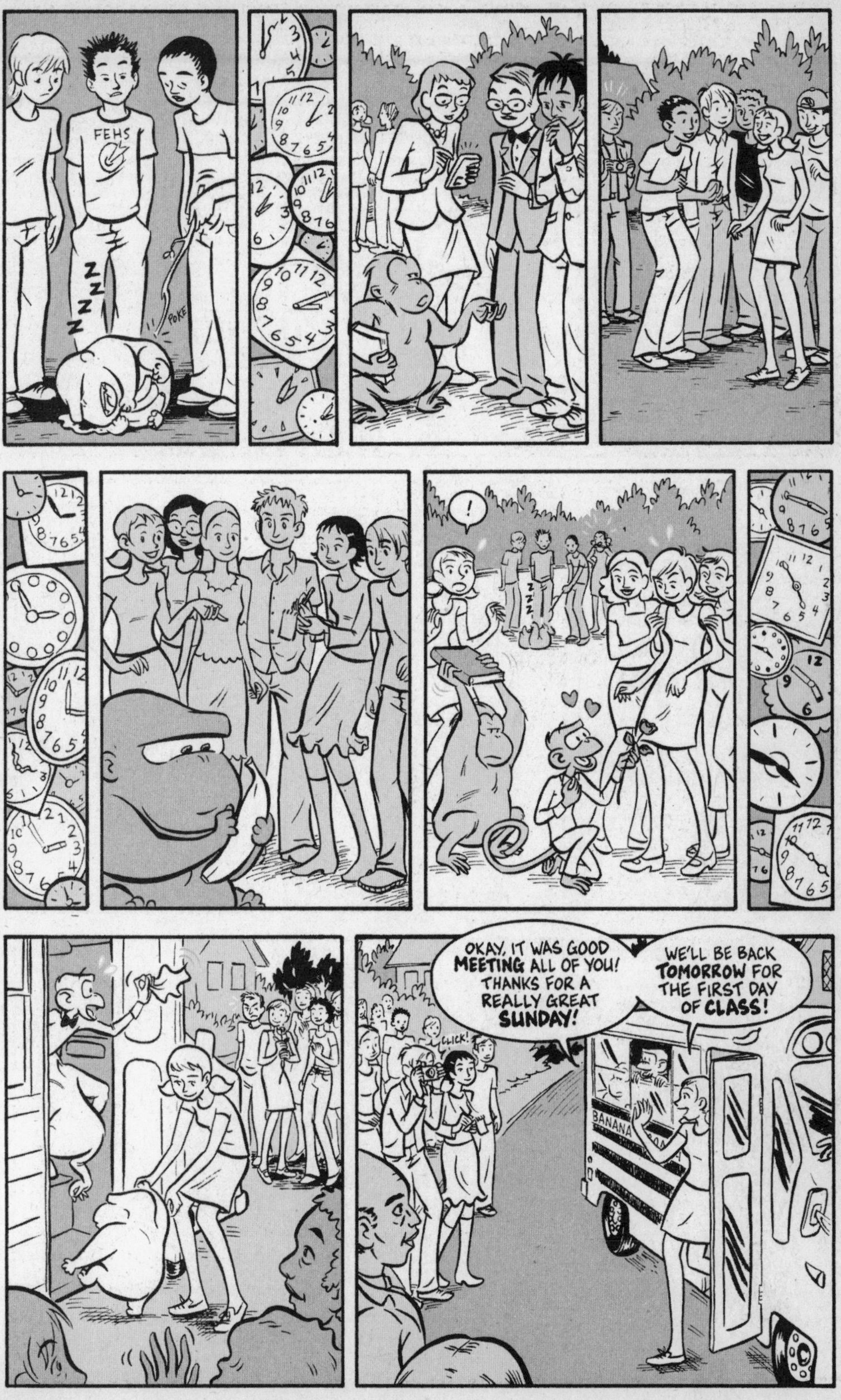
FEHS
ZZZZ
POKE
!
ZZZ
CLICK!
OKAY, IT WAS GOOD MEETING ALL OF YOU! THANKS FOR A REALLY GREAT SUNDAY!
WE'LL BE BACK TOMORROW FOR THE FIRST DAY OF CLASS!
BANANA

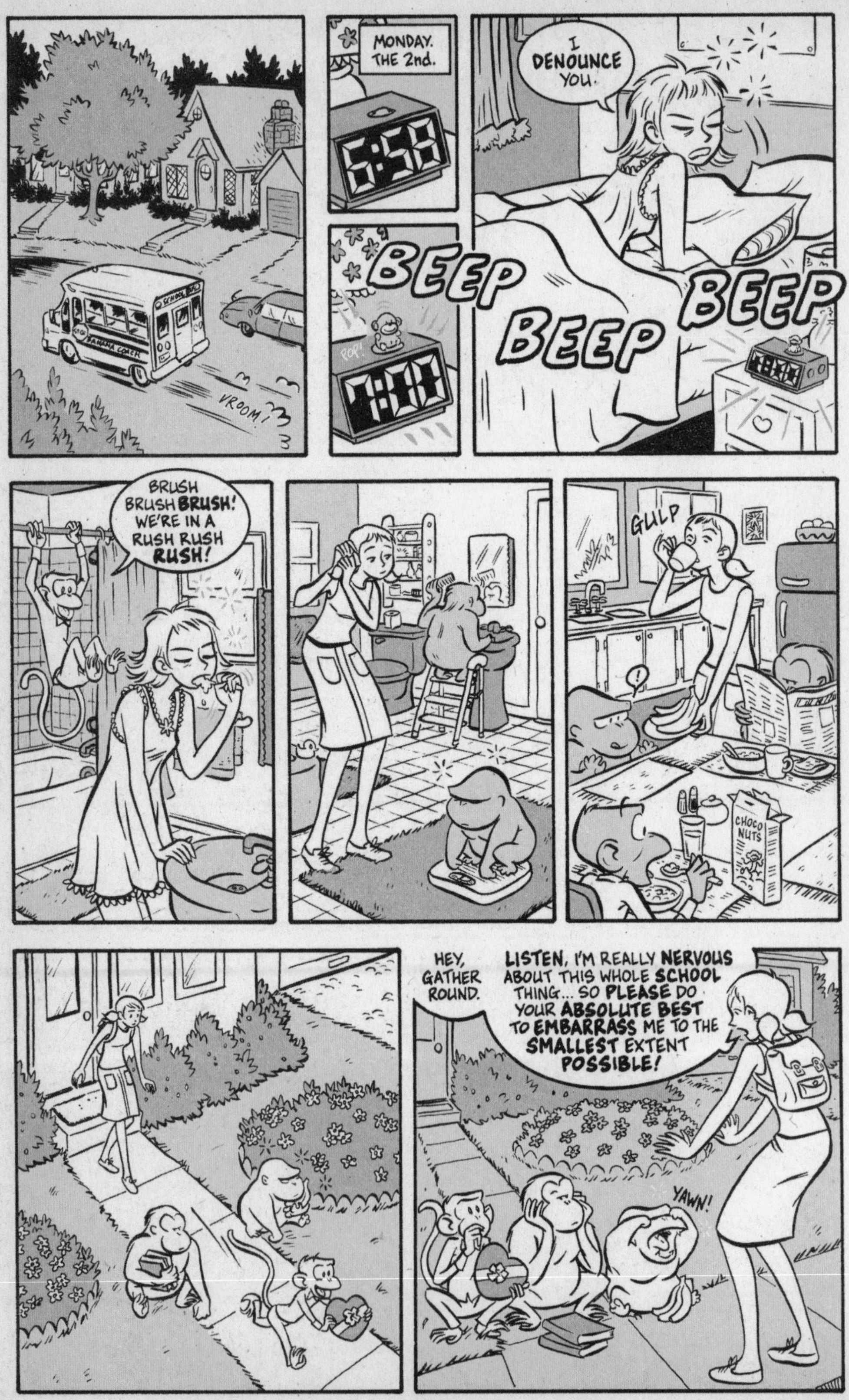

SCHOOL BUS
BANANA COACH
VROOM!
MONDAY. THE 2nd.
5:59
I DENOUNCE YOU.
BEEP
BEEP
BEEP
POP!
7:00
BRUSH BRUSH BRUSH! WE'RE IN A RUSH RUSH RUSH!
GULP
!
CHOCO NUTS
HEY, GATHER ROUND.
LISTEN, I'M REALLY NERVOUS ABOUT THIS WHOLE SCHOOL THING... SO PLEASE DO YOUR ABSOLUTE BEST TO EMBARRASS ME TO THE SMALLEST EXTENT POSSIBLE!
YAWN!

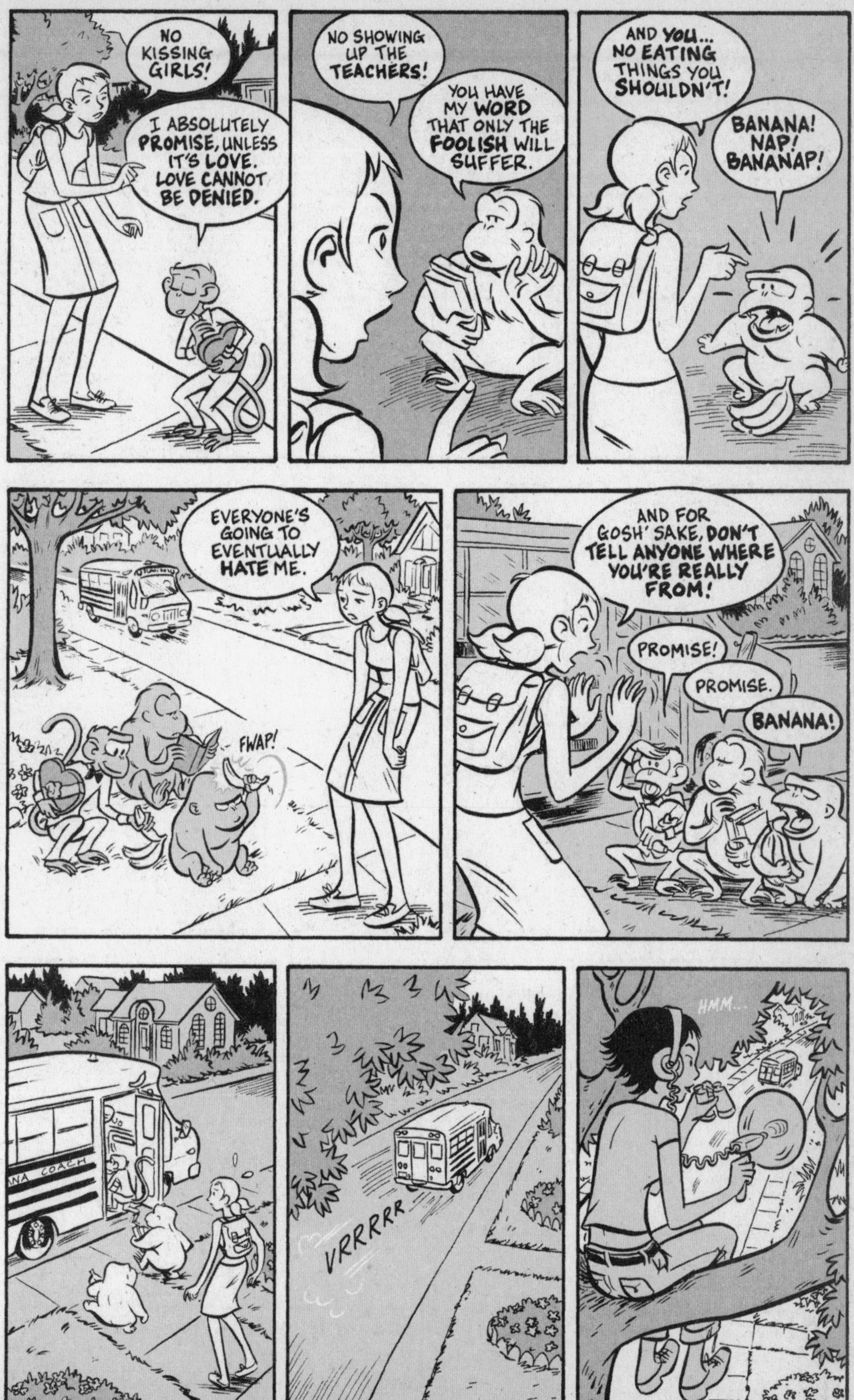
NO KISSING GIRLS!
I ABSOLUTELY PROMISE, UNLESS IT'S LOVE. LOVE CANNOT BE DENIED.
NO SHOWING UP THE TEACHERS!
YOU HAVE MY WORD THAT ONLY THE FOOLISH WILL SUFFER.
AND YOU... NO EATING THINGS YOU SHOULDN'T!
BANANA! NAP! BANANAP!
EVERYONE'S GOING TO EVENTUALLY HATE ME.
FWAP!
AND FOR GOSH' SAKE, DON'T TELL ANYONE WHERE YOU'RE REALLY FROM!
PROMISE!
PROMISE.
BANANA!
VRRRRR
HMM...

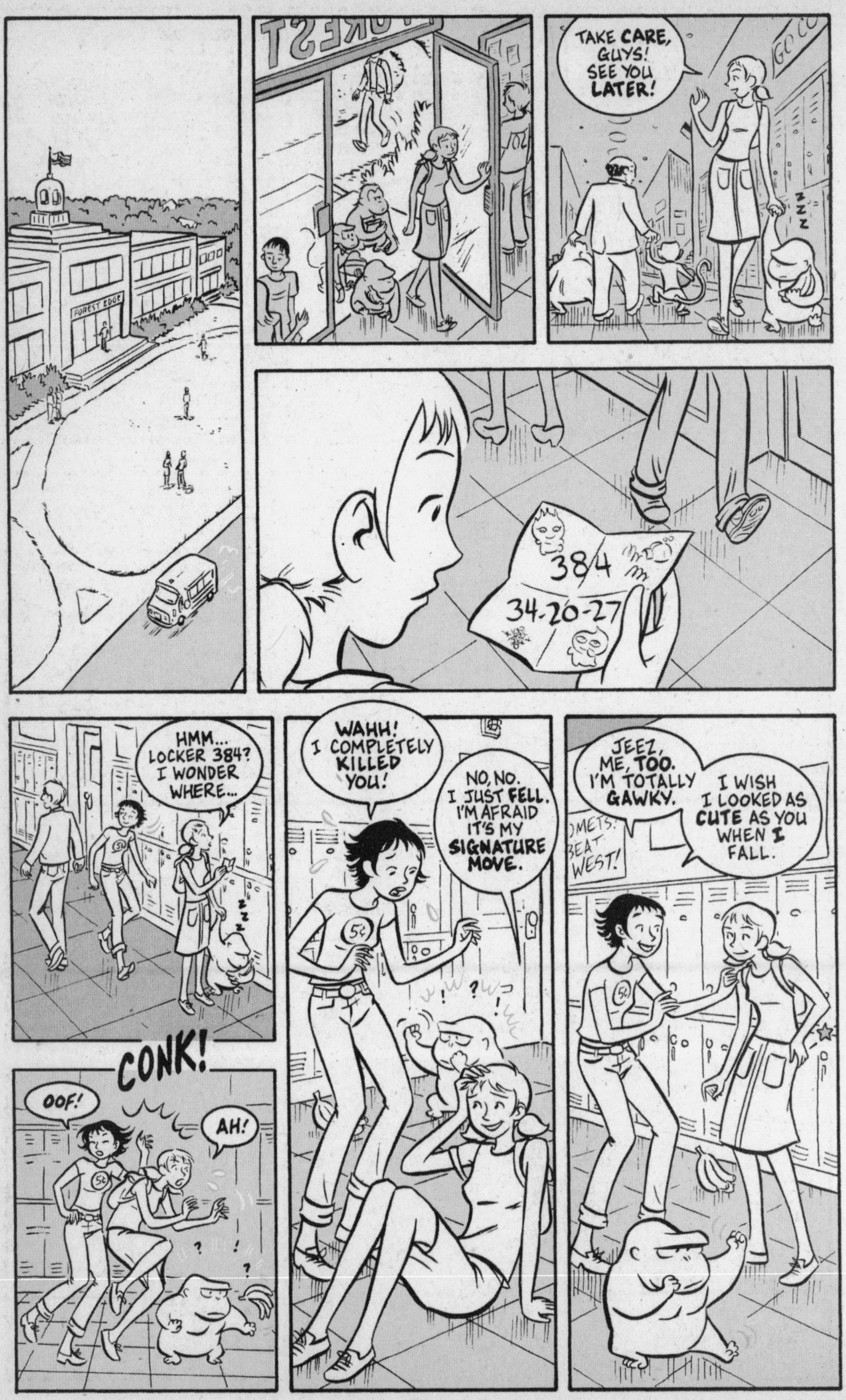
FOREST EDGE
TAKE CARE, GUYS! SEE YOU LATER!
384
34-20-27
HMM... LOCKER 384? I WONDER WHERE...
CONK!
OOF!
AH!
WAHH! I COMPLETELY KILLED YOU!
NO, NO. I JUST FELL. I'M AFRAID IT'S MY SIGNATURE MOVE.
JEEZ, ME, TOO. I'M TOTALLY GAWKY.
I WISH I LOOKED AS CUTE AS YOU WHEN I FALL.

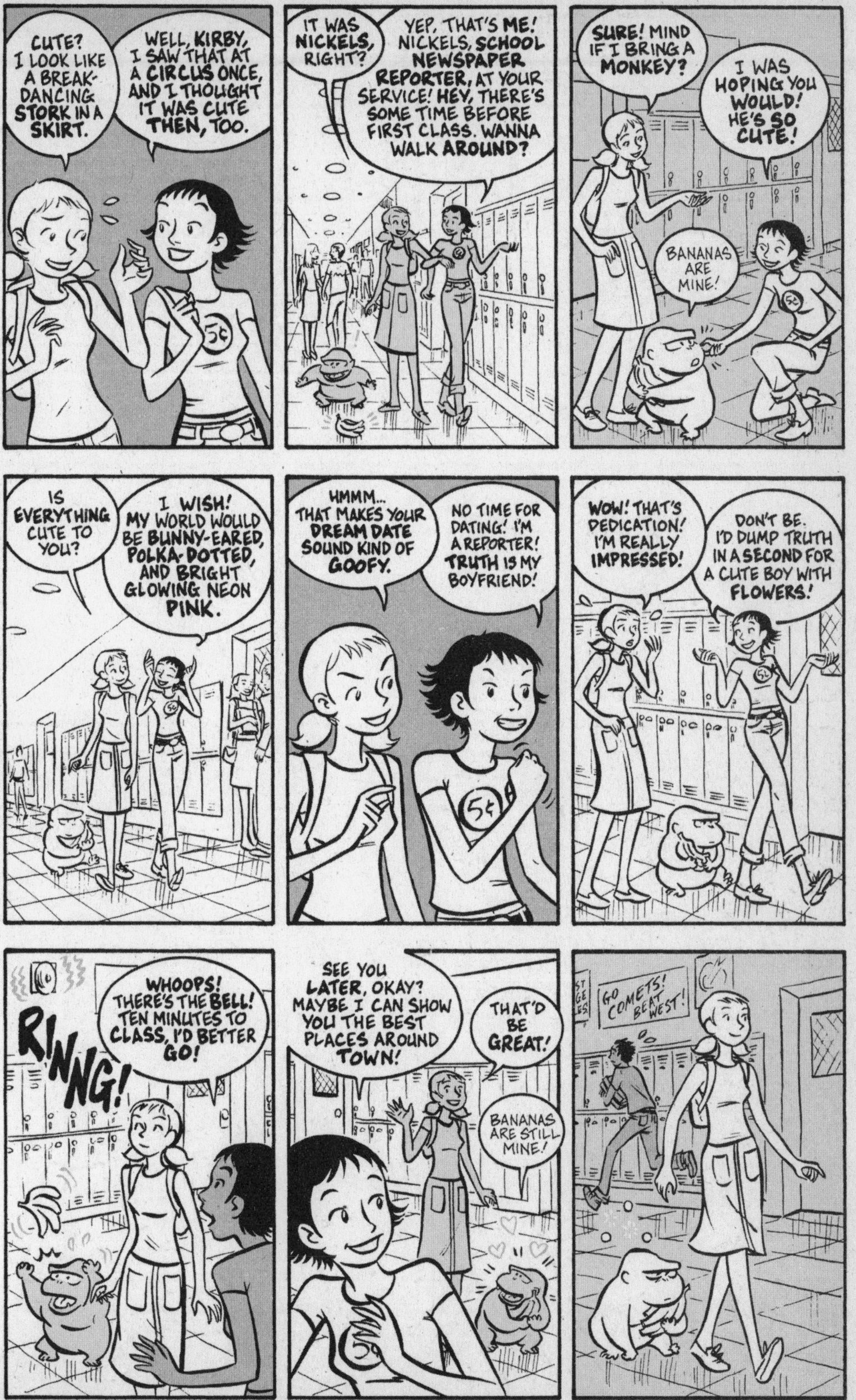
CUTE? I LOOK LIKE A BREAK-DANCING STORK IN A SKIRT.
WELL, KIRBY, I SAW THAT AT A CIRCUS ONCE, AND I THOUGHT IT WAS CUTE THEN, TOO.
IT WAS NICKELS, RIGHT?
YEP, THAT'S ME! NICKELS, SCHOOL NEWSPAPER REPORTER, AT YOUR SERVICE! HEY, THERE'S SOME TIME BEFORE FIRST CLASS. WANNA WALK AROUND?
SURE! MIND IF I BRING A MONKEY?
I WAS HOPING YOU WOULD! HE'S SO CUTE!
BANANAS ARE MINE!
IS EVERYTHING CUTE TO YOU?
I WISH! MY WORLD WOULD BE BUNNY-EARED, POLKA-DOTTED, AND BRIGHT GLOWING NEON PINK.
HMMM... THAT MAKES YOUR DREAM DATE SOUND KIND OF GOOFY.
NO TIME FOR DATING! I'M A REPORTER! TRUTH IS MY BOYFRIEND!
WOW! THAT'S DEDICATION! I'M REALLY IMPRESSED!
DON'T BE. I'D DUMP TRUTH IN A SECOND FOR A CUTE BOY WITH FLOWERS!
RINNG!
WHOOPS! THERE'S THE BELL! TEN MINUTES TO CLASS, I'D BETTER GO!
SEE YOU LATER, OKAY? MAYBE I CAN SHOW YOU THE BEST PLACES AROUND TOWN!
THAT'D BE GREAT!
BANANAS ARE STILL MINE!
GO COMETS! BEAT WEST!

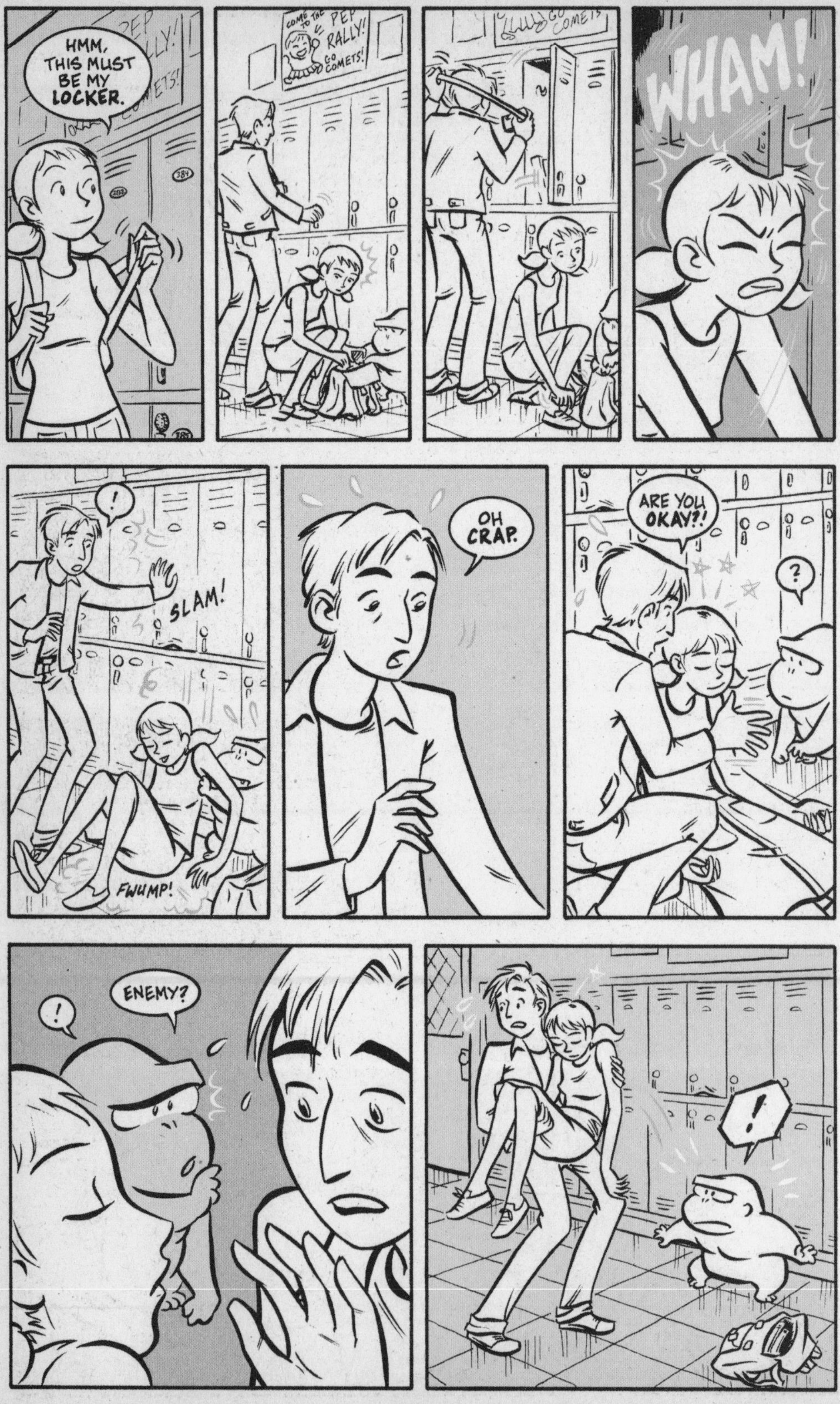

HMM, THIS MUST BE MY LOCKER.
COME TO THE PEP RALLY! GO COMETS!
WHAM!
!
SLAM!
FWUMP!
OH CRAP.
ARE YOU OKAY?!
?
!
ENEMY?
!

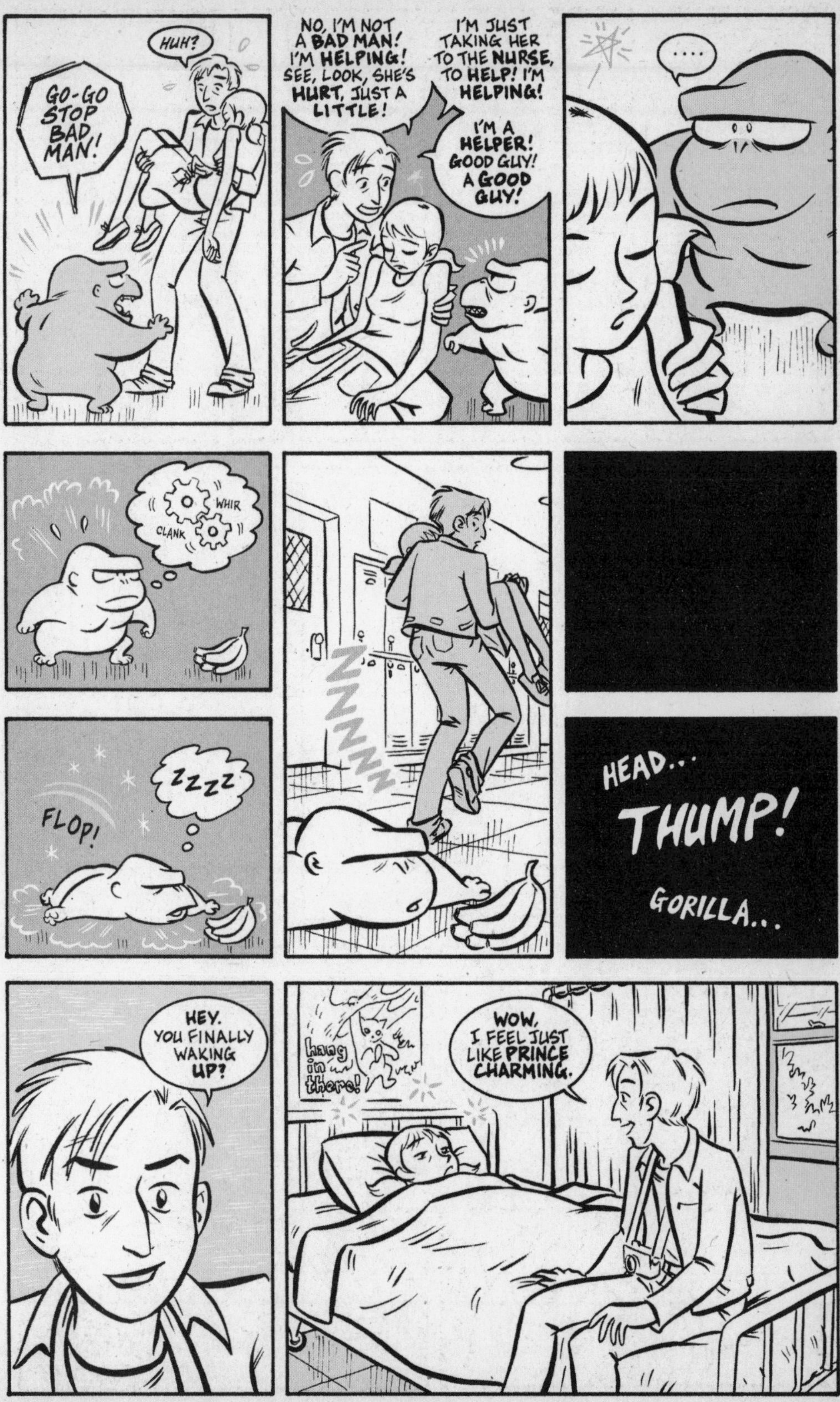
HUH?
GO-GO STOP BAD MAN!
NO, I'M NOT A BAD MAN! I'M HELPING! SEE, LOOK, SHE'S HURT, JUST A LITTLE!
I'M JUST TAKING HER TO THE NURSE, TO HELP! I'M HELPING!
I'M A HELPER! GOOD GUY! A GOOD GUY!
....
WHIR
CLANK
ZZZZ
FLOP!
ZZZZZ
HEAD...
THUMP!
GORILLA...
HEY. YOU FINALLY WAKING UP?
hang in there!
WOW, I FEEL JUST LIKE PRINCE CHARMING.

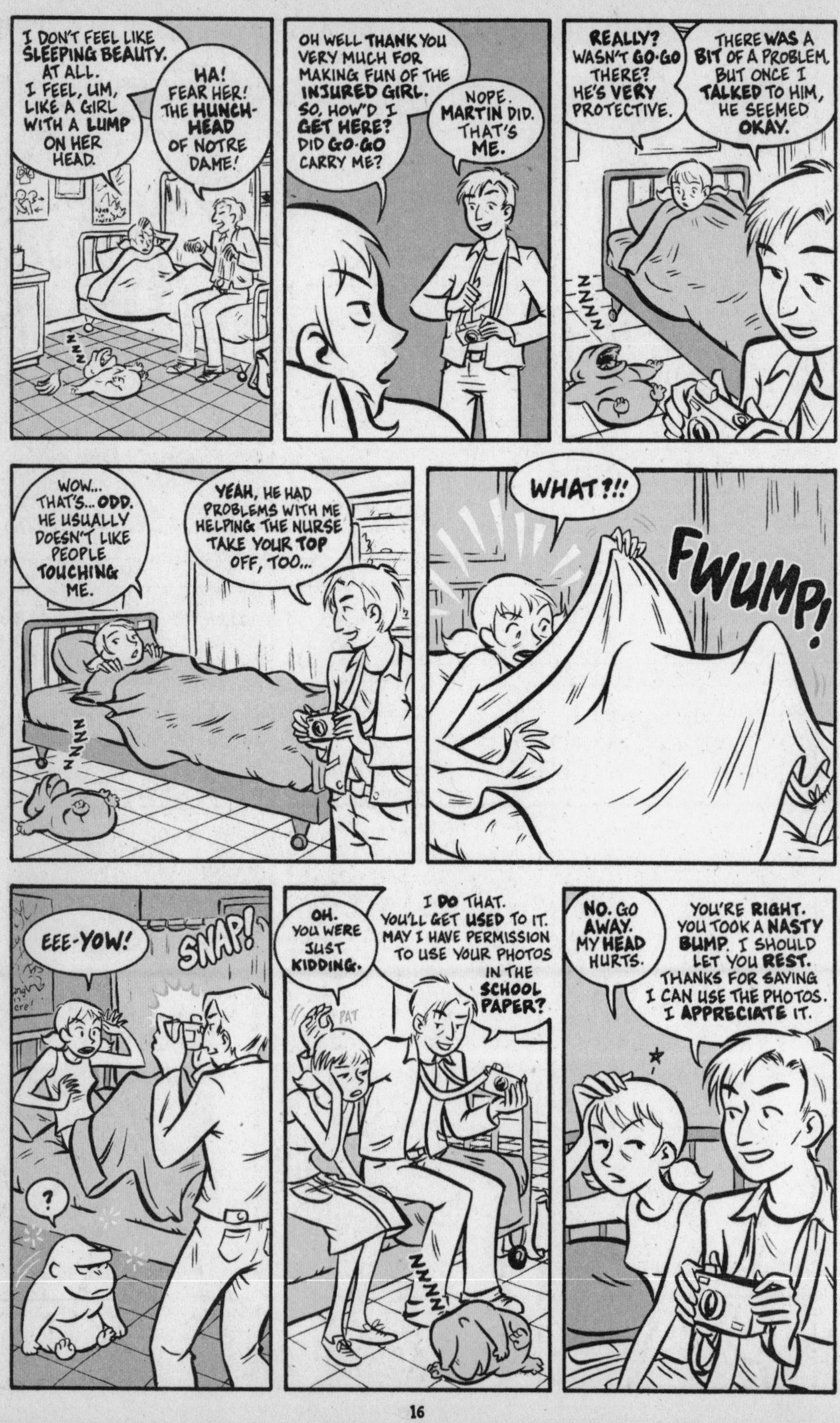
I DON'T FEEL LIKE SLEEPING BEAUTY. AT ALL. I FEEL, UM, LIKE A GIRL WITH A LUMP ON HER HEAD.
HA! FEAR HER! THE HUNCH-HEAD OF NOTRE DAME!
Z Z Z
OH WELL THANK YOU VERY MUCH FOR MAKING FUN OF THE INJURED GIRL. SO, HOW'D I GET HERE? DID GO-GO CARRY ME?
NOPE. MARTIN DID. THAT'S ME.
REALLY? WASN'T GO-GO THERE? HE'S VERY PROTECTIVE.
THERE WAS A BIT OF A PROBLEM, BUT ONCE I TALKED TO HIM, HE SEEMED OKAY.
ZZZZZ
WOW... THAT'S... ODD. HE USUALLY DOESN'T LIKE PEOPLE TOUCHING ME.
YEAH, HE HAD PROBLEMS WITH ME HELPING THE NURSE TAKE YOUR TOP OFF, TOO...
ZZZZ
WHAT?!!
FWUMP!
EEE-YOW!
SNAP!
?
OH. YOU WERE JUST KIDDING.
I DO THAT. YOU'LL GET USED TO IT. MAY I HAVE PERMISSION TO USE YOUR PHOTOS IN THE SCHOOL PAPER?
PAT
ZZZZ
NO. GO AWAY. MY HEAD HURTS.
YOU'RE RIGHT. YOU TOOK A NASTY BUMP. I SHOULD LET YOU REST. THANKS FOR SAYING I CAN USE THE PHOTOS. I APPRECIATE IT.

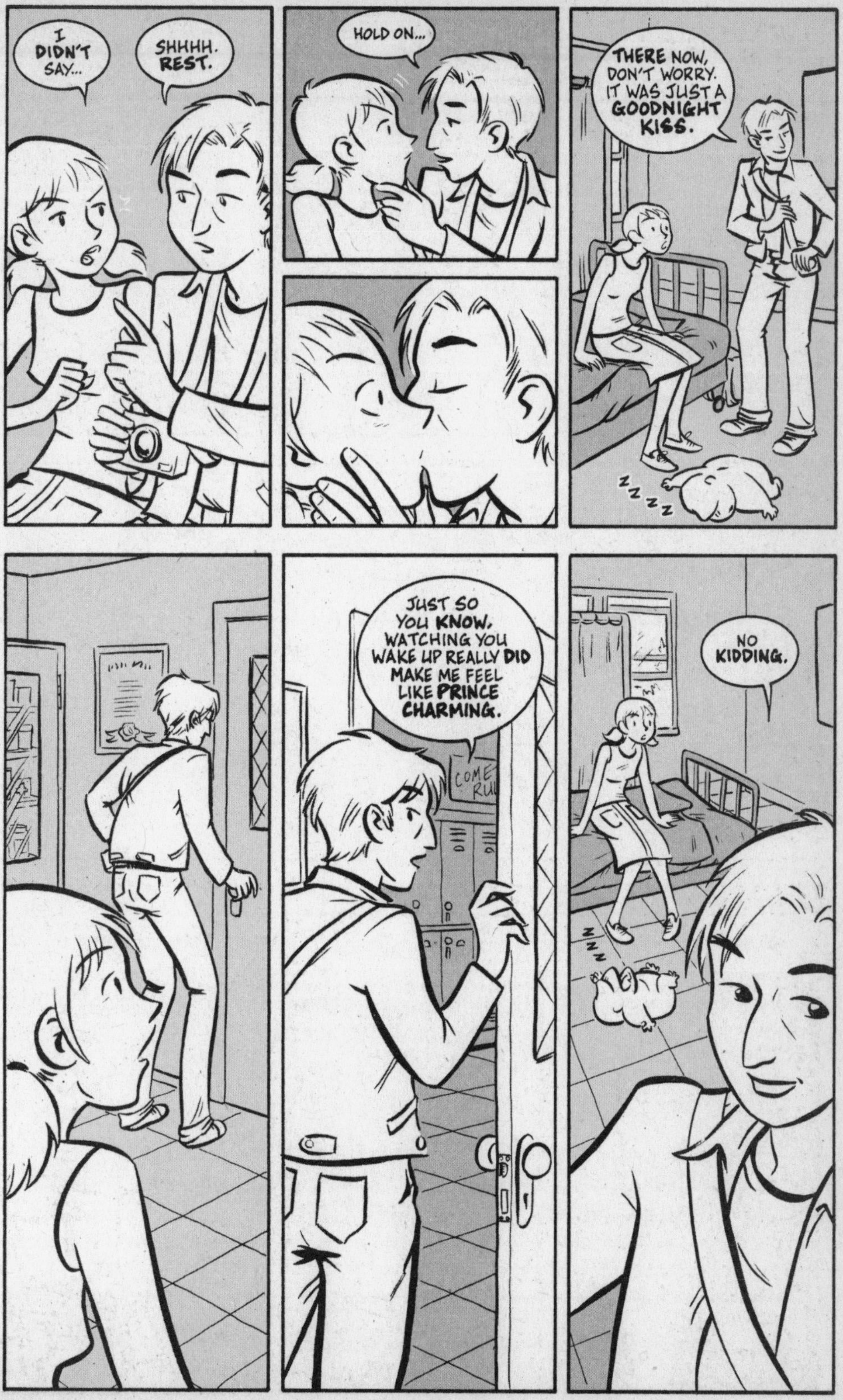

I DIDN'T SAY...
SHHHH. REST.
HOLD ON...
THERE NOW, DON'T WORRY. IT WAS JUST A GOODNIGHT KISS.
Z Z Z Z
JUST SO YOU KNOW, WATCHING YOU WAKE UP REALLY DID MAKE ME FEEL LIKE PRINCE CHARMING.
NO KIDDING.
Z Z Z

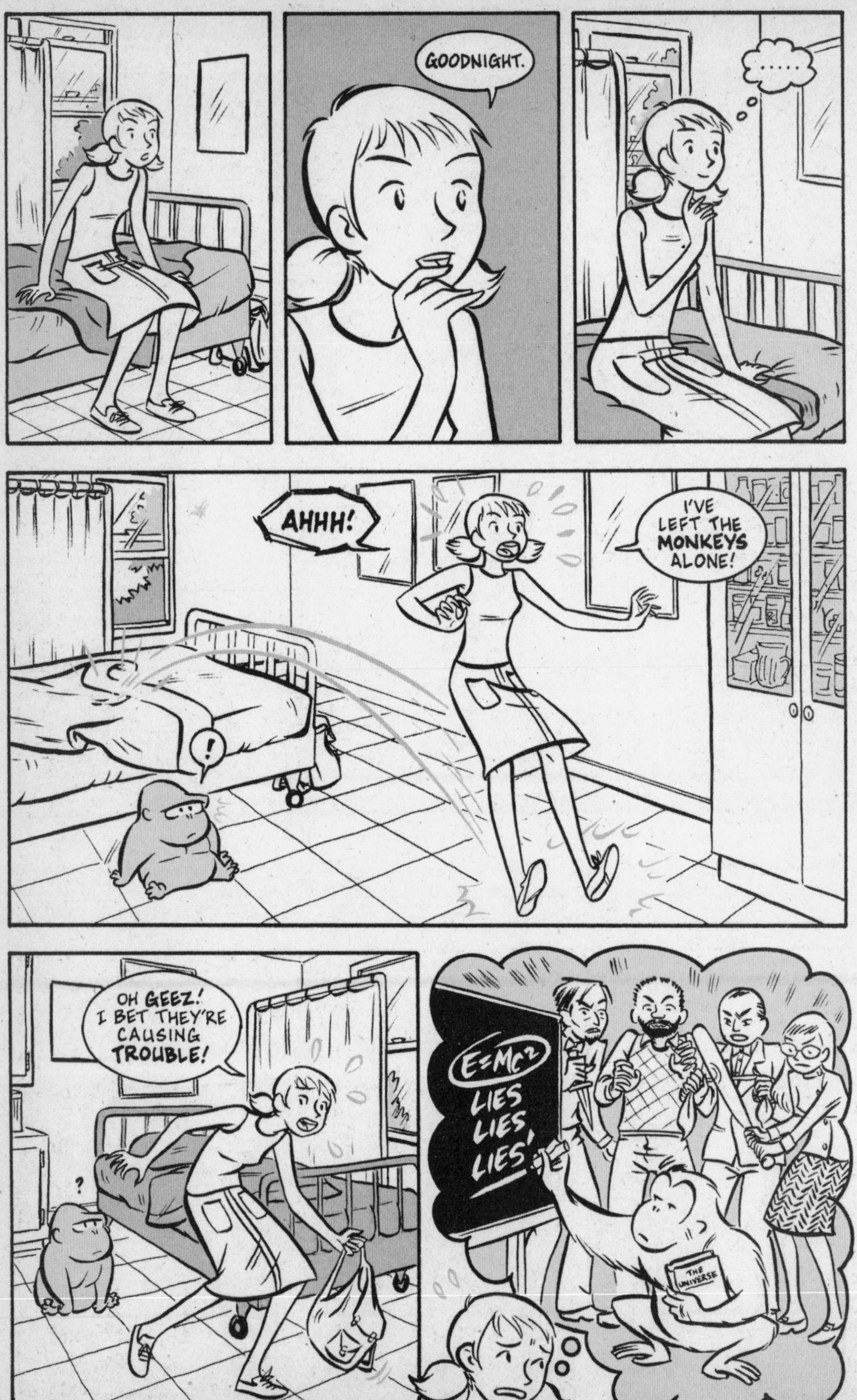
GOODNIGHT.
......
AHHH!
I'VE LEFT THE MONKEYS ALONE!
!
OH GEEZ! I BET THEY'RE CAUSING TROUBLE!
?
E=MC2
LIES LIES LIES!
THE UNIVERSE

GIRLS LOCKER ROOM

COMETS SOFTBALL SCHEDULE:

COMETS

?

ZZZZZ

OH, WAIT. *GO-GO,* YOU'RE *RIGHT HERE!*

OKAY. NOW WHERE ARE THE *OTHERS?*

YAWN!

HOKE HAKTPIBIG, THAI'S FIIV...

MAKI'IC IT KIRBY'S FATHER SC FIIPI'D MONKEYS...

HMM...

19

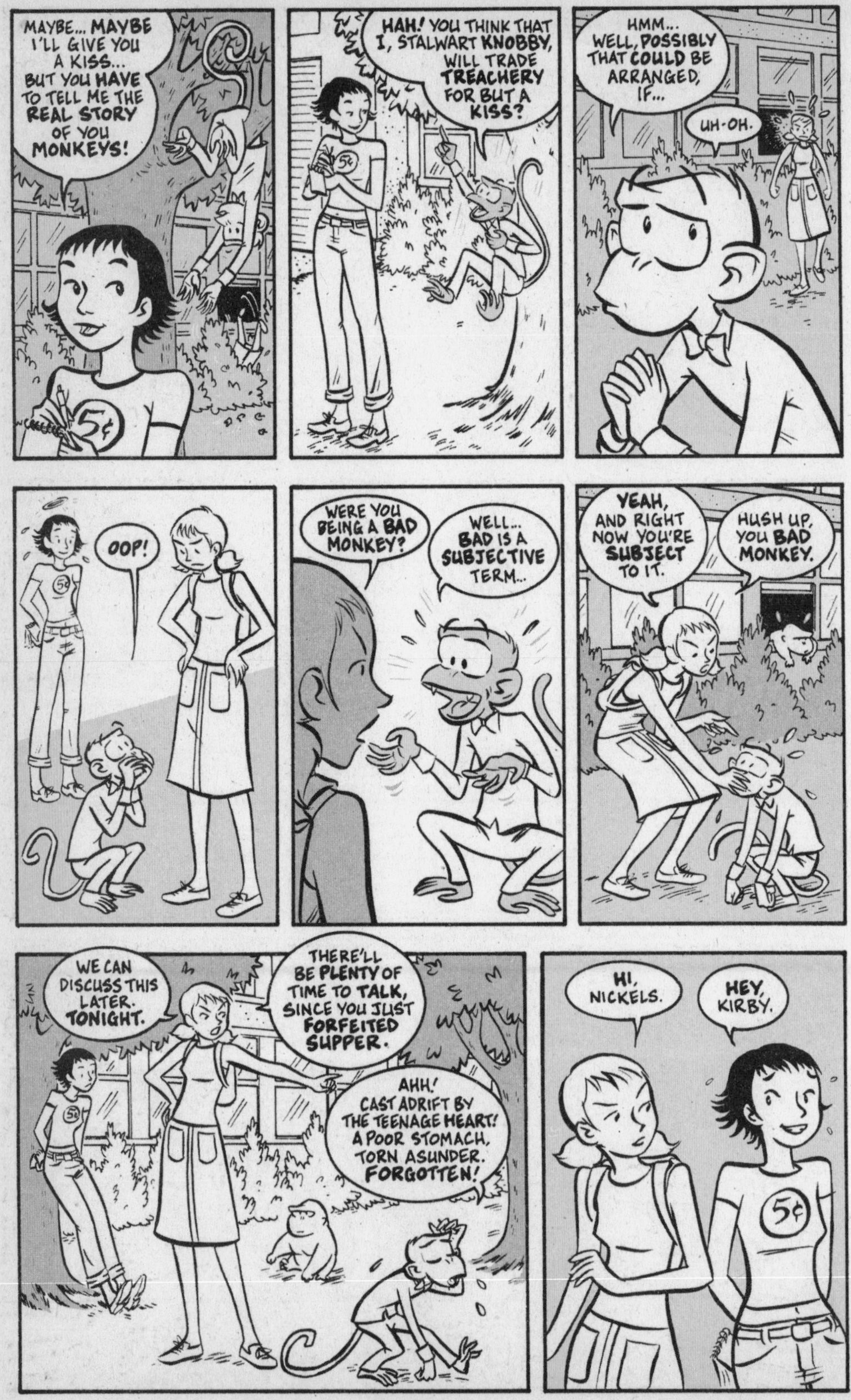
MAYBE... MAYBE I'LL GIVE YOU A KISS... BUT YOU HAVE TO TELL ME THE REAL STORY OF YOU MONKEYS!
HAH! YOU THINK THAT I, STALWART KNOBBY, WILL TRADE TREACHERY FOR BUT A KISS?
HMM... WELL, POSSIBLY THAT COULD BE ARRANGED, IF...
UH-OH.
OOP!
WERE YOU BEING A BAD MONKEY?
WELL... BAD IS A SUBJECTIVE TERM...
YEAH, AND RIGHT NOW YOU'RE SUBJECT TO IT.
HUSH UP, YOU BAD MONKEY.
WE CAN DISCUSS THIS LATER. TONIGHT.
THERE'LL BE PLENTY OF TIME TO TALK, SINCE YOU JUST FORFEITED SUPPER.
AHH! CAST ADRIFT BY THE TEENAGE HEART! A POOR STOMACH, TORN ASUNDER. FORGOTTEN!
HI, NICKELS.
HEY, KIRBY.

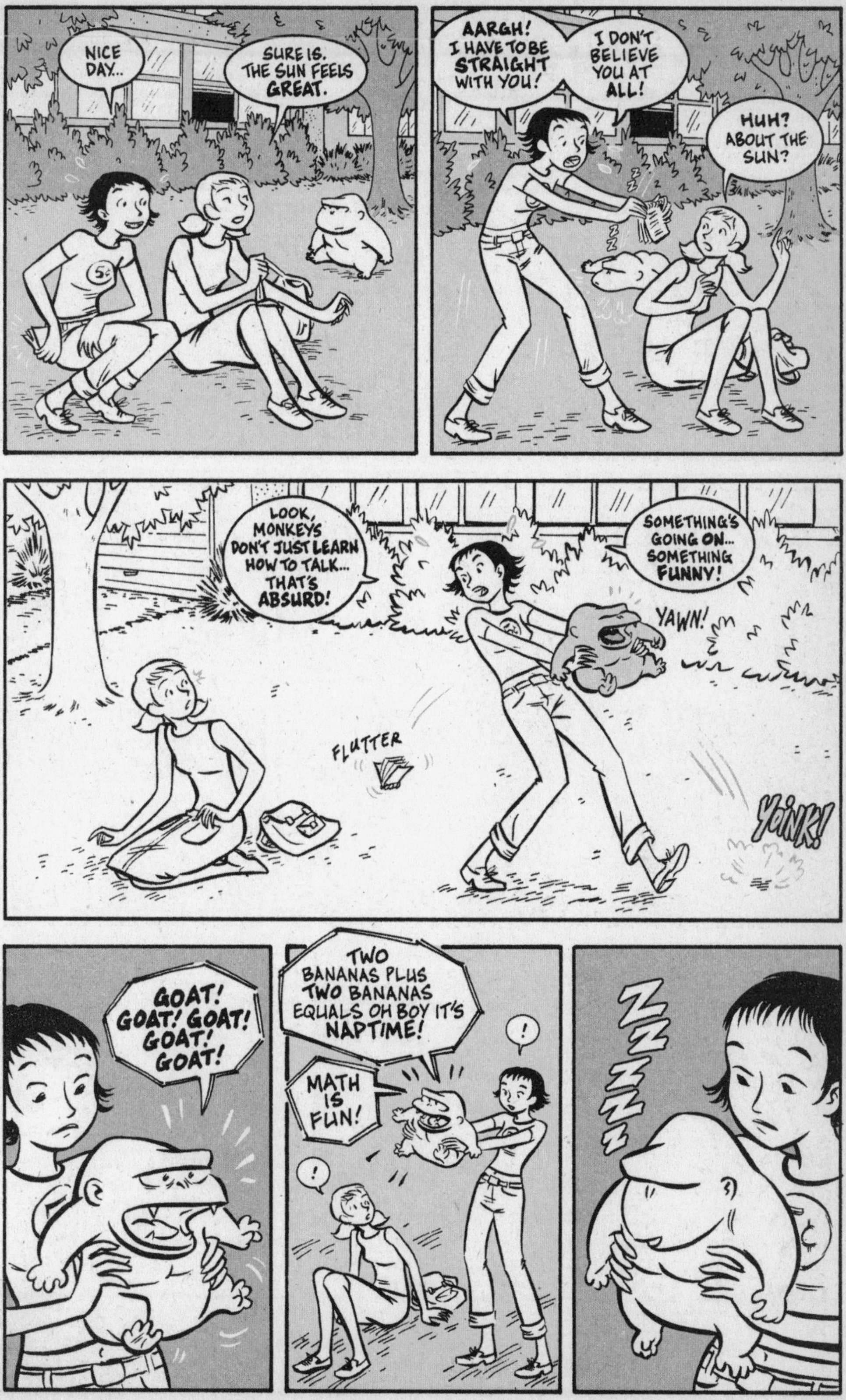
NICE DAY...
SURE IS. THE SUN FEELS GREAT.
AARGH! I HAVE TO BE STRAIGHT WITH YOU!
I DON'T BELIEVE YOU AT ALL!
HUH? ABOUT THE SUN?
LOOK, MONKEYS DON'T JUST LEARN HOW TO TALK... THAT'S ABSURD!
SOMETHING'S GOING ON... SOMETHING FUNNY!
YAWN!
FLUTTER
YOINK!
GOAT! GOAT! GOAT! GOAT! GOAT!
TWO BANANAS PLUS TWO BANANAS EQUALS OH BOY IT'S NAPTIME!
MATH IS FUN!
!
!
ZZZZZ

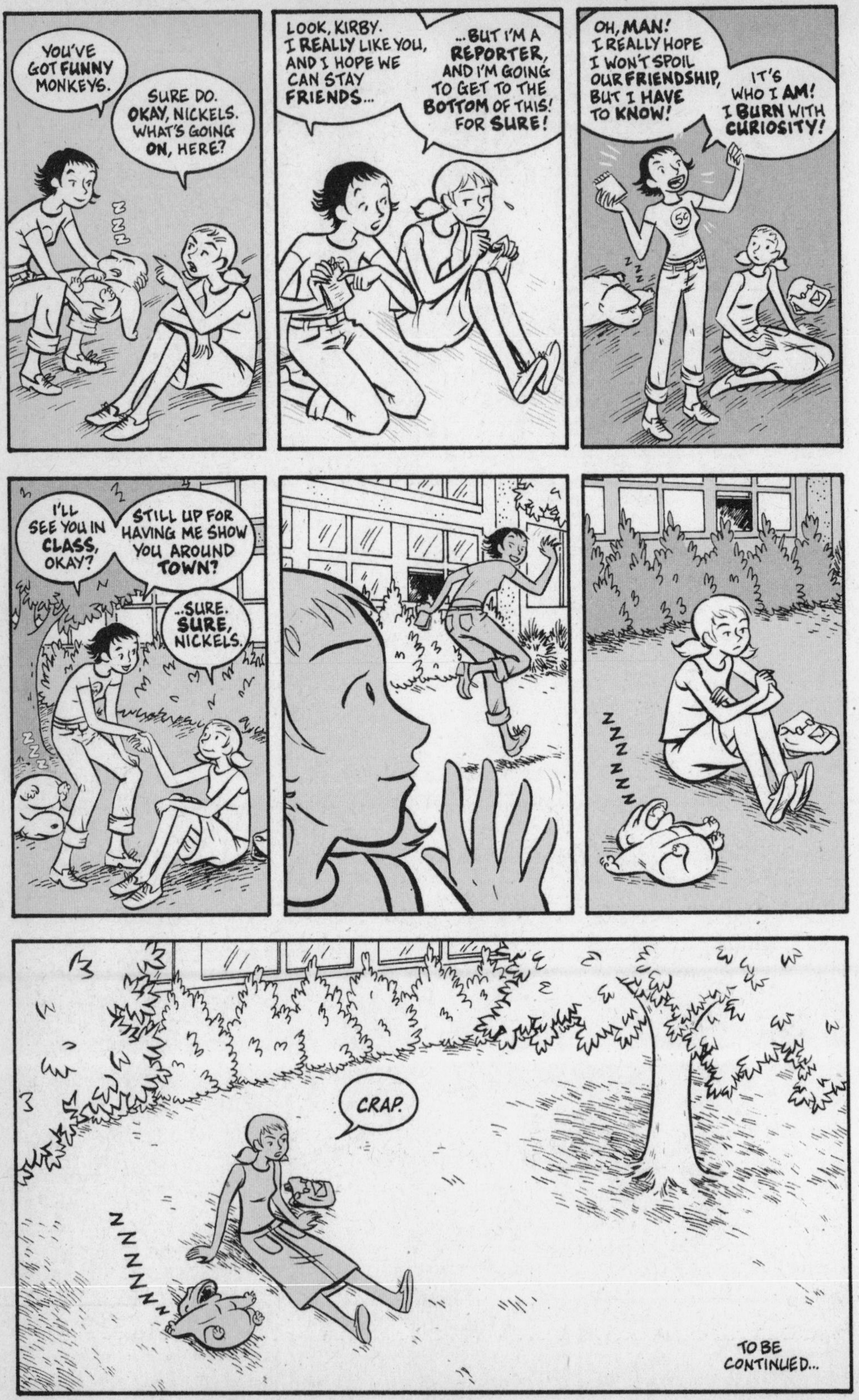
YOU'VE GOT FUNNY MONKEYS.
SURE DO. OKAY, NICKELS. WHAT'S GOING ON, HERE?
Z Z Z
LOOK, KIRBY. I REALLY LIKE YOU, AND I HOPE WE CAN STAY FRIENDS...
...BUT I'M A REPORTER, AND I'M GOING TO GET TO THE BOTTOM OF THIS! FOR SURE!
OH, MAN! I REALLY HOPE I WON'T SPOIL OUR FRIENDSHIP, BUT I HAVE TO KNOW!
IT'S WHO I AM! I BURN WITH CURIOSITY!
I'LL SEE YOU IN CLASS, OKAY?
STILL UP FOR HAVING ME SHOW YOU AROUND TOWN?
...SURE. SURE, NICKELS.
CRAP.
TO BE CONTINUED...

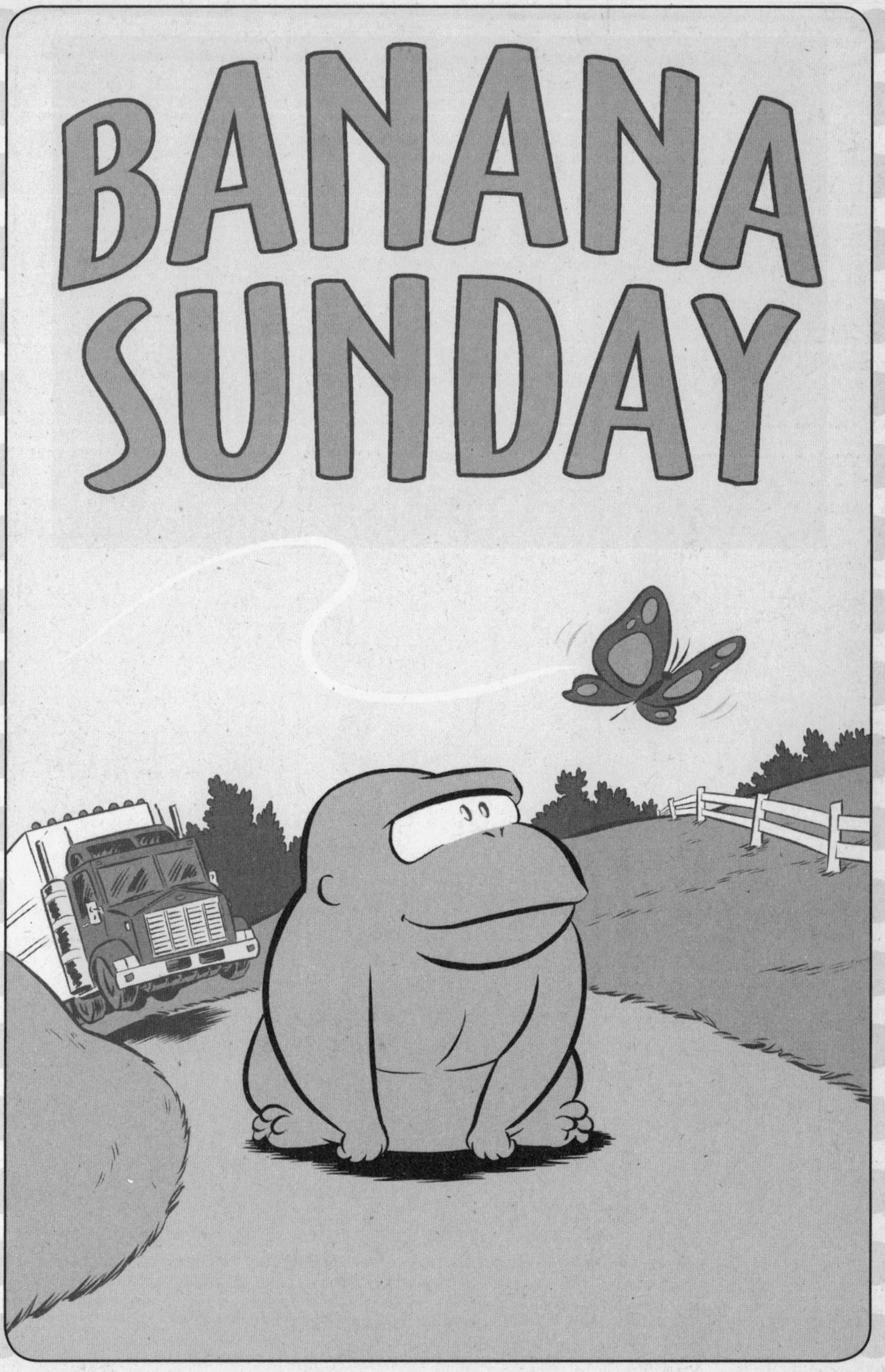
BANANA
SUNDAY

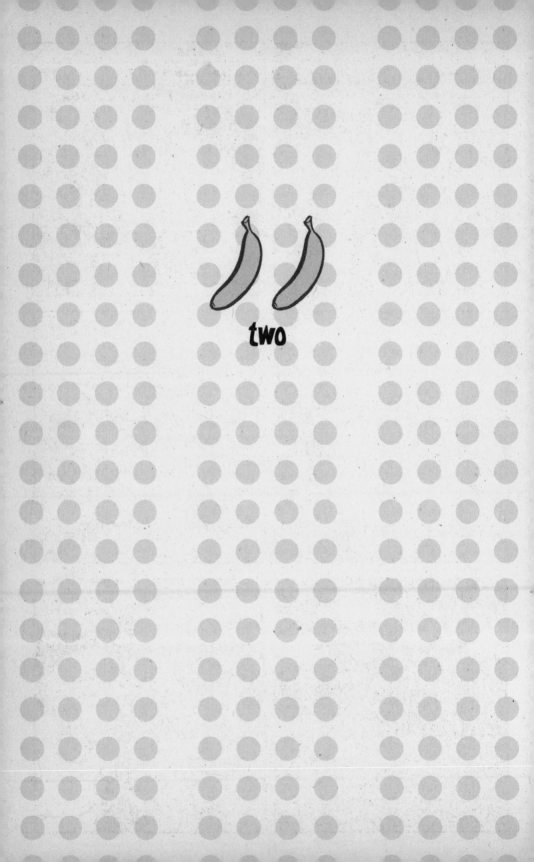

two

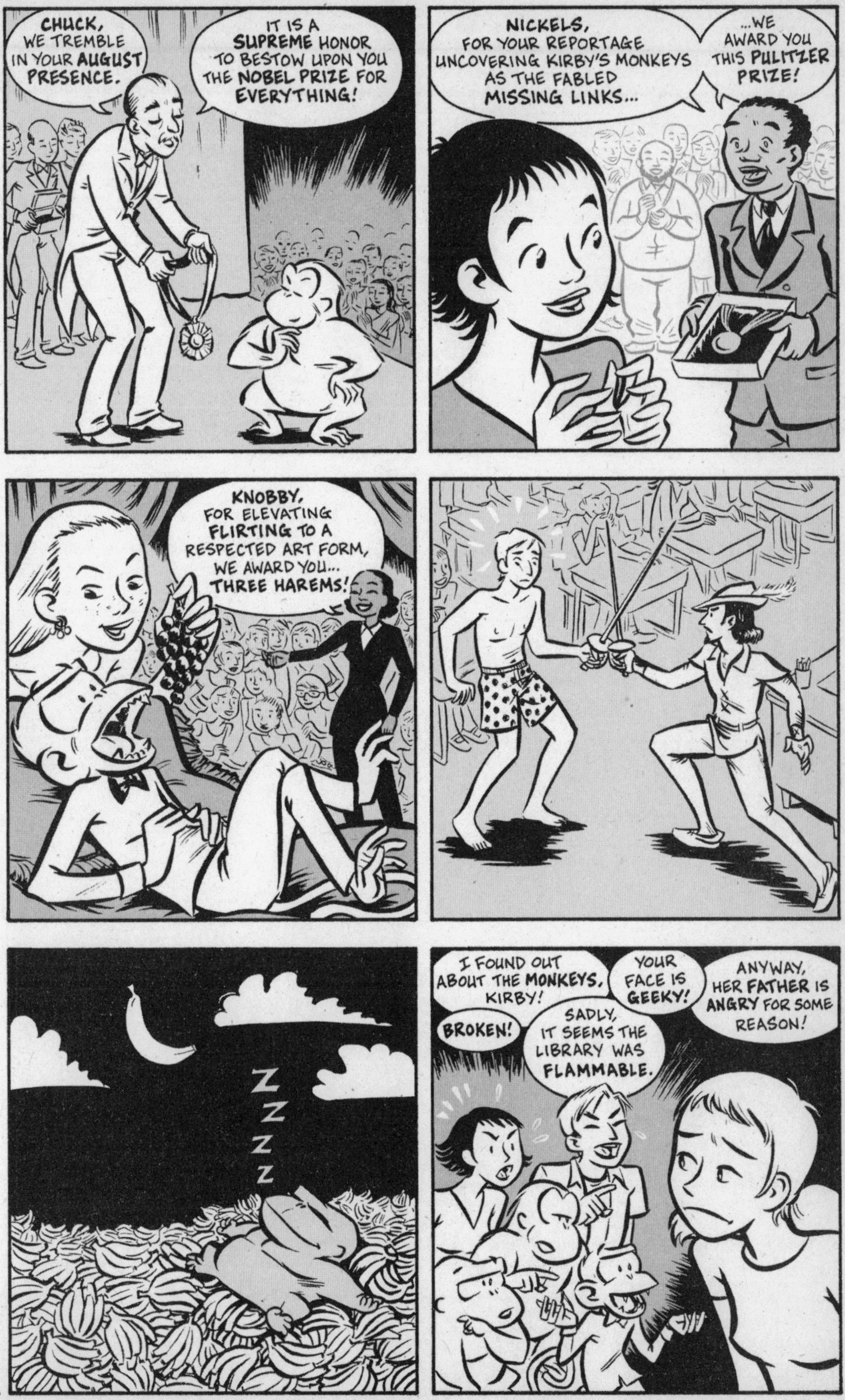
CHUCK, WE TREMBLE IN YOUR AUGUST PRESENCE.
IT IS A SUPREME HONOR TO BESTOW UPON YOU THE NOBEL PRIZE FOR EVERYTHING!
NICKELS, FOR YOUR REPORTAGE UNCOVERING KIRBY'S MONKEYS AS THE FABLED MISSING LINKS...
...WE AWARD YOU THIS PULITZER PRIZE!
KNOBBY, FOR ELEVATING FLIRTING TO A RESPECTED ART FORM, WE AWARD YOU... THREE HAREMS!
Z Z Z Z
I FOUND OUT ABOUT THE MONKEYS, KIRBY!
YOUR FACE IS GEEKY!
ANYWAY, HER FATHER IS ANGRY FOR SOME REASON!
BROKEN!
SADLY, IT SEEMS THE LIBRARY WAS FLAMMABLE.

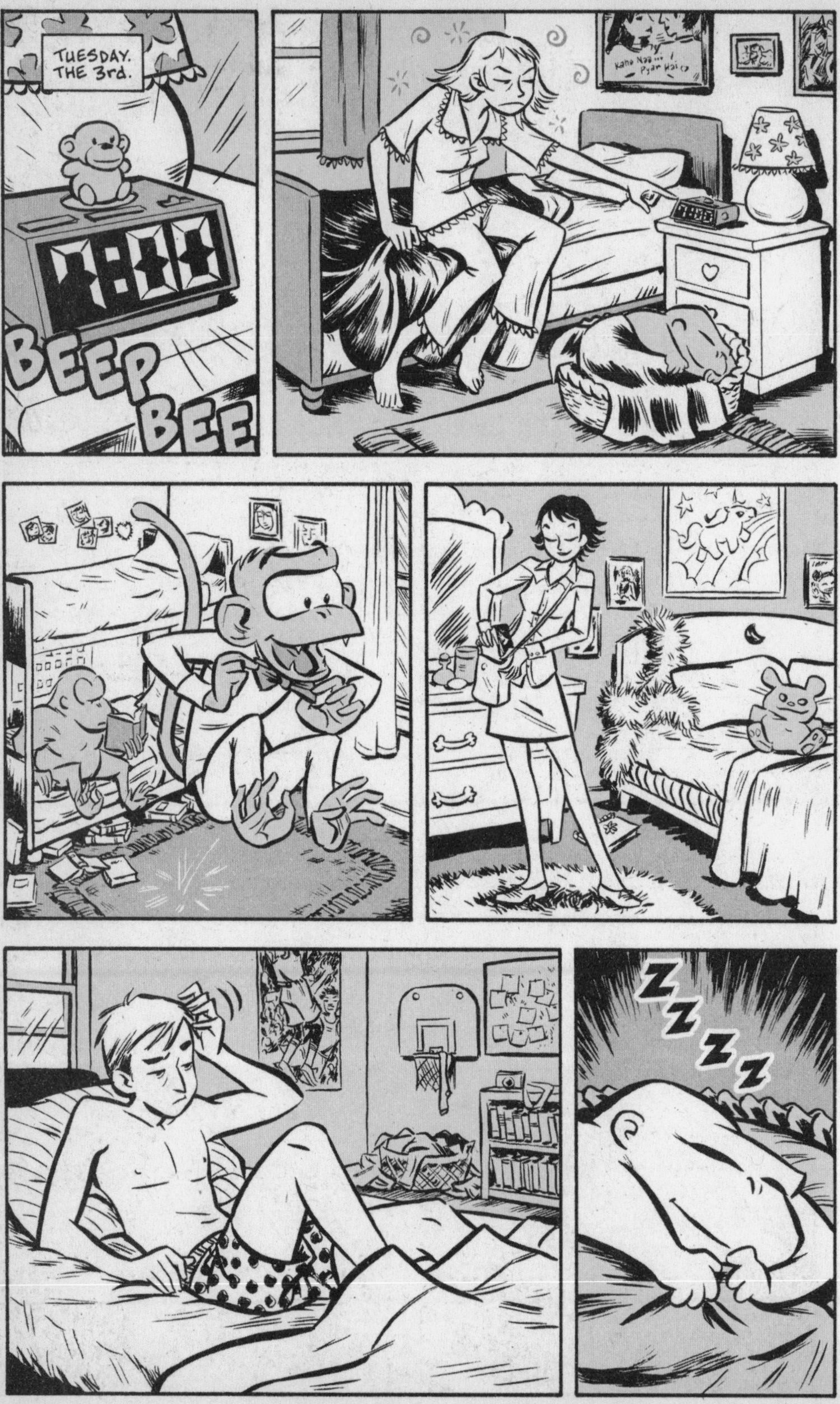
TUESDAY. THE 3rd.
BEEP
BEE
ZZZZ

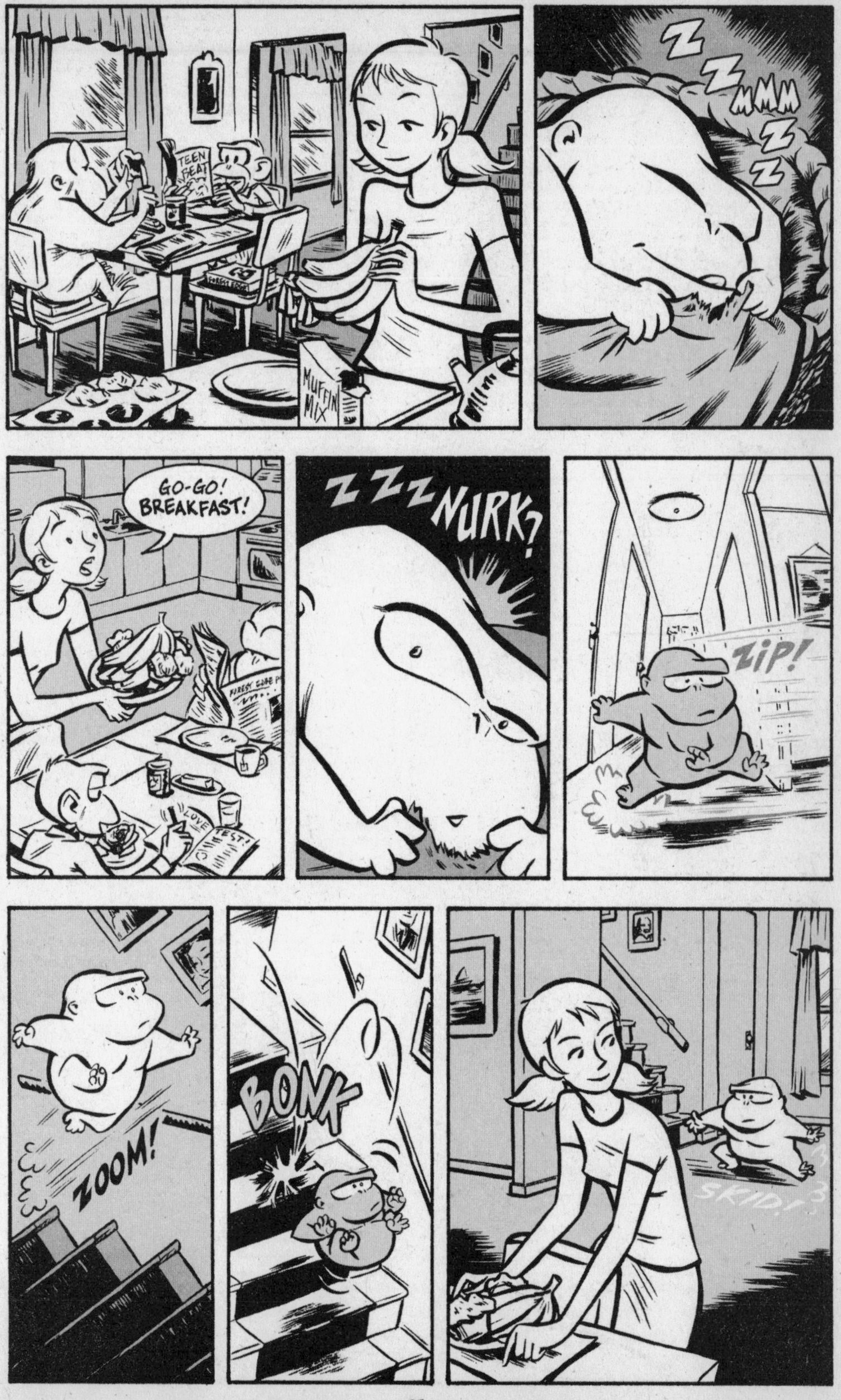
TEEN BEAT
MUFFIN MIX
ZZMMM
ZZ
GO-GO! BREAKFAST!
LOVE TEST!
ZZZNURK?
ZIP!
ZOOM!
BONK
SKID!

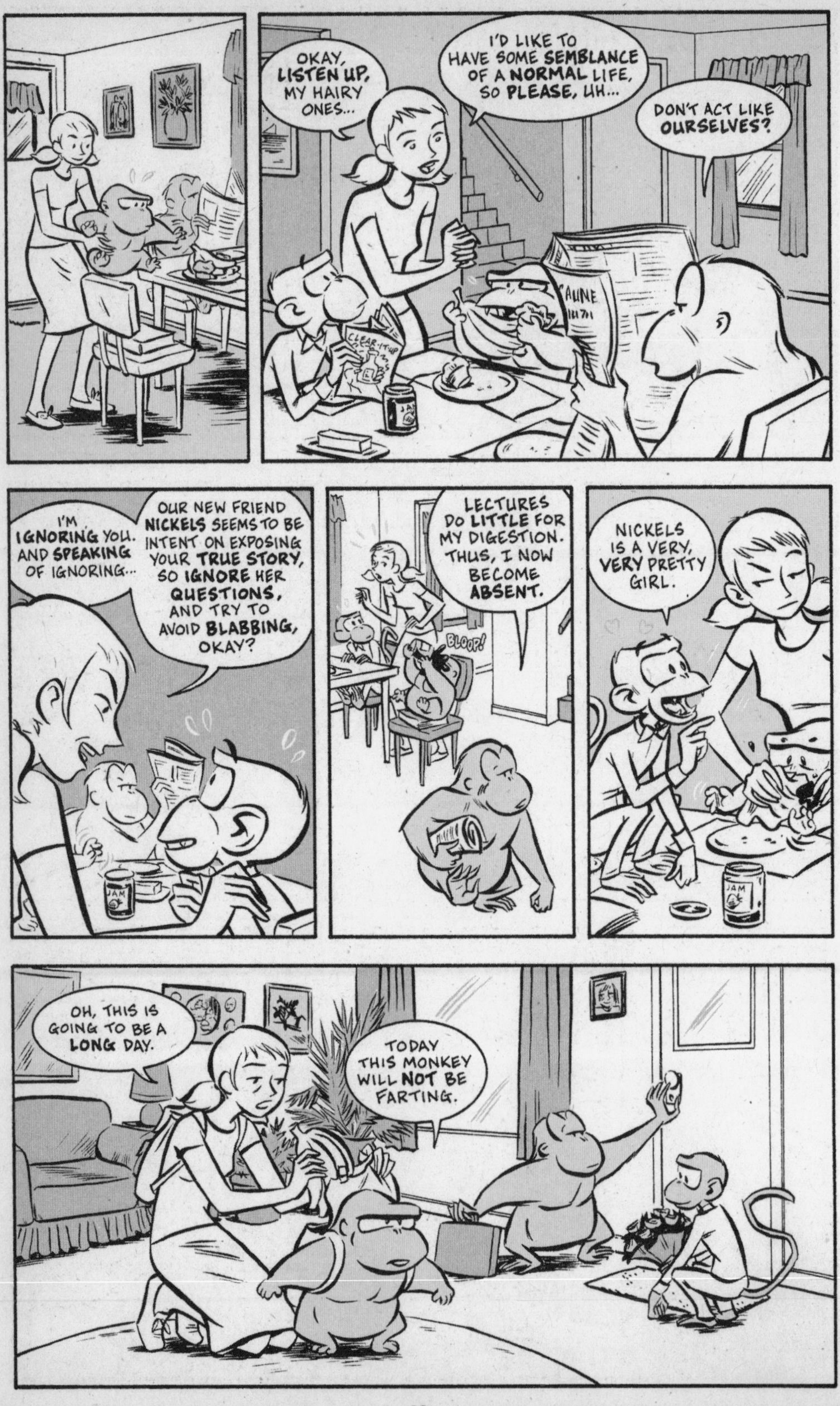
OKAY, LISTEN UP, MY HAIRY ONES...
I'D LIKE TO HAVE SOME SEMBLANCE OF A NORMAL LIFE, SO PLEASE, UH...
DON'T ACT LIKE OURSELVES?
JAM
I'M IGNORING YOU. AND SPEAKING OF IGNORING...
OUR NEW FRIEND NICKELS SEEMS TO BE INTENT ON EXPOSING YOUR TRUE STORY, SO IGNORE HER QUESTIONS, AND TRY TO AVOID BLABBING, OKAY?
LECTURES DO LITTLE FOR MY DIGESTION. THUS, I NOW BECOME ABSENT.
BLOOP!
NICKELS IS A VERY, VERY PRETTY GIRL.
OH, THIS IS GOING TO BE A LONG DAY.
TODAY THIS MONKEY WILL NOT BE FARTING.

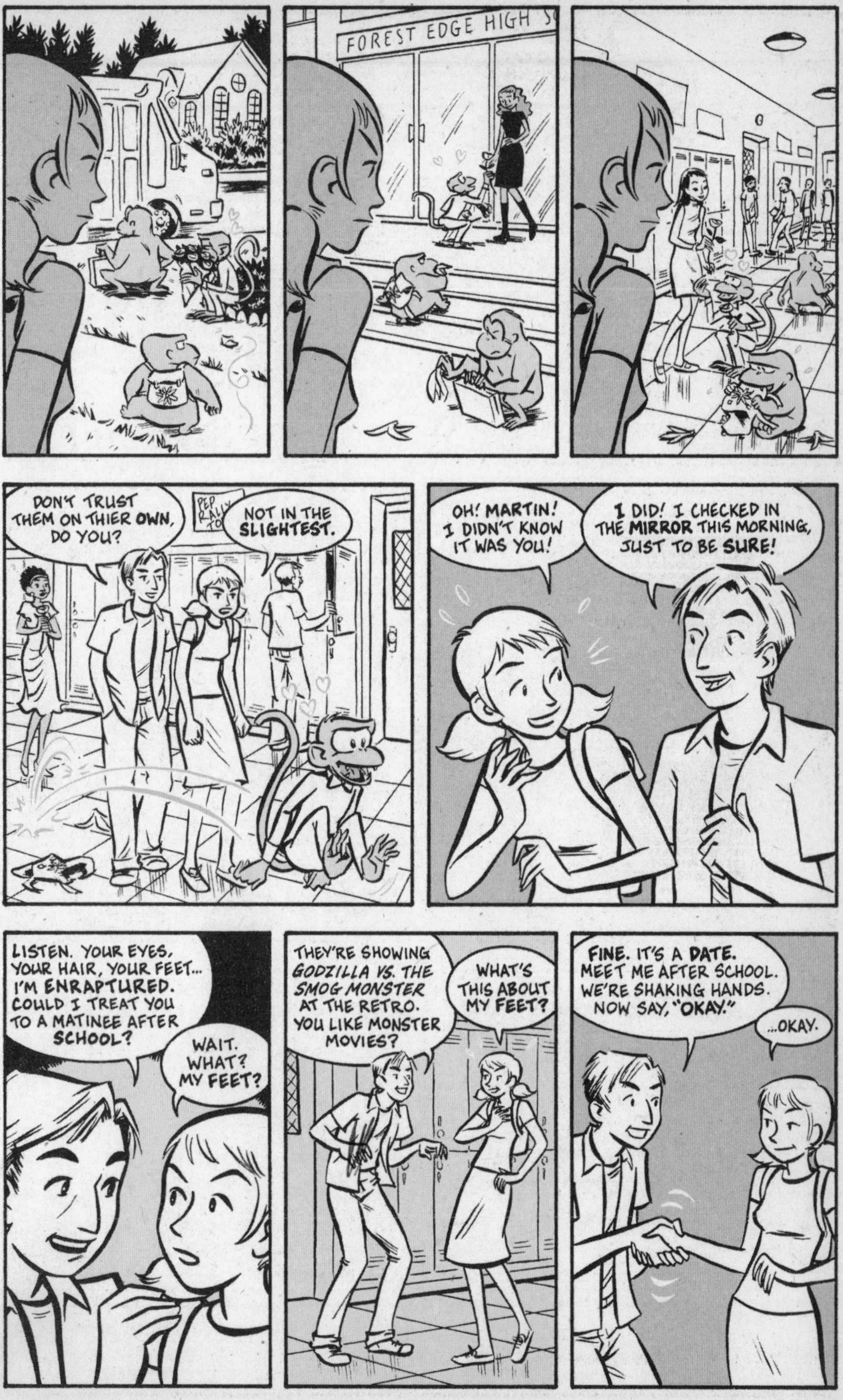
FOREST EDGE HIGH S
DON'T TRUST THEM ON THIER OWN, DO YOU?
PEP RALLY TO
NOT IN THE SLIGHTEST.
OH! MARTIN! I DIDN'T KNOW IT WAS YOU!
I DID! I CHECKED IN THE MIRROR THIS MORNING, JUST TO BE SURE!
LISTEN. YOUR EYES, YOUR HAIR, YOUR FEET... I'M ENRAPTURED. COULD I TREAT YOU TO A MATINEE AFTER SCHOOL?
WAIT. WHAT? MY FEET?
THEY'RE SHOWING GODZILLA VS. THE SMOG MONSTER AT THE RETRO. YOU LIKE MONSTER MOVIES?
WHAT'S THIS ABOUT MY FEET?
FINE. IT'S A DATE. MEET ME AFTER SCHOOL. WE'RE SHAKING HANDS. NOW SAY, "OKAY."
...OKAY.

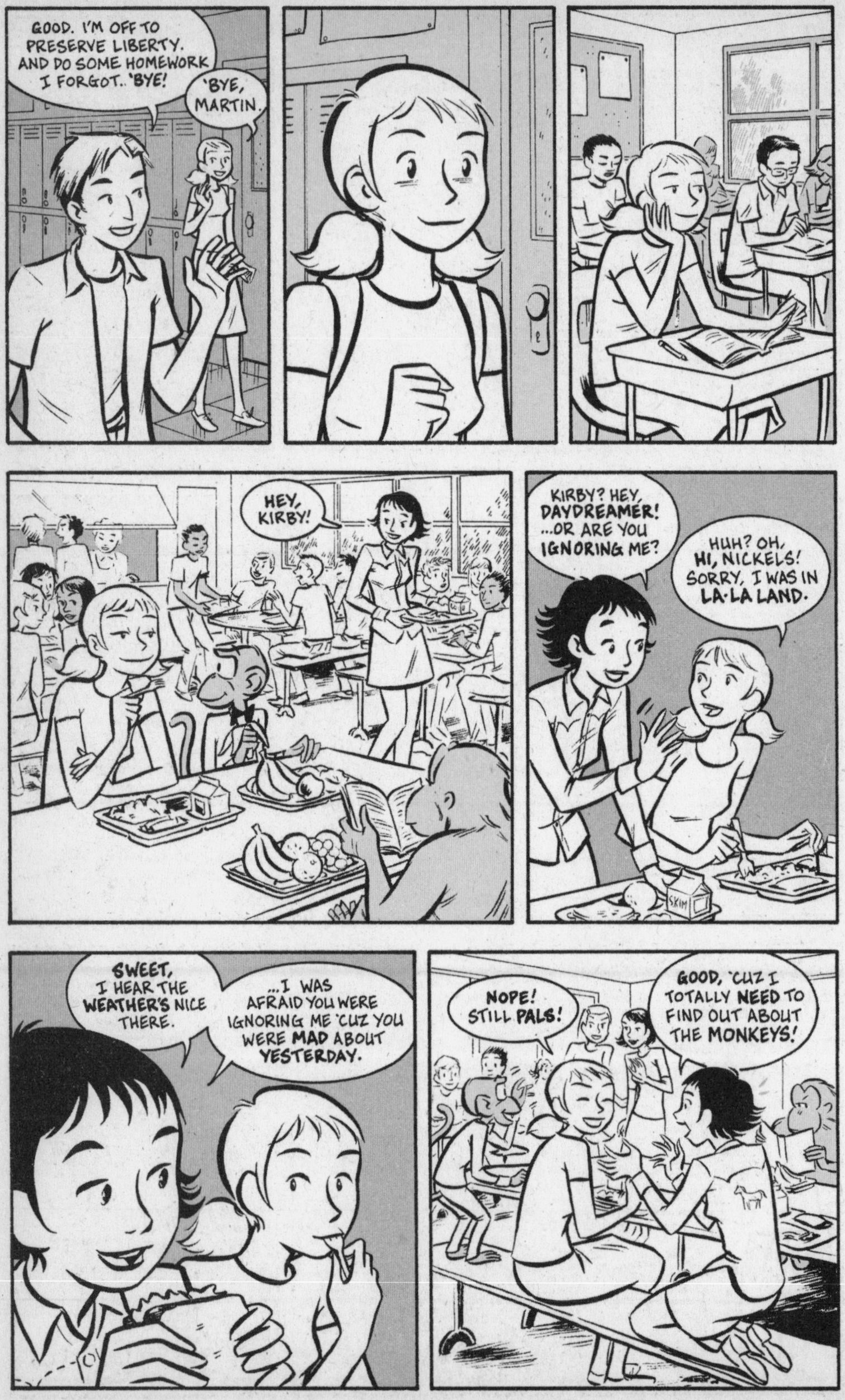
GOOD. I'M OFF TO PRESERVE LIBERTY. AND DO SOME HOMEWORK I FORGOT.. 'BYE!
'BYE, MARTIN.
HEY, KIRBY!
KIRBY? HEY, DAYDREAMER! ...OR ARE YOU IGNORING ME?
HUH? OH, HI, NICKELS! SORRY, I WAS IN LA-LA LAND.
SKIM
SWEET, I HEAR THE WEATHER'S NICE THERE.
...I WAS AFRAID YOU WERE IGNORING ME 'CUZ YOU WERE MAD ABOUT YESTERDAY.
NOPE! STILL PALS!
GOOD, 'CUZ I TOTALLY NEED TO FIND OUT ABOUT THE MONKEYS!

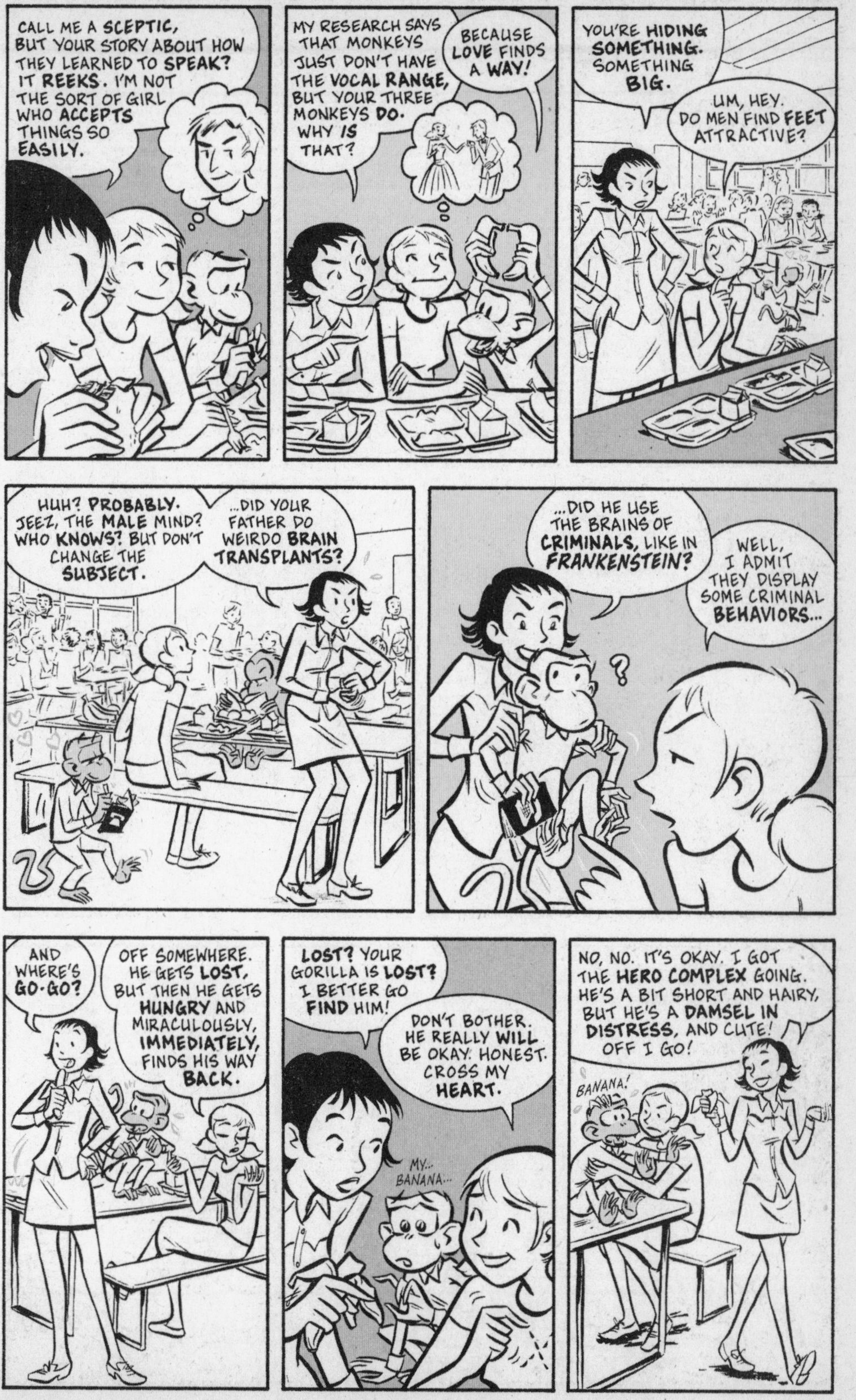
CALL ME A SCEPTIC, BUT YOUR STORY ABOUT HOW THEY LEARNED TO SPEAK? IT REEKS. I'M NOT THE SORT OF GIRL WHO ACCEPTS THINGS SO EASILY.
MY RESEARCH SAYS THAT MONKEYS JUST DON'T HAVE THE VOCAL RANGE, BUT YOUR THREE MONKEYS DO. WHY IS THAT?
BECAUSE LOVE FINDS A WAY!
YOU'RE HIDING SOMETHING. SOMETHING BIG.
UM, HEY. DO MEN FIND FEET ATTRACTIVE?
HUH? PROBABLY. JEEZ, THE MALE MIND? WHO KNOWS? BUT DON'T CHANGE THE SUBJECT.
...DID YOUR FATHER DO WEIRDO BRAIN TRANSPLANTS?
...DID HE USE THE BRAINS OF CRIMINALS, LIKE IN FRANKENSTEIN?
WELL, I ADMIT THEY DISPLAY SOME CRIMINAL BEHAVIORS...
?
AND WHERE'S GO-GO?
OFF SOMEWHERE. HE GETS LOST, BUT THEN HE GETS HUNGRY AND MIRACULOUSLY, IMMEDIATELY, FINDS HIS WAY BACK.
LOST? YOUR GORILLA IS LOST? I BETTER GO FIND HIM!
DON'T BOTHER. HE REALLY WILL BE OKAY. HONEST. CROSS MY HEART.
MY... BANANA...
NO, NO. IT'S OKAY. I GOT THE HERO COMPLEX GOING. HE'S A BIT SHORT AND HAIRY, BUT HE'S A DAMSEL IN DISTRESS, AND CUTE! OFF I GO!
BANANA!

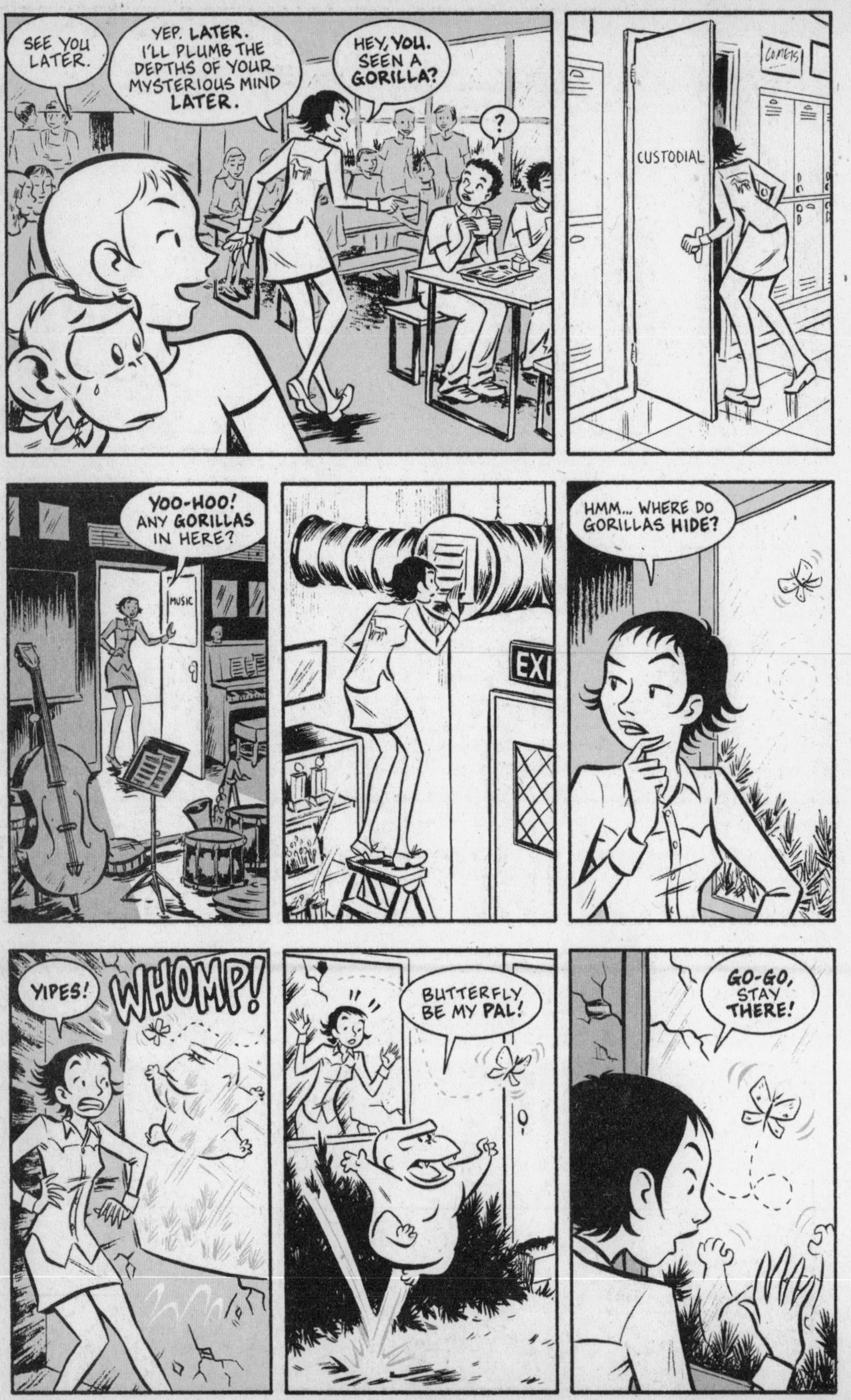
SEE YOU LATER.
YEP. LATER. I'LL PLUMB THE DEPTHS OF YOUR MYSTERIOUS MIND LATER.
HEY, YOU. SEEN A GORILLA?
?
CUSTODIAL
YOO-HOO! ANY GORILLAS IN HERE?
MUSIC
EXI
HMM... WHERE DO GORILLAS HIDE?
YIPES!
WHOMP!
BUTTERFLY BE MY PAL!
GO-GO, STAY THERE!

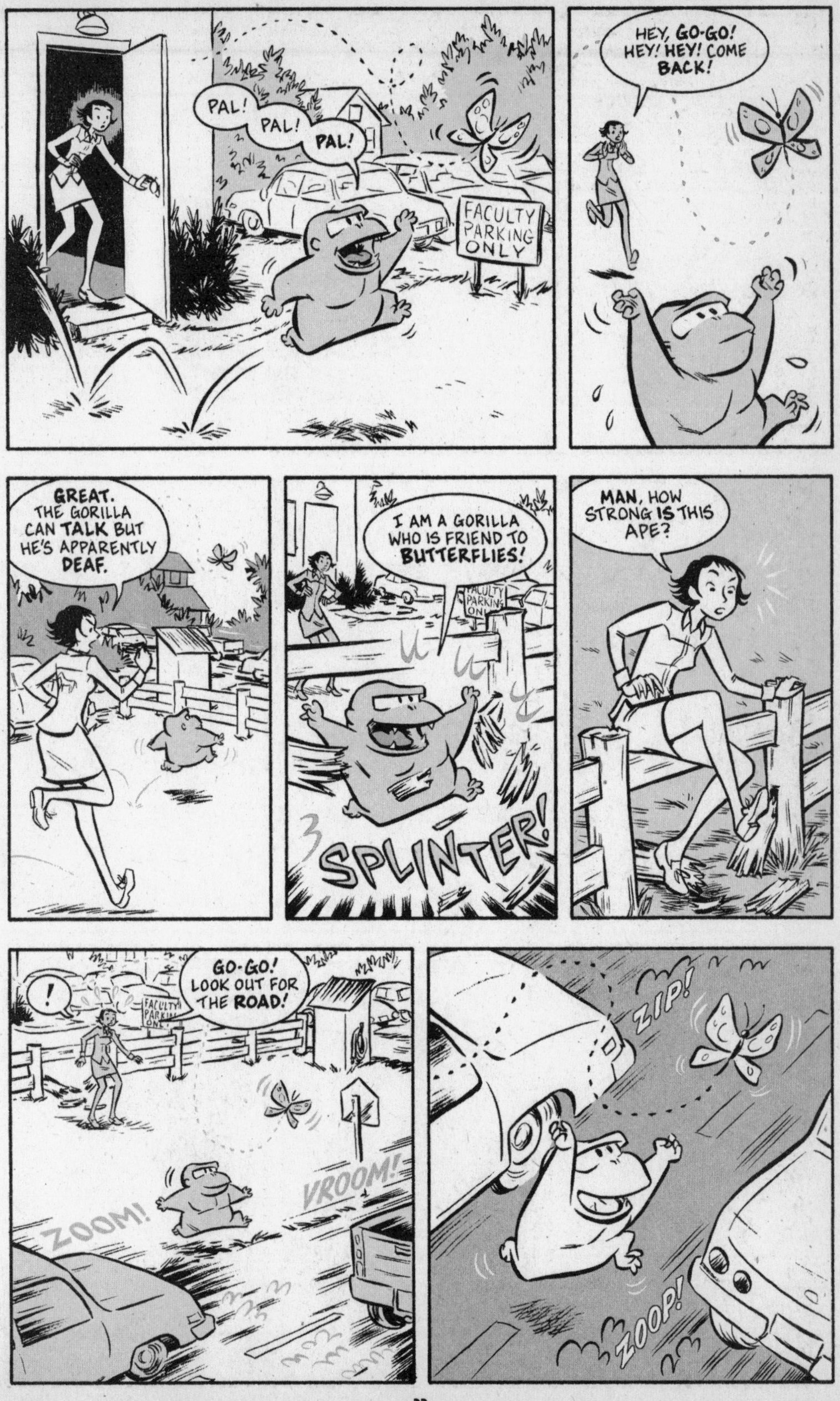
PAL!
PAL!
PAL!
FACULTY PARKING ONLY
HEY, GO-GO! HEY! HEY! COME BACK!
GREAT. THE GORILLA CAN TALK BUT HE'S APPARENTLY DEAF.
I AM A GORILLA WHO IS FRIEND TO BUTTERFLIES!
SPLINTER!
MAN, HOW STRONG IS THIS APE?
!
GO-GO! LOOK OUT FOR THE ROAD!
VROOM!
ZOOM!
ZIP!
ZOOP!

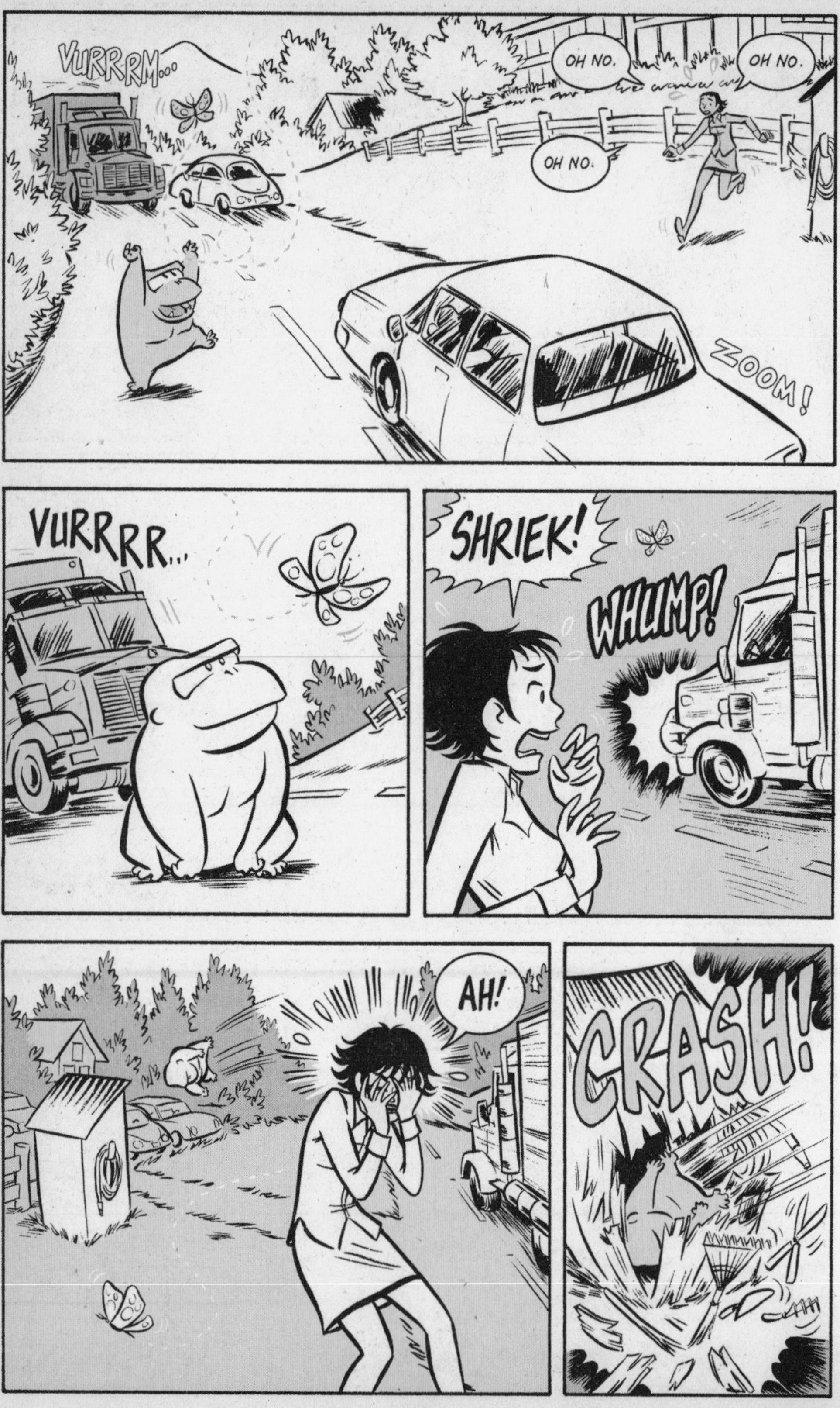
VURRRMooo
OH NO.
OH NO.
OH NO.
ZOOM!
VURRRR...
SHRIEK!
WHUMP!
AH!
CRASH!

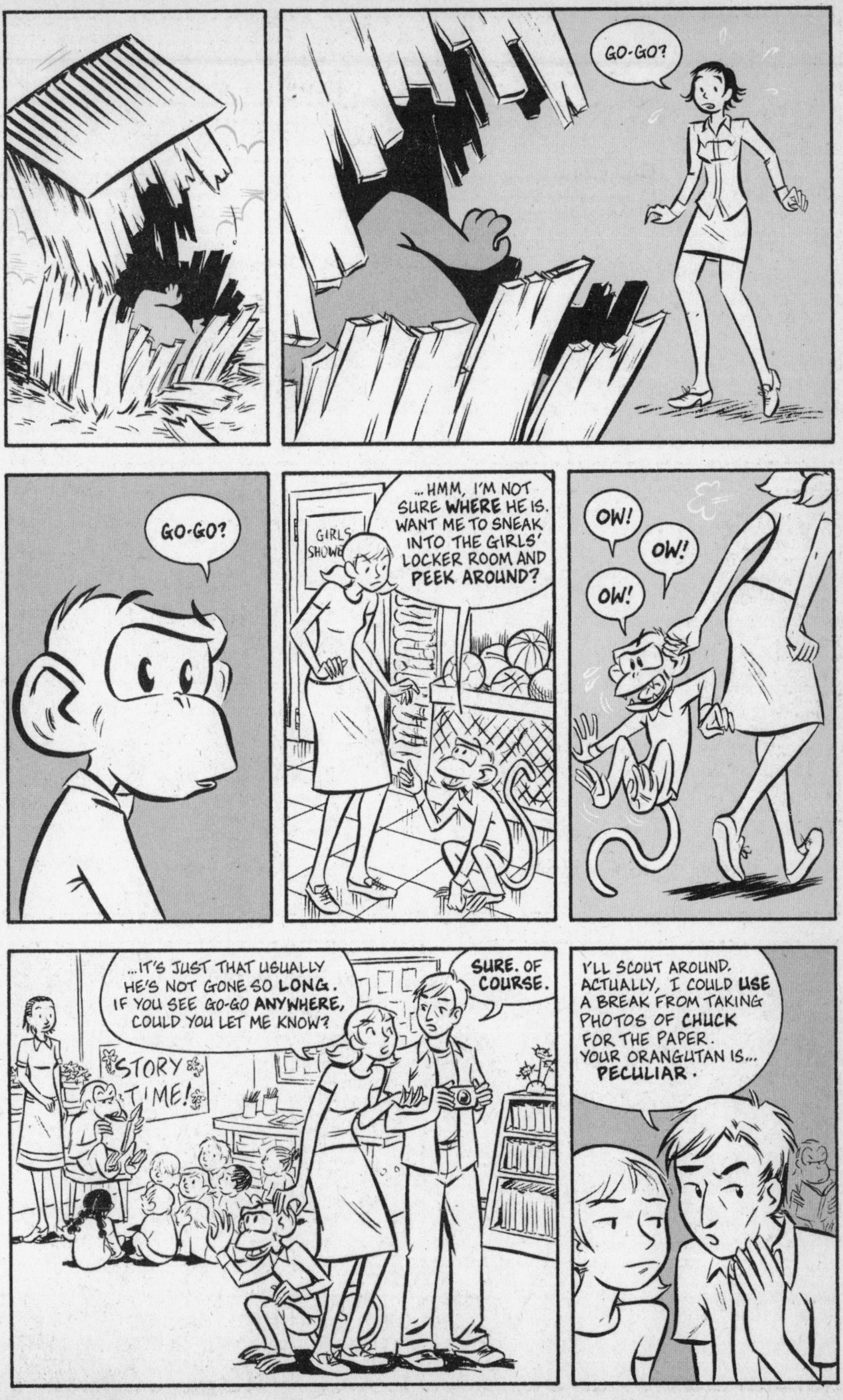
GO-GO?
GO-GO?
GIRLS SHOWE
...HMM, I'M NOT SURE WHERE HE IS. WANT ME TO SNEAK INTO THE GIRLS' LOCKER ROOM AND PEEK AROUND?
OW!
OW!
OW!
...IT'S JUST THAT USUALLY HE'S NOT GONE SO LONG. IF YOU SEE GO-GO ANYWHERE, COULD YOU LET ME KNOW?
SURE. OF COURSE.
STORY TIME!
I'LL SCOUT AROUND. ACTUALLY, I COULD USE A BREAK FROM TAKING PHOTOS OF CHUCK FOR THE PAPER. YOUR ORANGUTAN IS... PECULIAR.

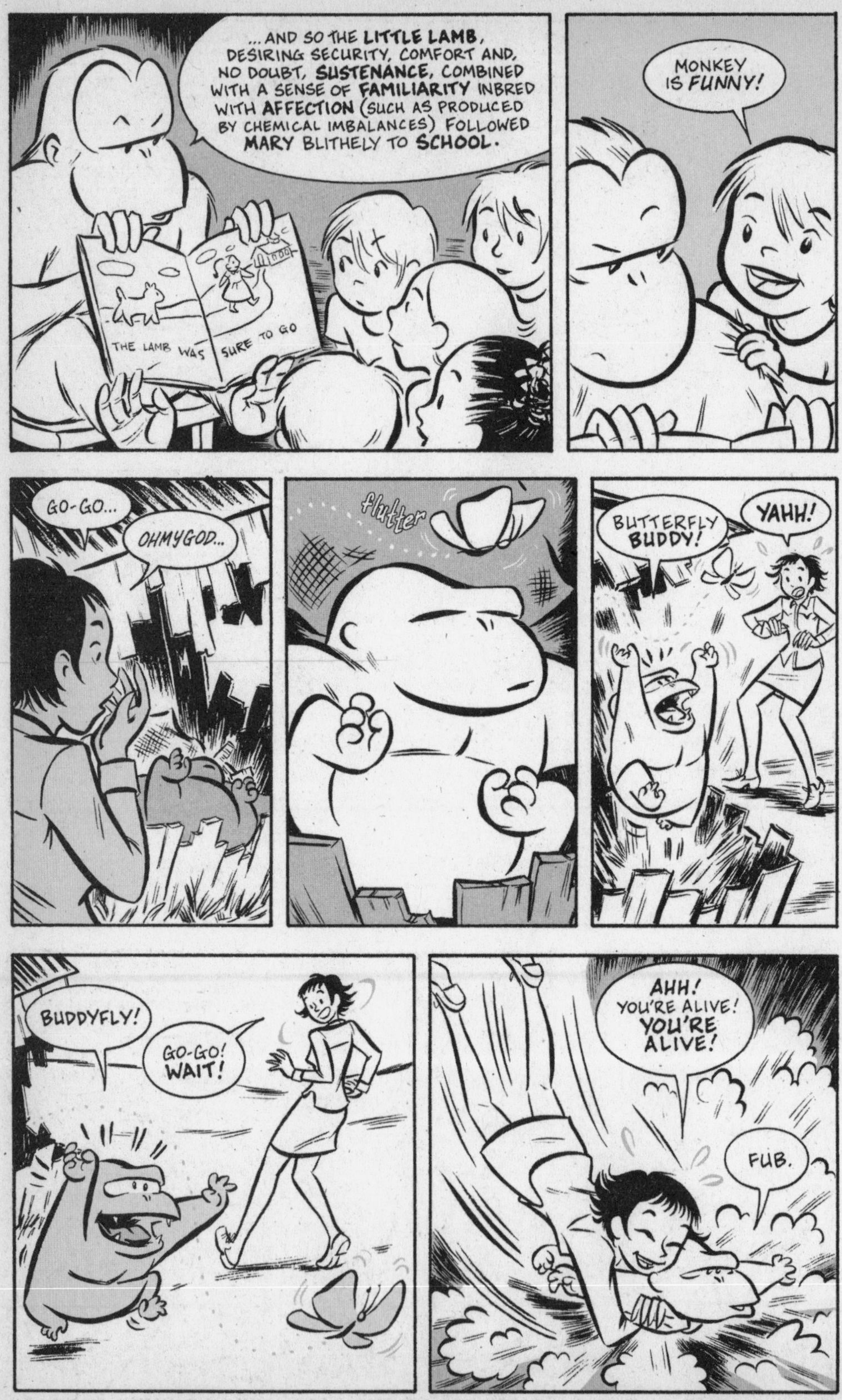
...AND SO THE LITTLE LAMB, DESIRING SECURITY, COMFORT AND, NO DOUBT, SUSTENANCE, COMBINED WITH A SENSE OF FAMILIARITY INBRED WITH AFFECTION (SUCH AS PRODUCED BY CHEMICAL IMBALANCES) FOLLOWED MARY BLITHELY TO SCHOOL.
THE LAMB WAS SURE TO GO
MONKEY IS FUNNY!
GO-GO...
OHMYGOD...
flutter
BUTTERFLY BUDDY!
YAHH!
BUDDYFLY!
GO-GO! WAIT!
AHH! YOU'RE ALIVE! YOU'RE ALIVE!
FUB.

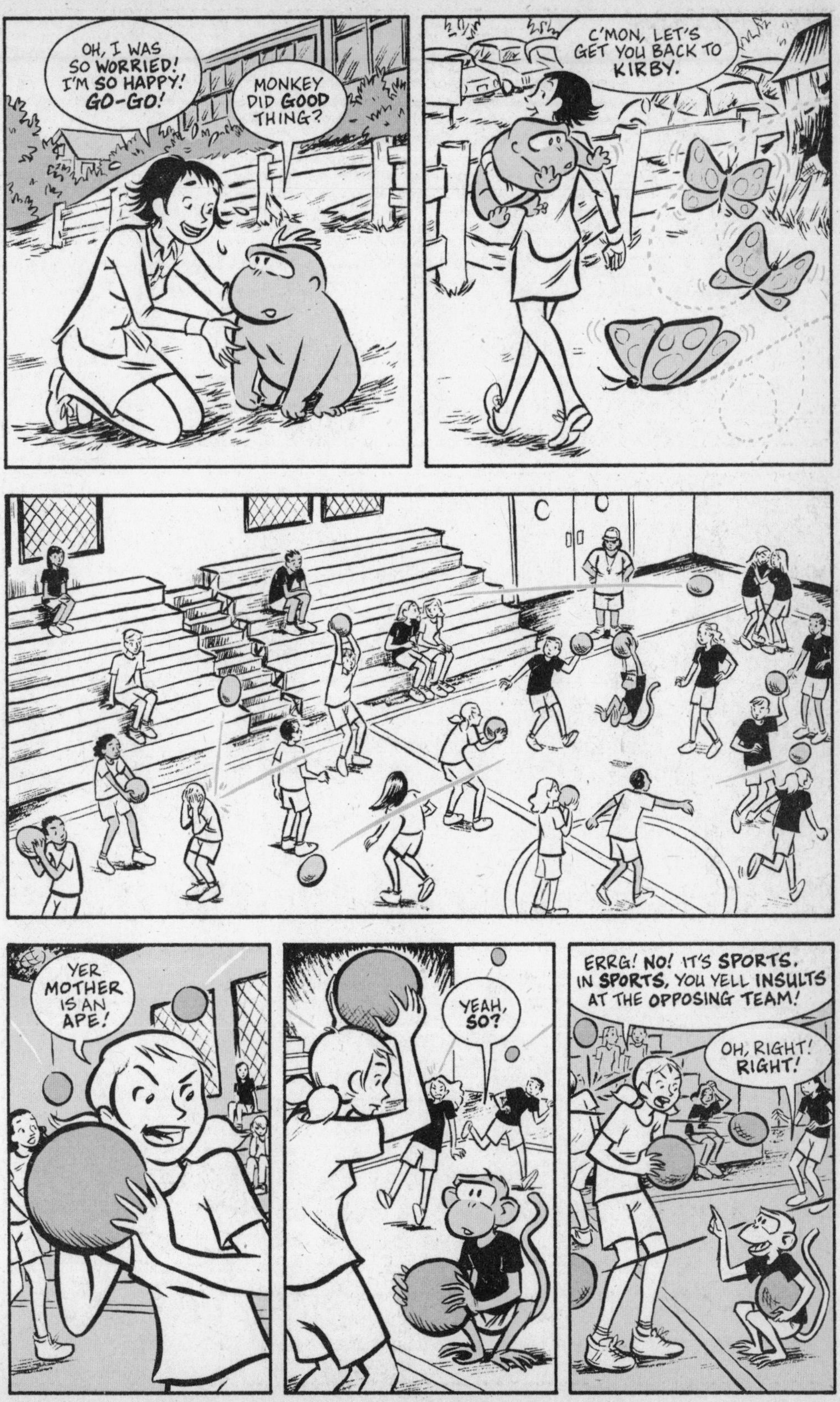

OH, I WAS SO WORRIED! I'M SO HAPPY! GO-GO!
MONKEY DID GOOD THING?
C'MON, LET'S GET YOU BACK TO KIRBY.
YER MOTHER IS AN APE!
YEAH, SO?
ERRG! NO! IT'S SPORTS. IN SPORTS, YOU YELL INSULTS AT THE OPPOSING TEAM!
OH, RIGHT! RIGHT!

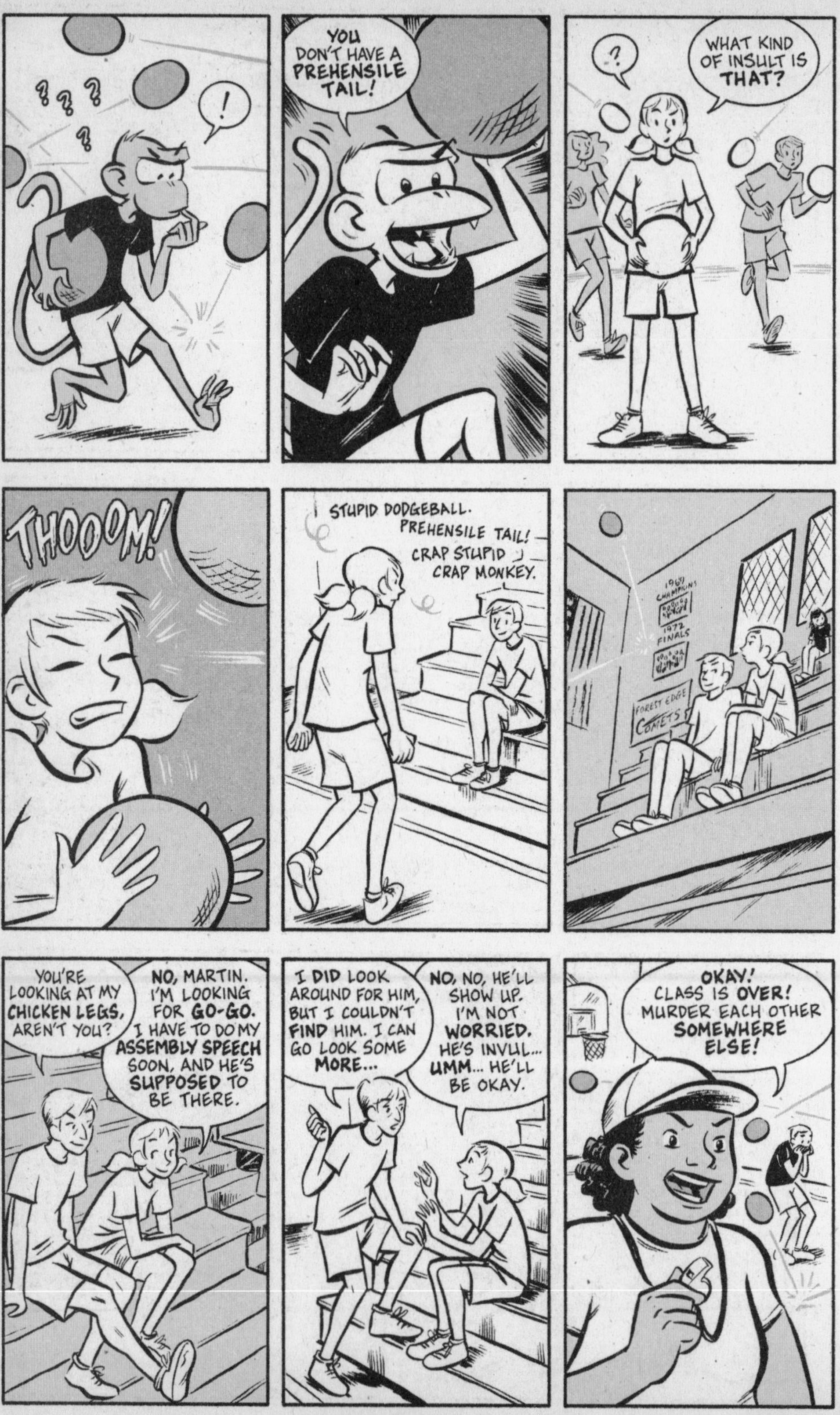
?
?
?
?
!
YOU DON'T HAVE A PREHENSILE TAIL!
?
WHAT KIND OF INSULT IS THAT?
THOOOM!
STUPID DODGEBALL.
PREHENSILE TAIL!
CRAP STUPID
CRAP MONKEY.
1972 FINALS
FOREST EDGE COMETS
YOU'RE LOOKING AT MY CHICKEN LEGS, AREN'T YOU?
NO, MARTIN. I'M LOOKING FOR GO-GO. I HAVE TO DO MY ASSEMBLY SPEECH SOON, AND HE'S SUPPOSED TO BE THERE.
I DID LOOK AROUND FOR HIM, BUT I COULDN'T FIND HIM. I CAN GO LOOK SOME MORE...
NO, NO, HE'LL SHOW UP. I'M NOT WORRIED. HE'S INVUL... UMM... HE'LL BE OKAY.
OKAY! CLASS IS OVER! MURDER EACH OTHER SOMEWHERE ELSE!

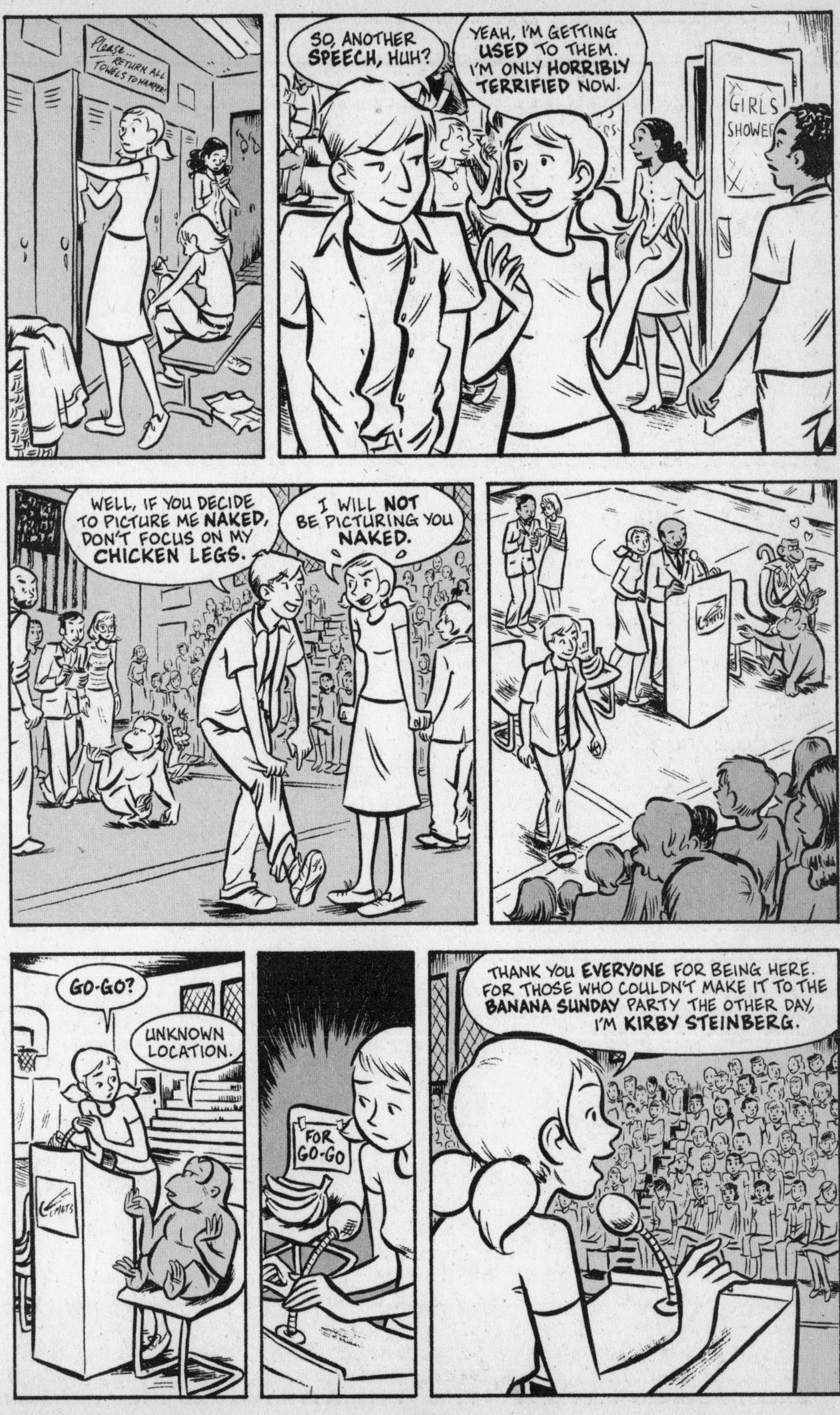
Please... RETURN ALL TOWELS TO HAMPER!
SO, ANOTHER SPEECH, HUH?
YEAH, I'M GETTING USED TO THEM. I'M ONLY HORRIBLY TERRIFIED NOW.
GIRLS SHOWE
WELL, IF YOU DECIDE TO PICTURE ME NAKED, DON'T FOCUS ON MY CHICKEN LEGS.
I WILL NOT BE PICTURING YOU NAKED.
GO-GO?
UNKNOWN LOCATION.
FOR GO-GO
THANK YOU EVERYONE FOR BEING HERE. FOR THOSE WHO COULDN'T MAKE IT TO THE BANANA SUNDAY PARTY THE OTHER DAY, I'M KIRBY STEINBERG.

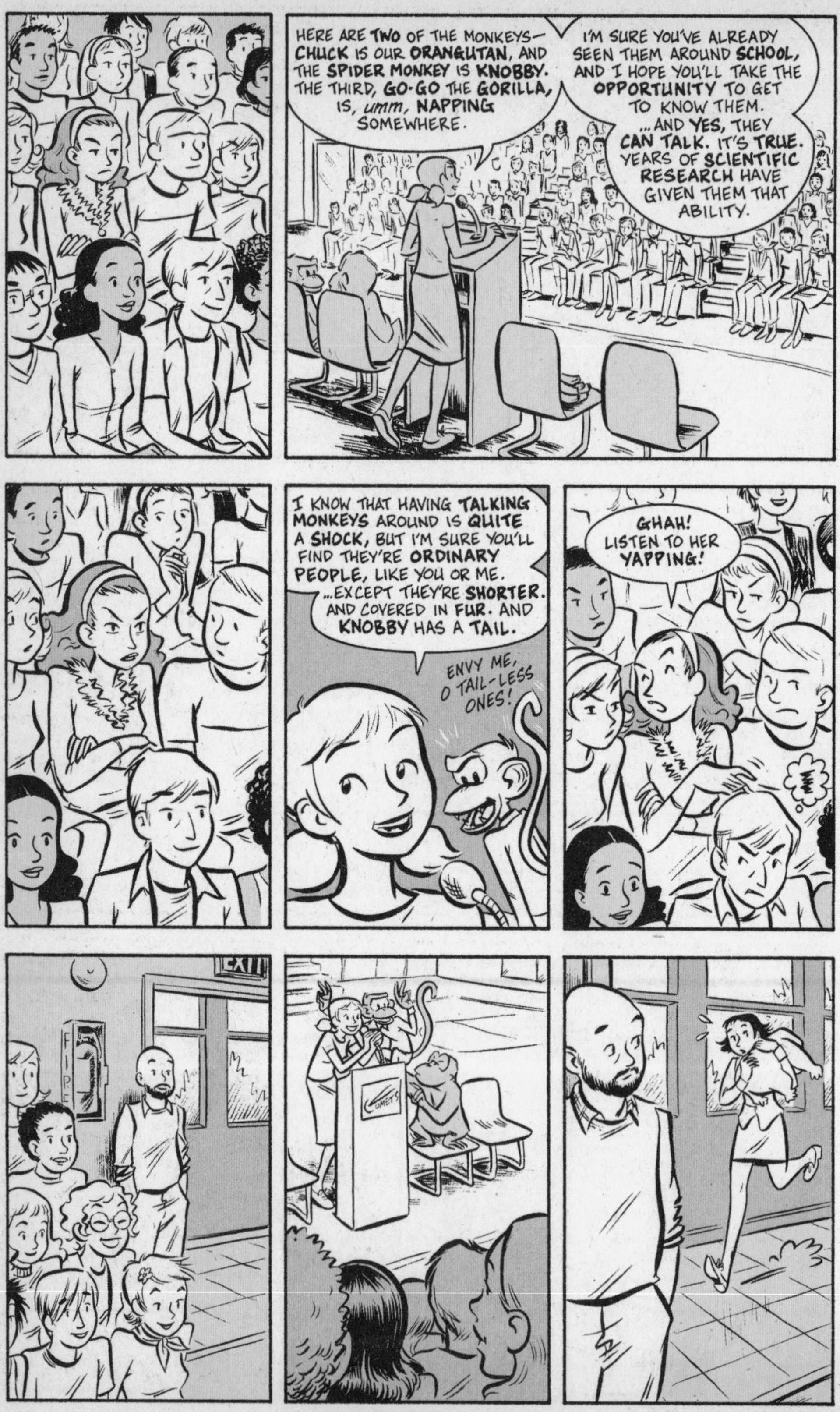
HERE ARE TWO OF THE MONKEYS— CHUCK IS OUR ORANGUTAN, AND THE SPIDER MONKEY IS KNOBBY. THE THIRD, GO-GO THE GORILLA, IS, *umm*, NAPPING SOMEWHERE.
I'M SURE YOU'VE ALREADY SEEN THEM AROUND SCHOOL, AND I HOPE YOU'LL TAKE THE OPPORTUNITY TO GET TO KNOW THEM.
...AND YES, THEY CAN TALK. IT'S TRUE. YEARS OF SCIENTIFIC RESEARCH HAVE GIVEN THEM THAT ABILITY.
I KNOW THAT HAVING TALKING MONKEYS AROUND IS QUITE A SHOCK, BUT I'M SURE YOU'LL FIND THEY'RE ORDINARY PEOPLE, LIKE YOU OR ME.
...EXCEPT THEY'RE SHORTER. AND COVERED IN FUR. AND KNOBBY HAS A TAIL.
ENVY ME, O TAIL-LESS ONES!
GHAH! LISTEN TO HER YAPPING!
EXIT

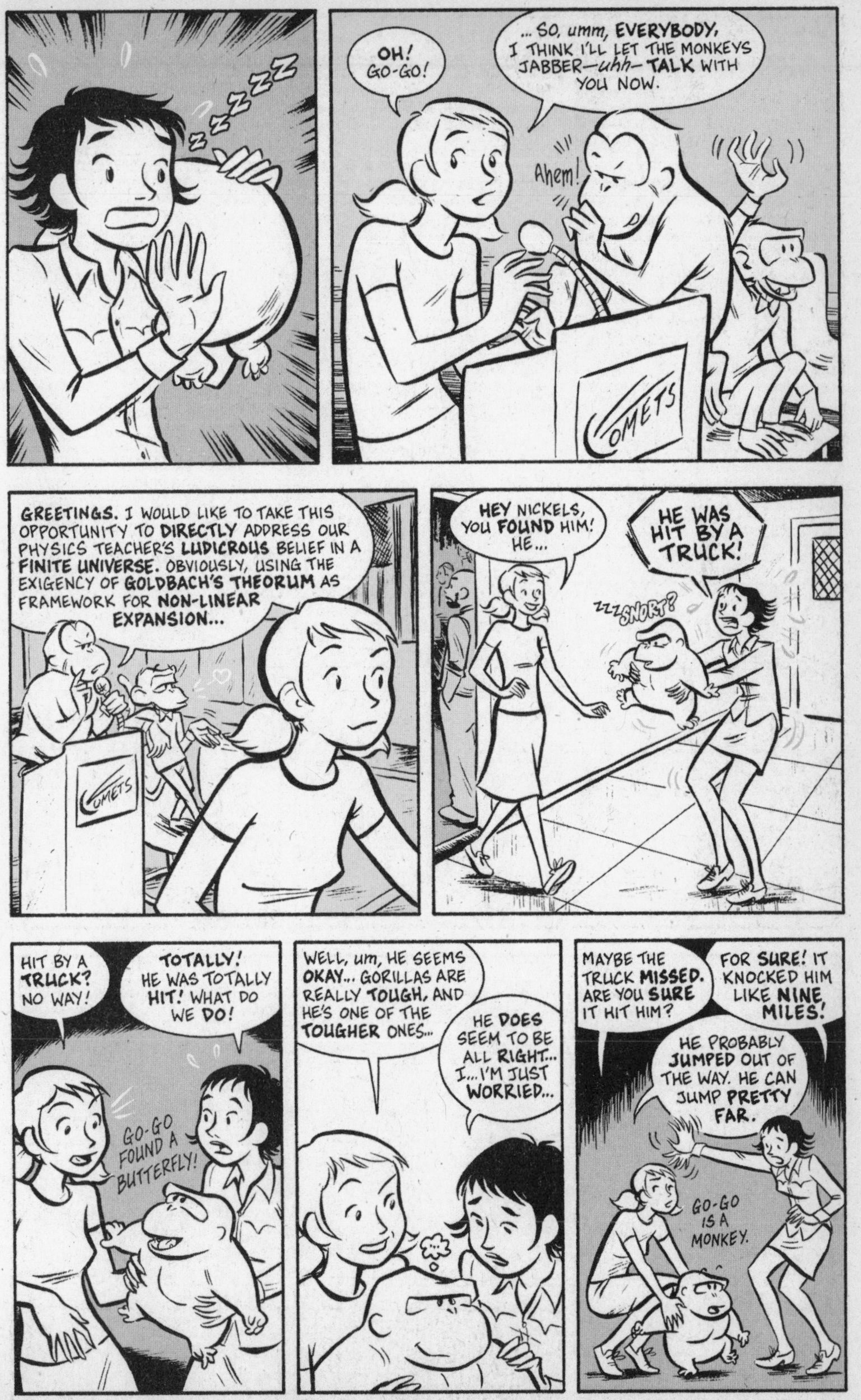
ZZZZZZ
OH! GO-GO!
... SO, umm, EVERYBODY, I THINK I'LL LET THE MONKEYS JABBER—uhh—TALK WITH YOU NOW.
Ahem!
COMETS
GREETINGS. I WOULD LIKE TO TAKE THIS OPPORTUNITY TO DIRECTLY ADDRESS OUR PHYSICS TEACHER'S LUDICROUS BELIEF IN A FINITE UNIVERSE. OBVIOUSLY, USING THE EXIGENCY OF GOLDBACH'S THEORUM AS FRAMEWORK FOR NON-LINEAR EXPANSION...
COMETS
HEY NICKELS, YOU FOUND HIM! HE...
HE WAS HIT BY A TRUCK!
ZZZSNORT?
HIT BY A TRUCK? NO WAY!
TOTALLY! HE WAS TOTALLY HIT! WHAT DO WE DO!
GO-GO FOUND A BUTTERFLY!
WELL, um, HE SEEMS OKAY... GORILLAS ARE REALLY TOUGH, AND HE'S ONE OF THE TOUGHER ONES...
HE DOES SEEM TO BE ALL RIGHT... I...I'M JUST WORRIED...
MAYBE THE TRUCK MISSED. ARE YOU SURE IT HIT HIM?
FOR SURE! IT KNOCKED HIM LIKE NINE MILES!
HE PROBABLY JUMPED OUT OF THE WAY. HE CAN JUMP PRETTY FAR.
GO-GO IS A MONKEY.

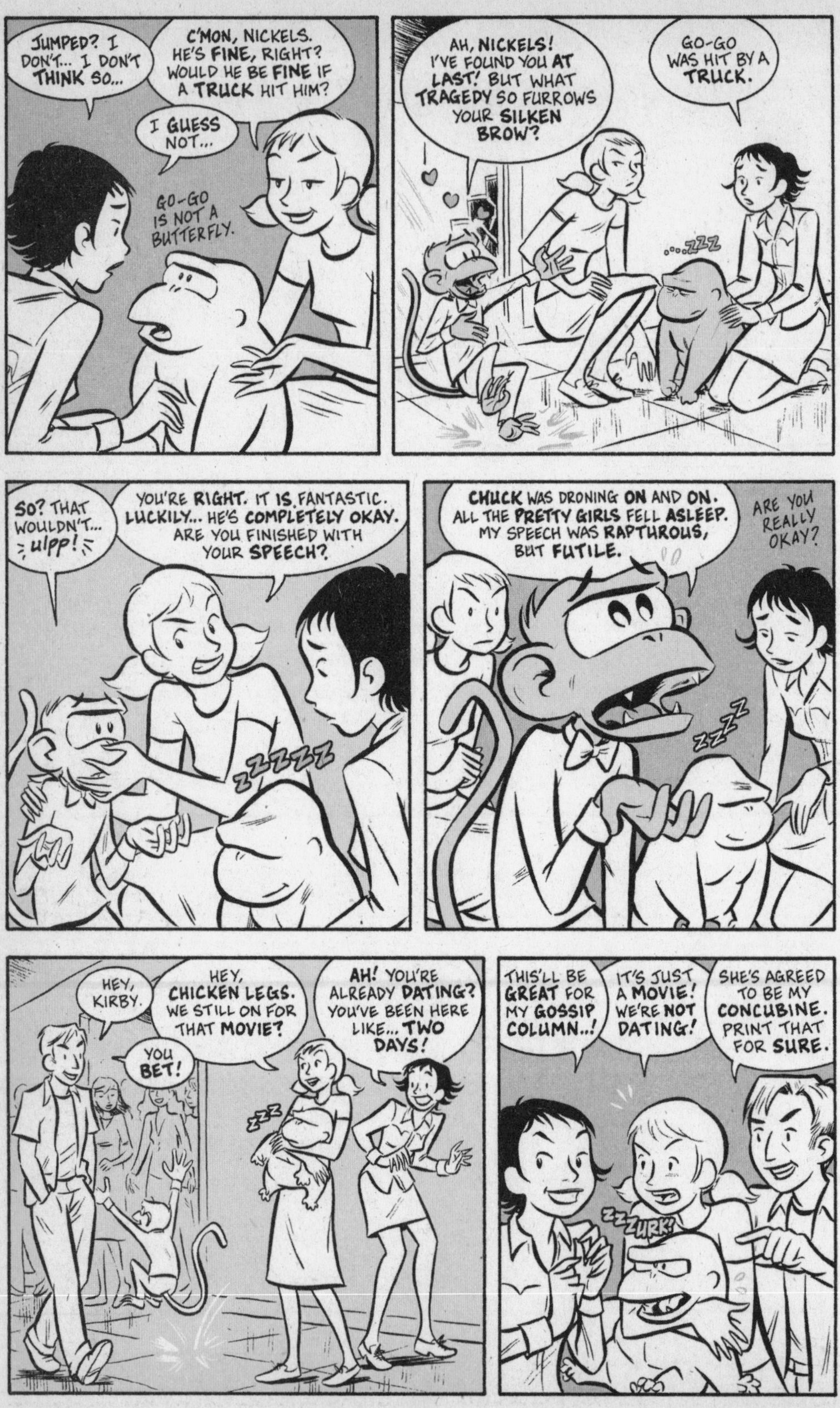
JUMPED? I DON'T... I DON'T THINK SO...
C'MON, NICKELS. HE'S FINE, RIGHT? WOULD HE BE FINE IF A TRUCK HIT HIM?
I GUESS NOT...
GO-GO IS NOT A BUTTERFLY.
AH, NICKELS! I'VE FOUND YOU AT LAST! BUT WHAT TRAGEDY SO FURROWS YOUR SILKEN BROW?
GO-GO WAS HIT BY A TRUCK.
...ZZZ
SO? THAT WOULDN'T... ULPP!
YOU'RE RIGHT. IT IS FANTASTIC. LUCKILY... HE'S COMPLETELY OKAY. ARE YOU FINISHED WITH YOUR SPEECH?
ZZZZZ
CHUCK WAS DRONING ON AND ON. ALL THE PRETTY GIRLS FELL ASLEEP. MY SPEECH WAS RAPTUROUS, BUT FUTILE.
ARE YOU REALLY OKAY?
ZZZZ
HEY, KIRBY.
HEY, CHICKEN LEGS. WE STILL ON FOR THAT MOVIE?
YOU BET!
AH! YOU'RE ALREADY DATING? YOU'VE BEEN HERE LIKE... TWO DAYS!
ZZZ
THIS'LL BE GREAT FOR MY GOSSIP COLUMN..!
IT'S JUST A MOVIE! WE'RE NOT DATING!
SHE'S AGREED TO BE MY CONCUBINE. PRINT THAT FOR SURE.
ZZZURK!

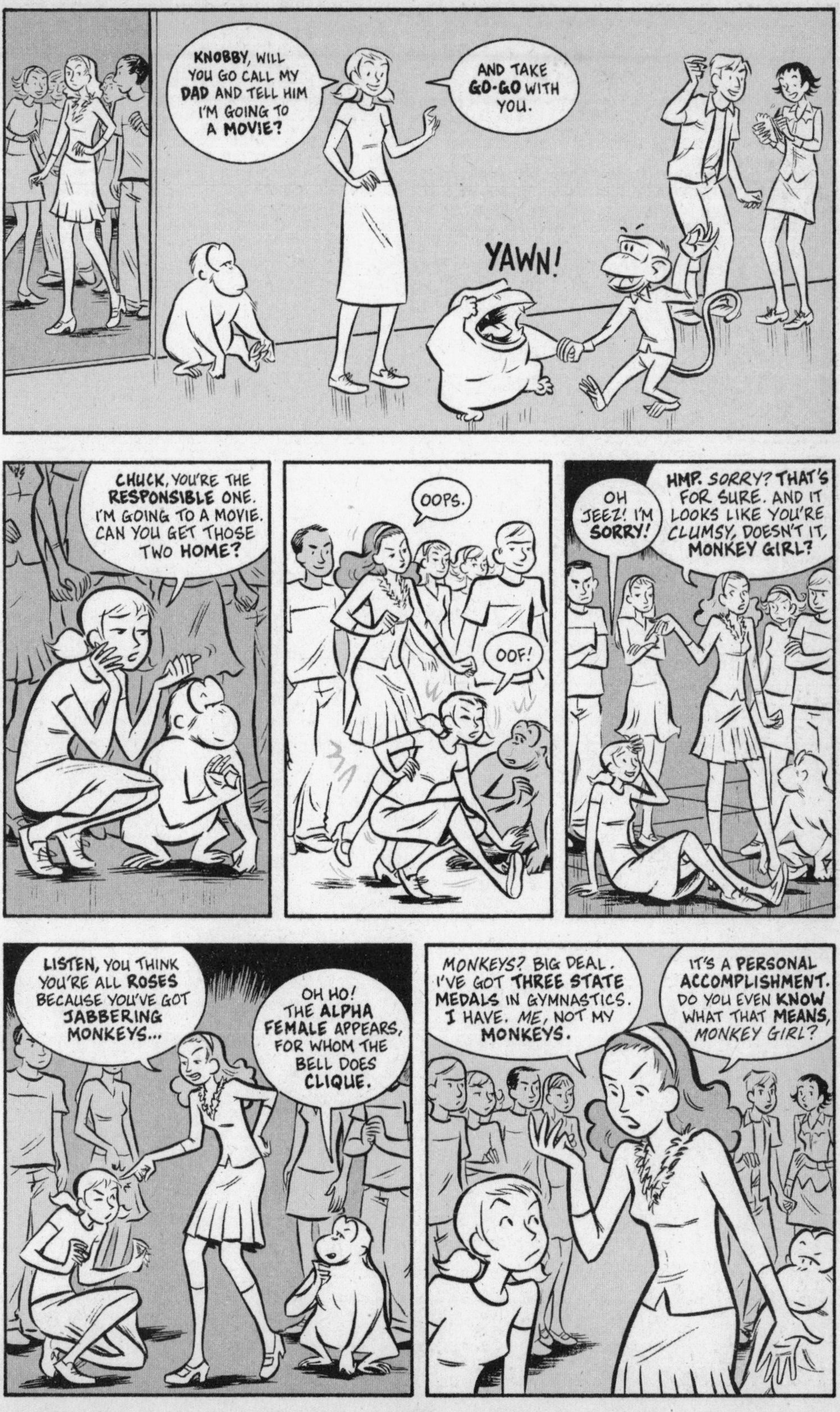
KNOBBY, WILL YOU GO CALL MY DAD AND TELL HIM I'M GOING TO A MOVIE?
AND TAKE GO-GO WITH YOU.
YAWN!
CHUCK, YOU'RE THE RESPONSIBLE ONE. I'M GOING TO A MOVIE. CAN YOU GET THOSE TWO HOME?
OOPS.
OOF!
OH JEEZ! I'M SORRY!
HMP. SORRY? THAT'S FOR SURE. AND IT LOOKS LIKE YOU'RE CLUMSY, DOESN'T IT, MONKEY GIRL?
LISTEN, YOU THINK YOU'RE ALL ROSES BECAUSE YOU'VE GOT JABBERING MONKEYS...
OH HO! THE ALPHA FEMALE APPEARS, FOR WHOM THE BELL DOES CLIQUE.
MONKEYS? BIG DEAL. I'VE GOT THREE STATE MEDALS IN GYMNASTICS. I HAVE. ME, NOT MY MONKEYS.
IT'S A PERSONAL ACCOMPLISHMENT. DO YOU EVEN KNOW WHAT THAT MEANS, MONKEY GIRL?

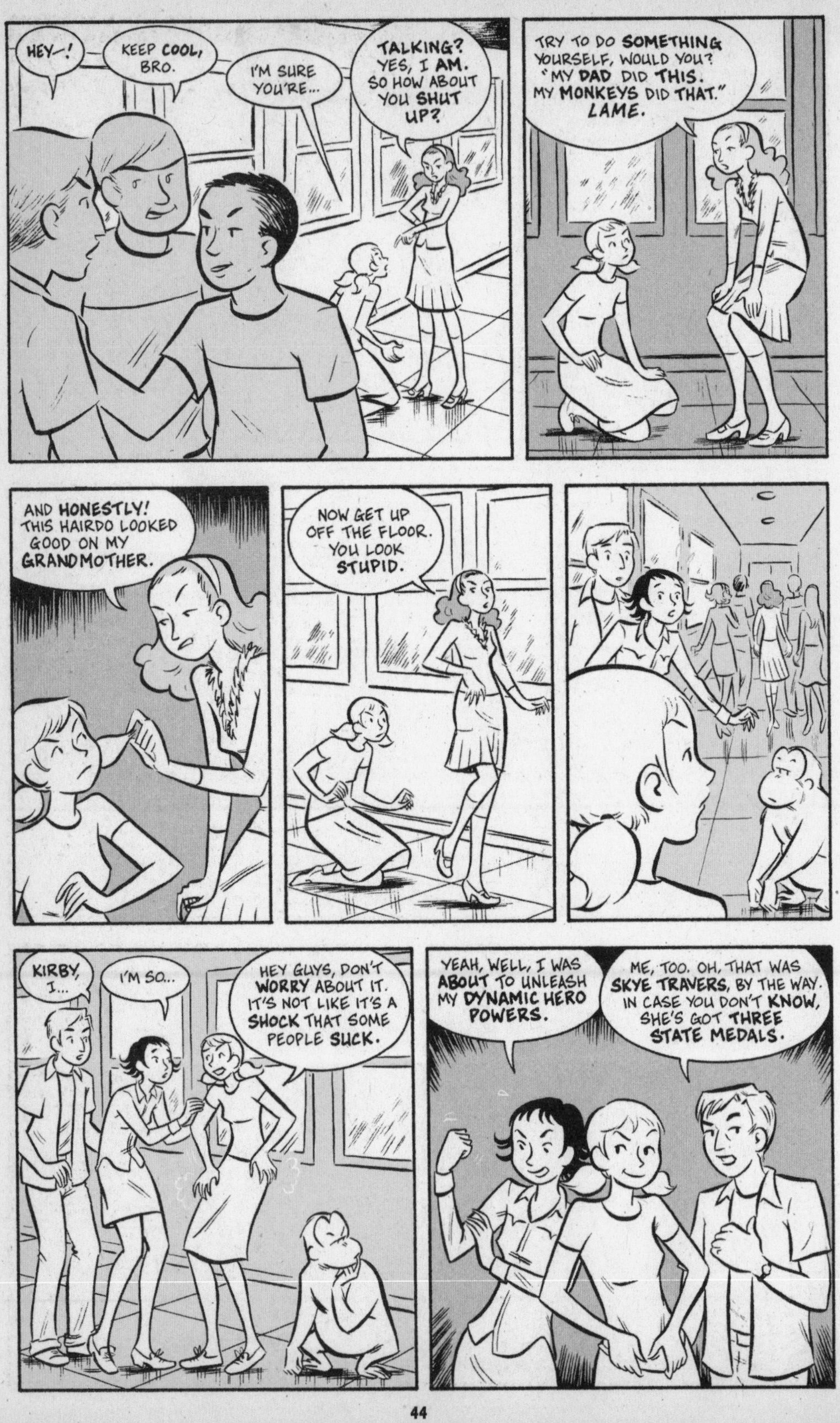
HEY—!
KEEP COOL, BRO.
I'M SURE YOU'RE...
TALKING? YES, I AM. SO HOW ABOUT YOU SHUT UP?
TRY TO DO SOMETHING YOURSELF, WOULD YOU? "MY DAD DID THIS. MY MONKEYS DID THAT." LAME.
AND HONESTLY! THIS HAIRDO LOOKED GOOD ON MY GRANDMOTHER.
NOW GET UP OFF THE FLOOR. YOU LOOK STUPID.
KIRBY, I...
I'M SO...
HEY GUYS, DON'T WORRY ABOUT IT. IT'S NOT LIKE IT'S A SHOCK THAT SOME PEOPLE SUCK.
YEAH, WELL, I WAS ABOUT TO UNLEASH MY DYNAMIC HERO POWERS.
ME, TOO. OH, THAT WAS SKYE TRAVERS, BY THE WAY. IN CASE YOU DON'T KNOW, SHE'S GOT THREE STATE MEDALS.

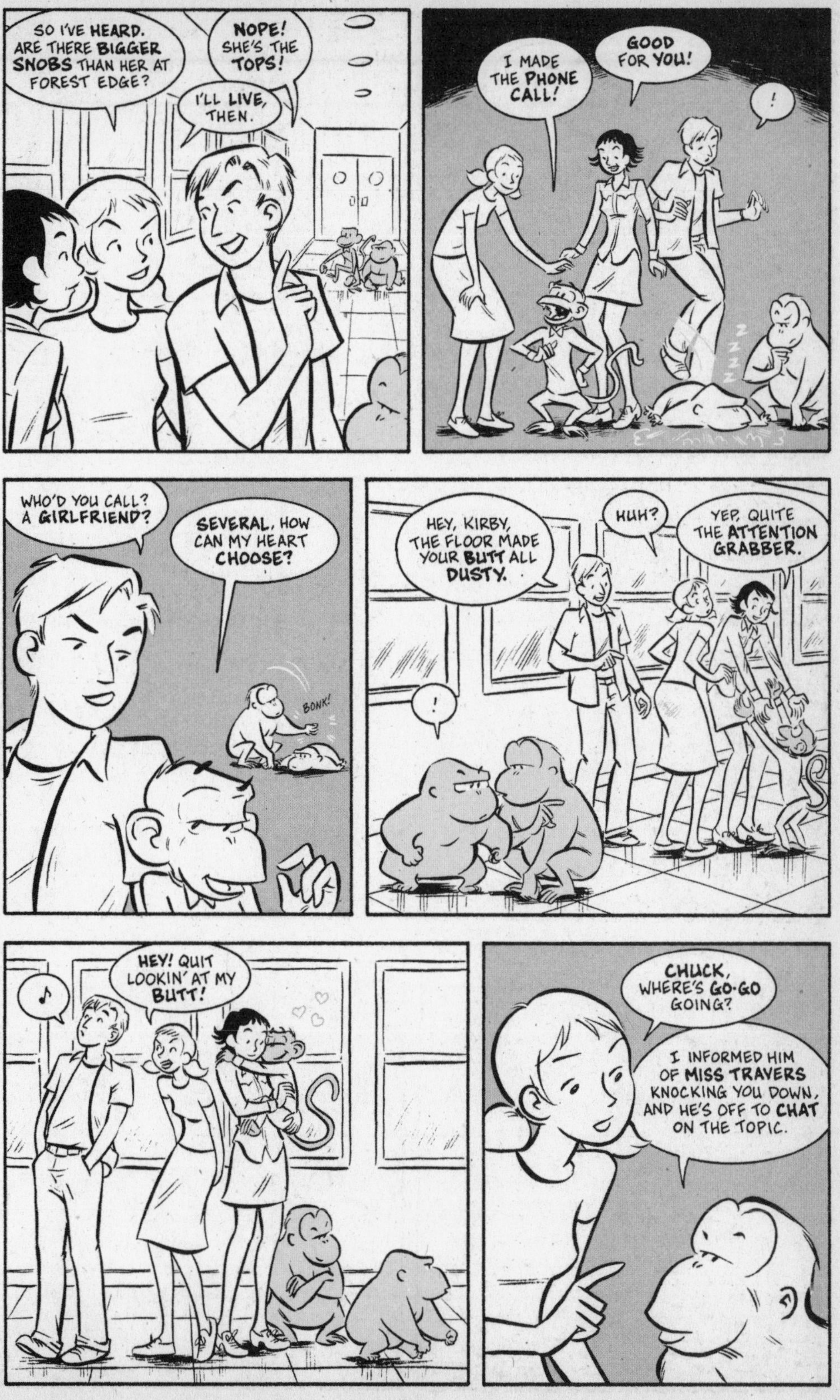
SO I'VE HEARD. ARE THERE BIGGER SNOBS THAN HER AT FOREST EDGE?
NOPE! SHE'S THE TOPS!
I'LL LIVE, THEN.
I MADE THE PHONE CALL!
GOOD FOR YOU!
!
WHO'D YOU CALL? A GIRLFRIEND?
SEVERAL. HOW CAN MY HEART CHOOSE?
BONK!
HEY, KIRBY, THE FLOOR MADE YOUR BUTT ALL DUSTY.
HUH?
YEP, QUITE THE ATTENTION GRABBER.
!
♪
HEY! QUIT LOOKIN' AT MY BUTT!
CHUCK, WHERE'S GO-GO GOING?
I INFORMED HIM OF MISS TRAVERS KNOCKING YOU DOWN, AND HE'S OFF TO CHAT ON THE TOPIC.

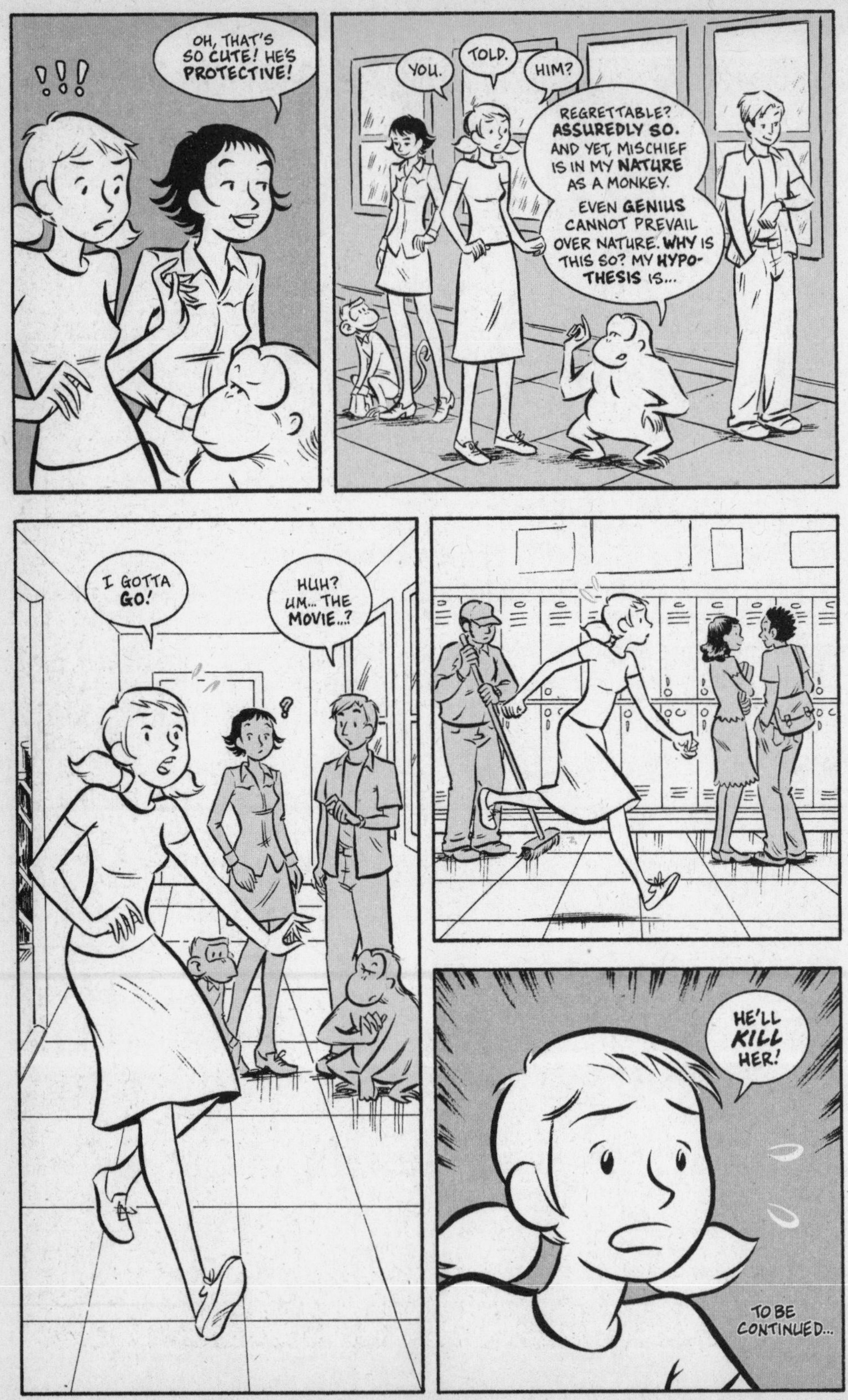
!!!
OH, THAT'S SO CUTE! HE'S PROTECTIVE!
YOU.
TOLD.
HIM?
REGRETTABLE? ASSUREDLY SO. AND YET, MISCHIEF IS IN MY NATURE AS A MONKEY.
EVEN GENIUS CANNOT PREVAIL OVER NATURE. WHY IS THIS SO? MY HYPOTHESIS IS...
I GOTTA GO!
HUH? UM... THE MOVIE...?
?
HE'LL KILL HER!
TO BE CONTINUED...

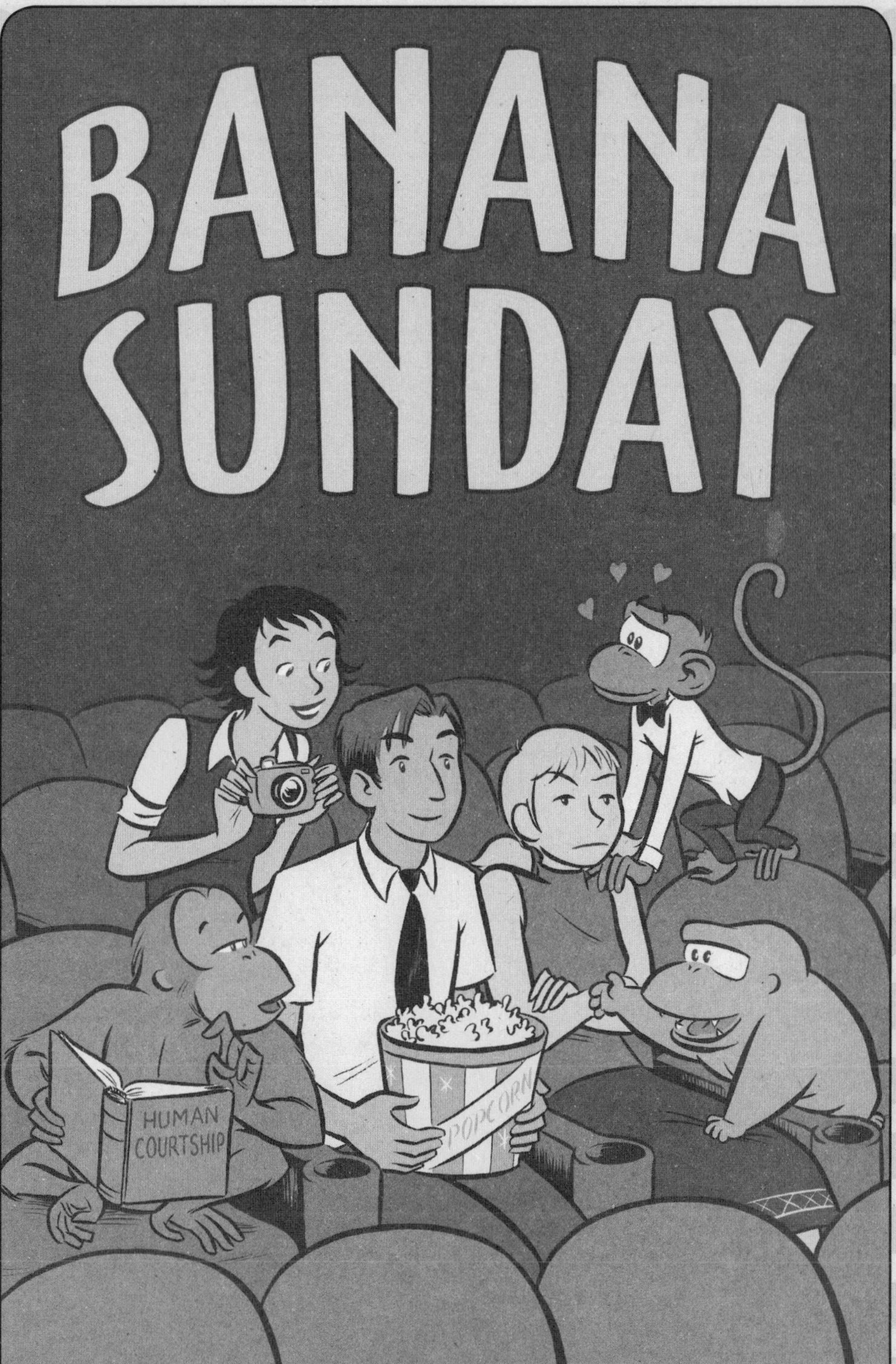
BANANA SUNDAY
HUMAN COURTSHIP
POPCORN

three

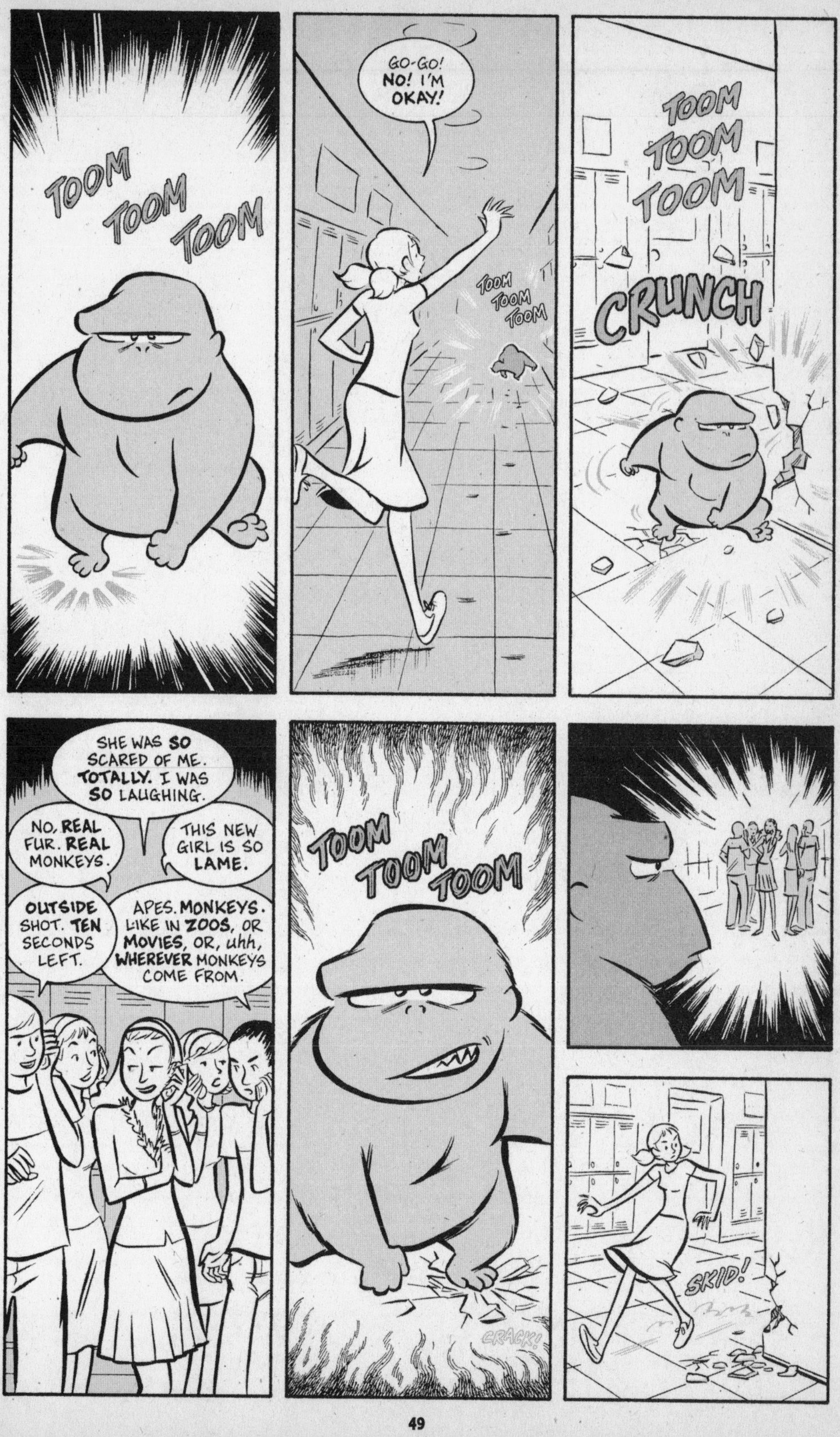
TOOM TOOM TOOM
GO-GO! NO! I'M OKAY!
TOOM TOOM TOOM
TOOM TOOM TOOM
CRUNCH
SHE WAS SO SCARED OF ME. TOTALLY. I WAS SO LAUGHING.
NO, REAL FUR. REAL MONKEYS.
THIS NEW GIRL IS SO LAME.
OUTSIDE SHOT. TEN SECONDS LEFT.
APES. MONKEYS. LIKE IN ZOOS, OR MOVIES, OR, uhh, WHEREVER MONKEYS COME FROM.
TOOM TOOM TOOM
CRACK!
SKID!

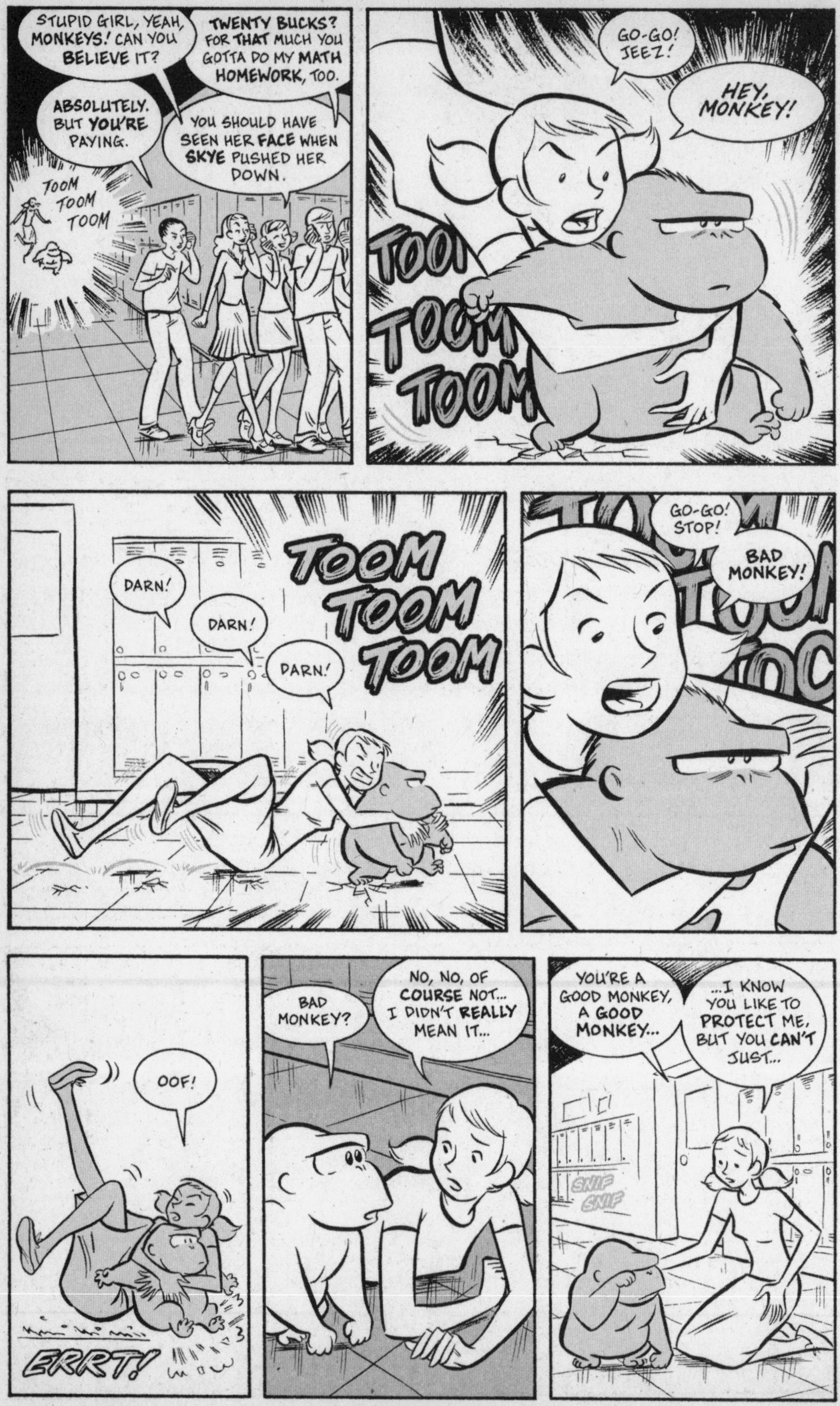
STUPID GIRL, YEAH, MONKEYS! CAN YOU BELIEVE IT?
TWENTY BUCKS? FOR THAT MUCH YOU GOTTA DO MY MATH HOMEWORK, TOO.
ABSOLUTELY. BUT YOU'RE PAYING.
YOU SHOULD HAVE SEEN HER FACE WHEN SKYE PUSHED HER DOWN.
TOOM TOOM TOOM
GO-GO! JEEZ!
HEY, MONKEY!
TOOM TOOM TOOM
DARN!
DARN!
DARN!
TOOM TOOM TOOM
GO-GO! STOP!
BAD MONKEY!
OOF!
ERRT!
BAD MONKEY?
NO, NO, OF COURSE NOT... I DIDN'T REALLY MEAN IT...
YOU'RE A GOOD MONKEY, A GOOD MONKEY...
...I KNOW YOU LIKE TO PROTECT ME, BUT YOU CAN'T JUST...
SNIF SNIF

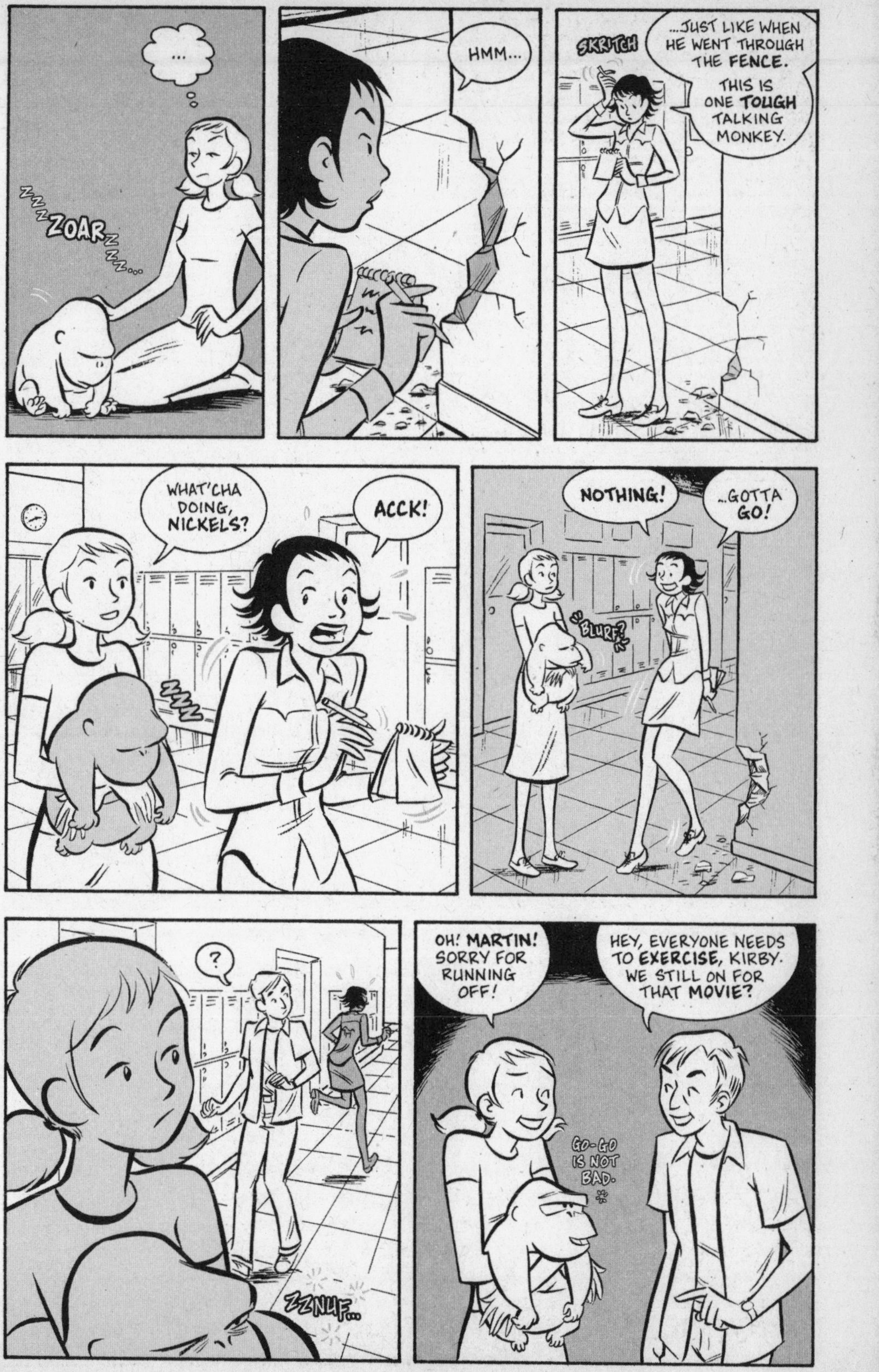
...
ZZZZOARZZZZ...
HMM...
SKRITCH
...JUST LIKE WHEN HE WENT THROUGH THE FENCE.
THIS IS ONE TOUGH TALKING MONKEY.
WHAT'CHA DOING, NICKELS?
ACCK!
ZZZ
NOTHING!
..GOTTA GO!
BLURF?
?
ZZNUF...
OH! MARTIN! SORRY FOR RUNNING OFF!
HEY, EVERYONE NEEDS TO EXERCISE, KIRBY. WE STILL ON FOR THAT MOVIE?
GO-GO IS NOT BAD.

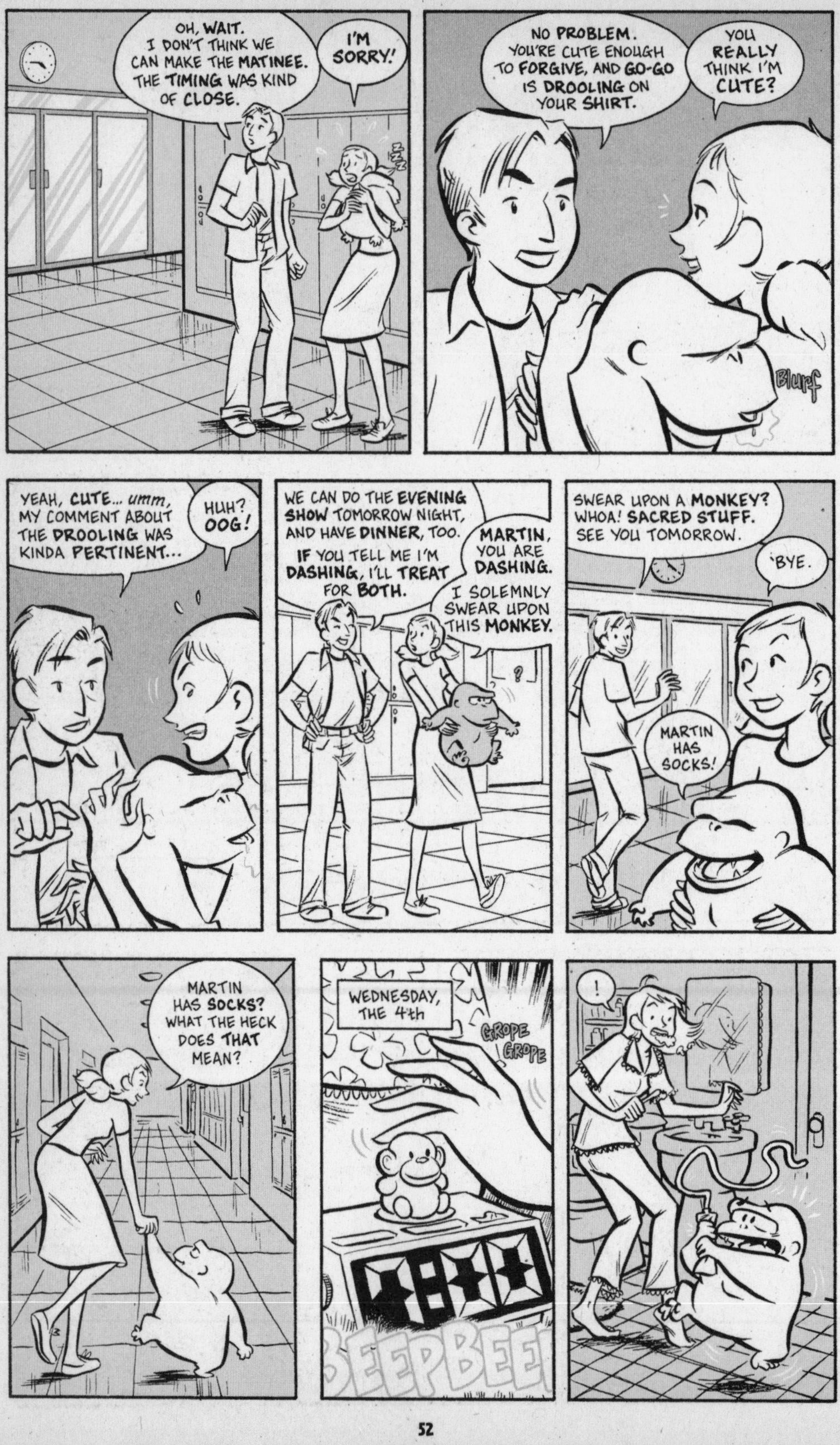
OH, WAIT. I DON'T THINK WE CAN MAKE THE MATINEE. THE TIMING WAS KIND OF CLOSE.
I'M SORRY!
NO PROBLEM. YOU'RE CUTE ENOUGH TO FORGIVE, AND GO-GO IS DROOLING ON YOUR SHIRT.
YOU REALLY THINK I'M CUTE?
Blurf
YEAH, CUTE... umm, MY COMMENT ABOUT THE DROOLING WAS KINDA PERTINENT...
HUH? OOG!
WE CAN DO THE EVENING SHOW TOMORROW NIGHT, AND HAVE DINNER, TOO.
IF YOU TELL ME I'M DASHING, I'LL TREAT FOR BOTH.
MARTIN, YOU ARE DASHING.
I SOLEMNLY SWEAR UPON THIS MONKEY.
?
SWEAR UPON A MONKEY? WHOA! SACRED STUFF. SEE YOU TOMORROW.
'BYE.
MARTIN HAS SOCKS!
MARTIN HAS SOCKS? WHAT THE HECK DOES THAT MEAN?
WEDNESDAY, THE 4th
GROPE GROPE
BEEPBEEP
!

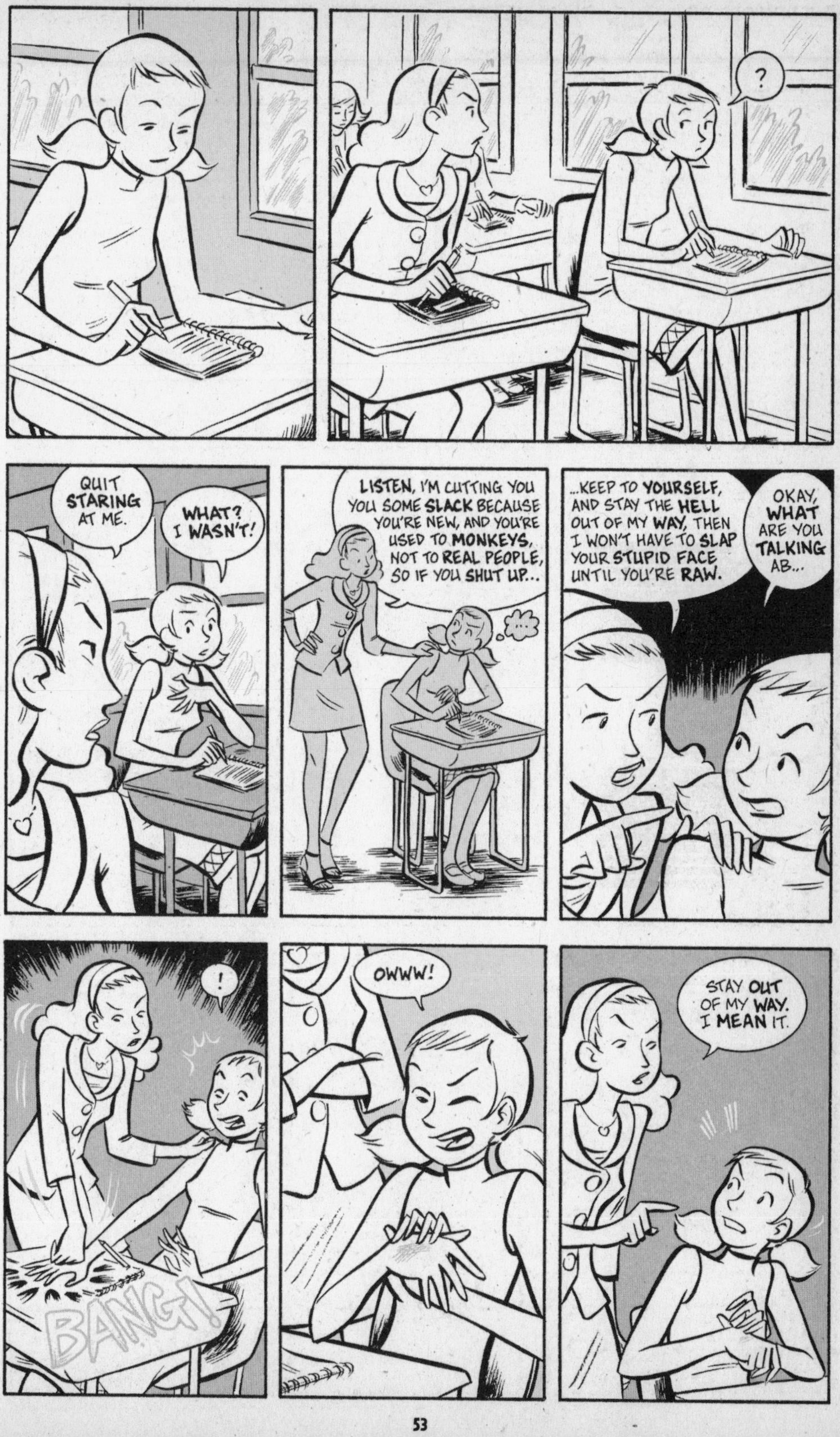
?
QUIT STARING AT ME.
WHAT? I WASN'T!
LISTEN, I'M CUTTING YOU YOU SOME SLACK BECAUSE YOU'RE NEW, AND YOU'RE USED TO MONKEYS, NOT TO REAL PEOPLE, SO IF YOU SHUT UP...
...
...KEEP TO YOURSELF, AND STAY THE HELL OUT OF MY WAY, THEN I WON'T HAVE TO SLAP YOUR STUPID FACE UNTIL YOU'RE RAW.
OKAY, WHAT ARE YOU TALKING AB...
!
BANG!
OWWW!
STAY OUT OF MY WAY. I MEAN IT.

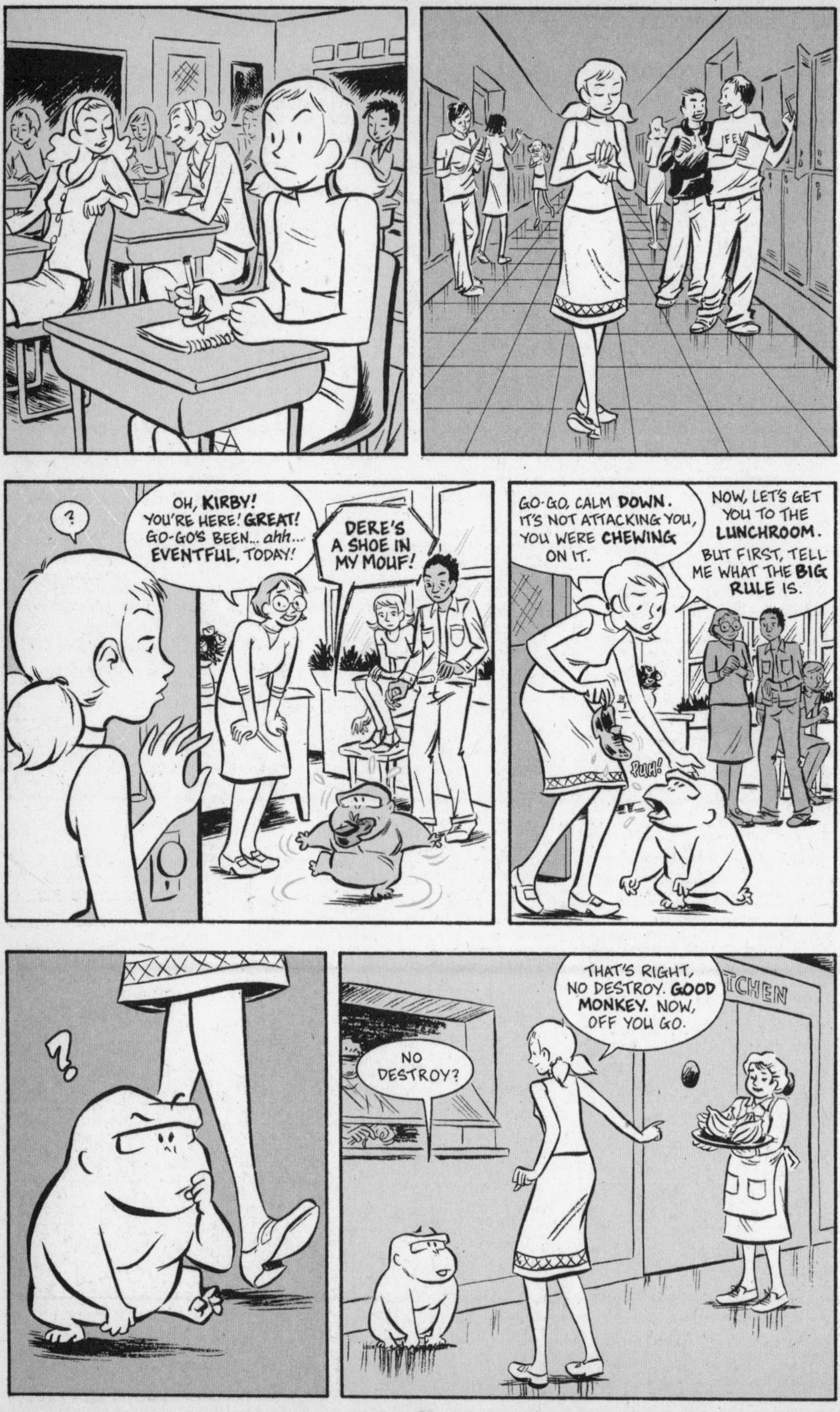
?
OH, KIRBY! YOU'RE HERE! GREAT! GO-GO'S BEEN... ahh... EVENTFUL, TODAY!
DERE'S A SHOE IN MY MOUF!
GO-GO, CALM DOWN. IT'S NOT ATTACKING YOU, YOU WERE CHEWING ON IT.
NOW, LET'S GET YOU TO THE LUNCHROOM.
BUT FIRST, TELL ME WHAT THE BIG RULE IS.
PUH!
?
NO DESTROY?
THAT'S RIGHT, NO DESTROY. GOOD MONKEY. NOW, OFF YOU GO.

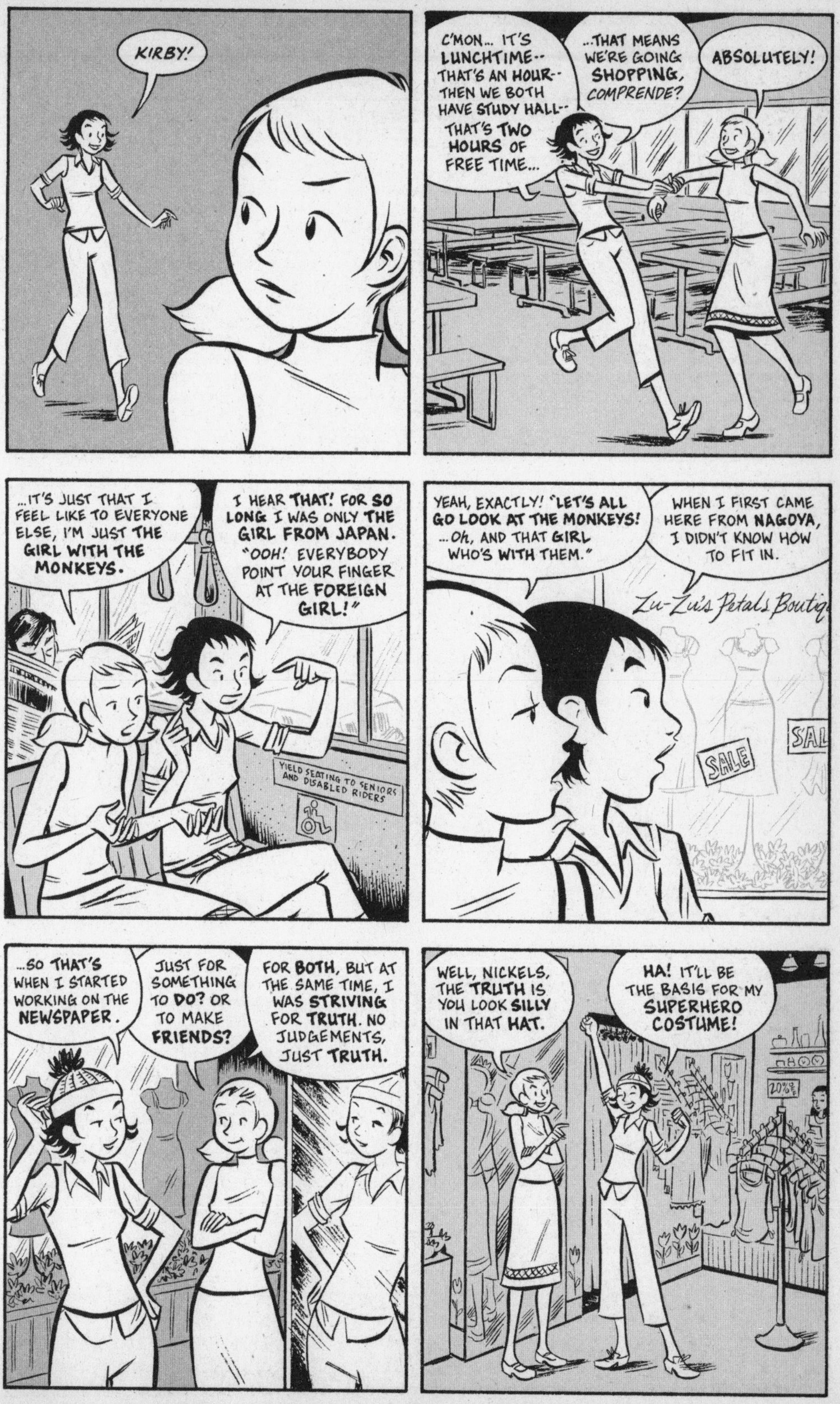
KIRBY!
C'MON... IT'S LUNCHTIME-- THAT'S AN HOUR-- THEN WE BOTH HAVE STUDY HALL-- THAT'S TWO HOURS OF FREE TIME...
...THAT MEANS WE'RE GOING SHOPPING, COMPRENDE?
ABSOLUTELY!
...IT'S JUST THAT I FEEL LIKE TO EVERYONE ELSE, I'M JUST THE GIRL WITH THE MONKEYS.
I HEAR THAT! FOR SO LONG I WAS ONLY THE GIRL FROM JAPAN. "OOH! EVERYBODY POINT YOUR FINGER AT THE FOREIGN GIRL!"
YIELD SEATING TO SENIORS AND DISABLED RIDERS
YEAH, EXACTLY! "LET'S ALL GO LOOK AT THE MONKEYS! ...Oh, AND THAT GIRL WHO'S WITH THEM."
WHEN I FIRST CAME HERE FROM NAGOYA, I DIDN'T KNOW HOW TO FIT IN.
Zu-Zu's Petals Boutiq
SALE
SAL
...SO THAT'S WHEN I STARTED WORKING ON THE NEWSPAPER.
JUST FOR SOMETHING TO DO? OR TO MAKE FRIENDS?
FOR BOTH, BUT AT THE SAME TIME, I WAS STRIVING FOR TRUTH. NO JUDGEMENTS, JUST TRUTH.
WELL, NICKELS, THE TRUTH IS YOU LOOK SILLY IN THAT HAT.
HA! IT'LL BE THE BASIS FOR MY SUPERHERO COSTUME!

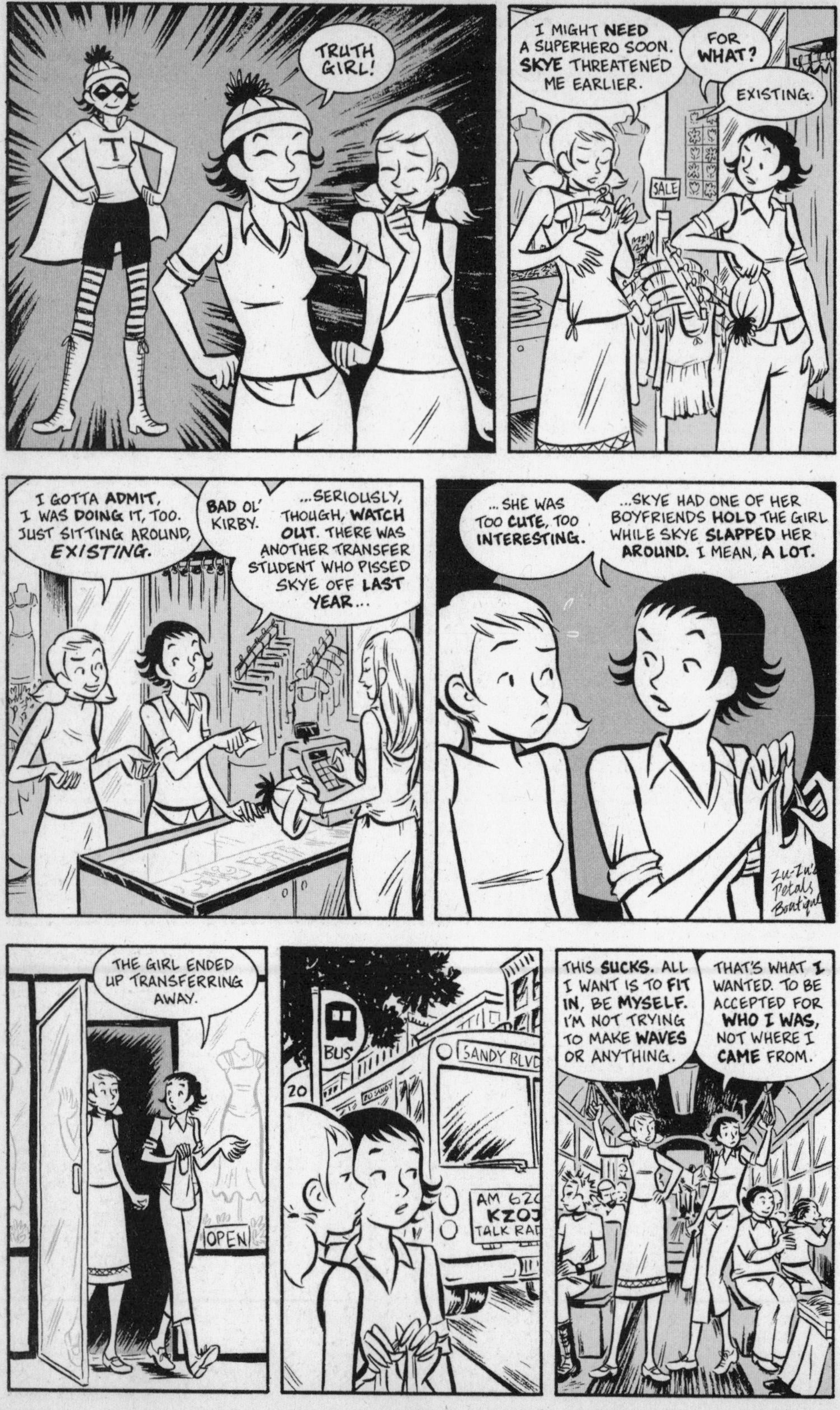
TRUTH GIRL!
I MIGHT NEED A SUPERHERO SOON. SKYE THREATENED ME EARLIER.
FOR WHAT?
EXISTING.
SALE
I GOTTA ADMIT, I WAS DOING IT, TOO. JUST SITTING AROUND, EXISTING.
BAD OL' KIRBY.
...SERIOUSLY, THOUGH, WATCH OUT. THERE WAS ANOTHER TRANSFER STUDENT WHO PISSED SKYE OFF LAST YEAR...
...SHE WAS TOO CUTE, TOO INTERESTING.
...SKYE HAD ONE OF HER BOYFRIENDS HOLD THE GIRL WHILE SKYE SLAPPED HER AROUND. I MEAN, A LOT.
Zu-Zu's Petals Boutique
THE GIRL ENDED UP TRANSFERRING AWAY.
OPEN
BUS
20
SANDY BLVD
AM 620 KZOJ TALK RAD
THIS SUCKS. ALL I WANT IS TO FIT IN, BE MYSELF. I'M NOT TRYING TO MAKE WAVES OR ANYTHING.
THAT'S WHAT I WANTED. TO BE ACCEPTED FOR WHO I WAS, NOT WHERE I CAME FROM.

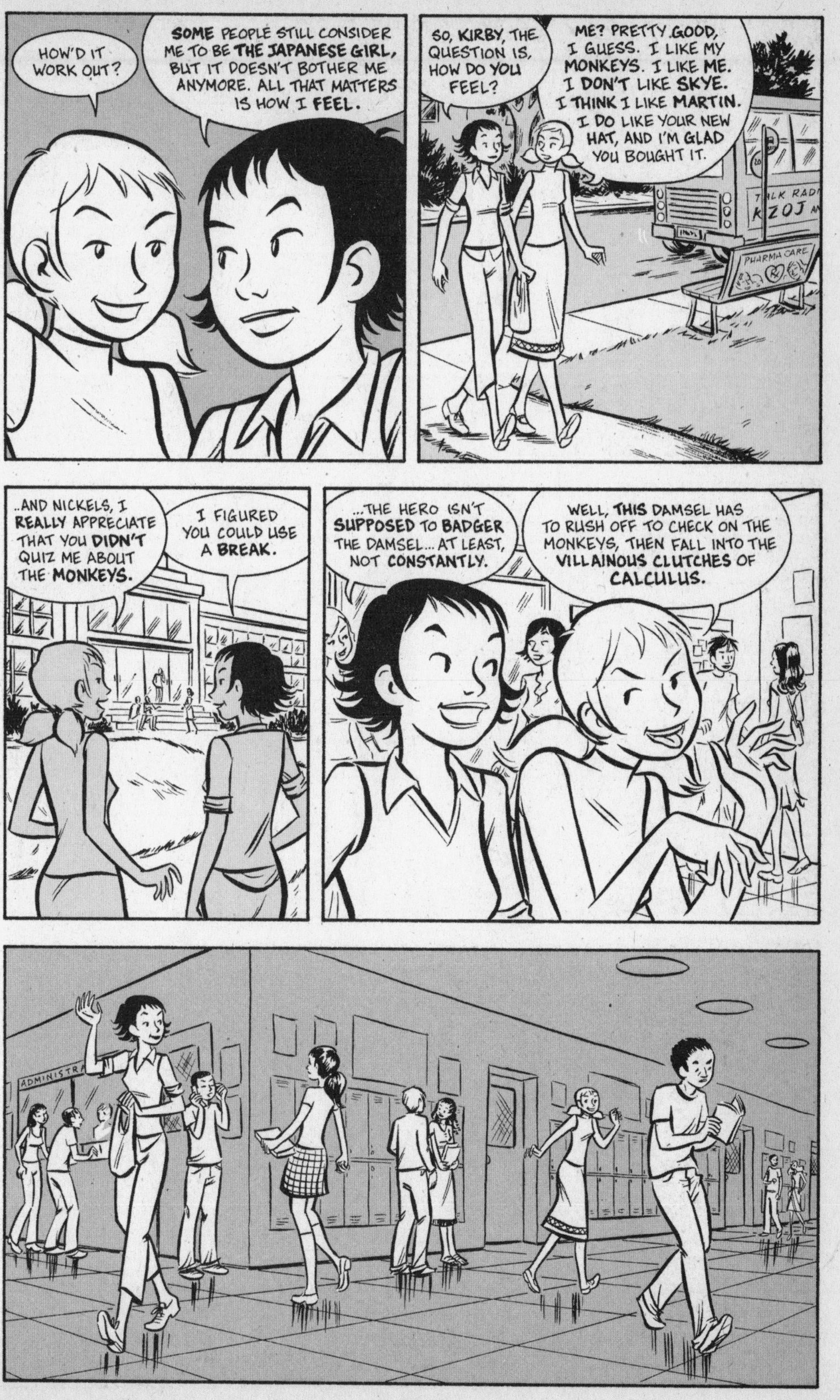

HOW'D IT WORK OUT?
SOME PEOPLE STILL CONSIDER ME TO BE THE JAPANESE GIRL, BUT IT DOESN'T BOTHER ME ANYMORE. ALL THAT MATTERS IS HOW I FEEL.
SO, KIRBY, THE QUESTION IS, HOW DO YOU FEEL?
ME? PRETTY GOOD, I GUESS. I LIKE MY MONKEYS. I LIKE ME. I DON'T LIKE SKYE. I THINK I LIKE MARTIN. I DO LIKE YOUR NEW HAT, AND I'M GLAD YOU BOUGHT IT.
PHARMA CARE
..AND NICKELS, I REALLY APPRECIATE THAT YOU DIDN'T QUIZ ME ABOUT THE MONKEYS.
I FIGURED YOU COULD USE A BREAK.
...THE HERO ISN'T SUPPOSED TO BADGER THE DAMSEL... AT LEAST, NOT CONSTANTLY.
WELL, THIS DAMSEL HAS TO RUSH OFF TO CHECK ON THE MONKEYS, THEN FALL INTO THE VILLAINOUS CLUTCHES OF CALCULUS.

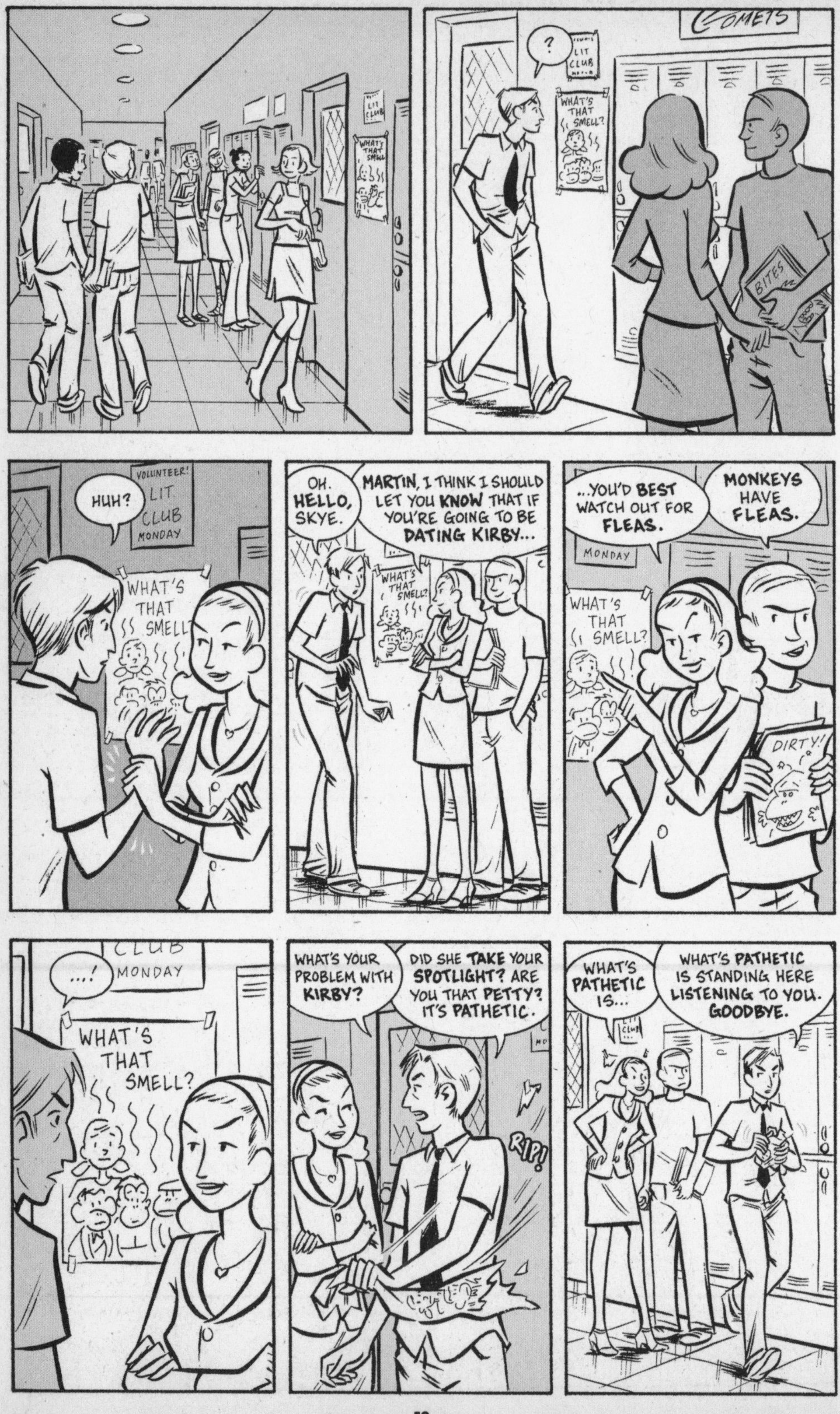

LIT CLUB
WHAT'S THAT SMELL
COMETS
?
LIT CLUB
WHAT'S THAT SMELL?
BITES
VOLUNTEER! LIT CLUB MONDAY
HUH?
WHAT'S THAT SMELL
OH. HELLO, SKYE.
MARTIN, I THINK I SHOULD LET YOU KNOW THAT IF YOU'RE GOING TO BE DATING KIRBY...
WHAT'S THAT SMELL?
...YOU'D BEST WATCH OUT FOR FLEAS.
MONKEYS HAVE FLEAS.
MONDAY
WHAT'S THAT SMELL?
DIRTY!
CLUB MONDAY
...!
WHAT'S THAT SMELL?
WHAT'S YOUR PROBLEM WITH KIRBY?
DID SHE TAKE YOUR SPOTLIGHT? ARE YOU THAT PETTY? IT'S PATHETIC.
RIP!
WHAT'S PATHETIC IS...
WHAT'S PATHETIC IS STANDING HERE LISTENING TO YOU. GOODBYE.

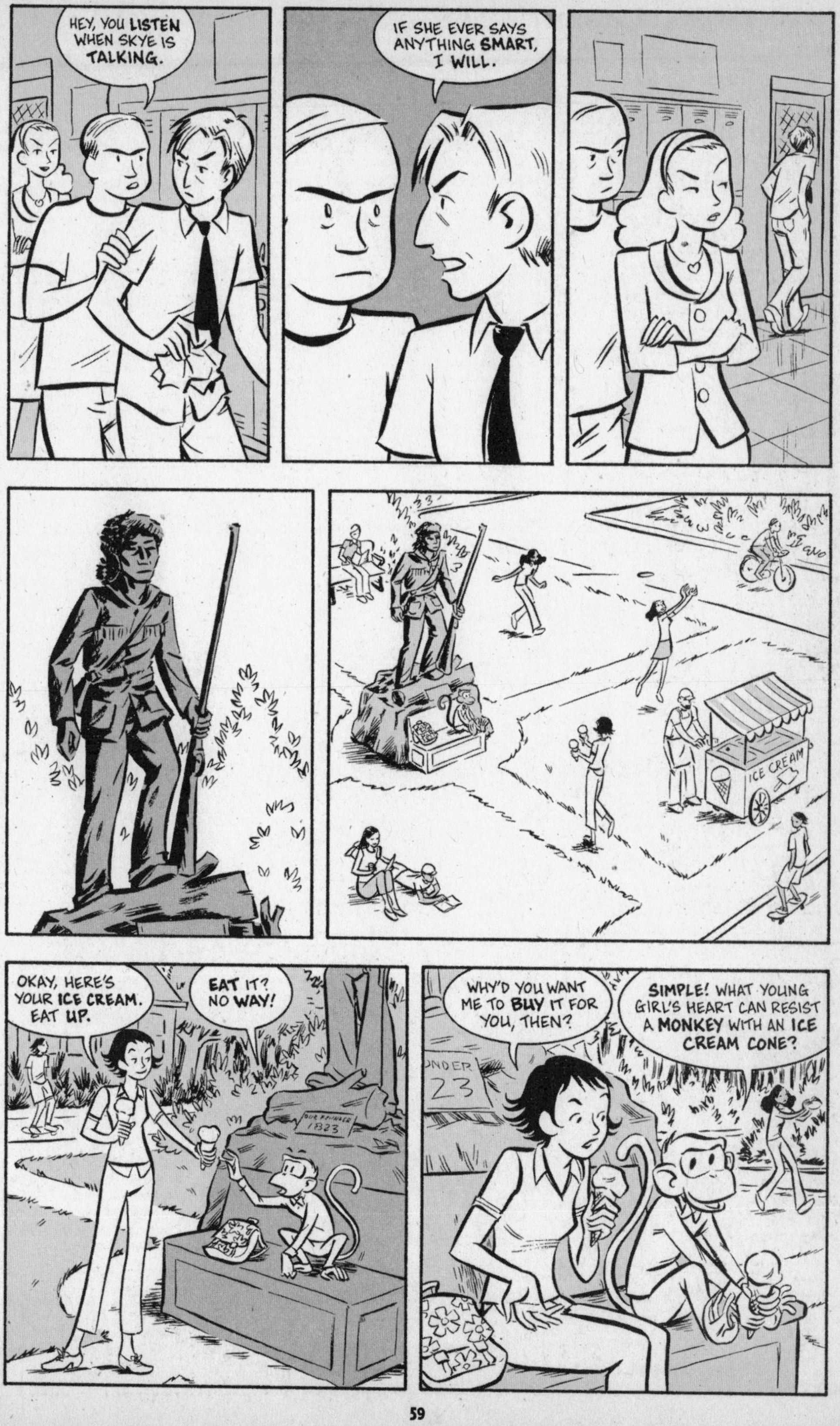
HEY, YOU LISTEN WHEN SKYE IS TALKING.
IF SHE EVER SAYS ANYTHING SMART, I WILL.
ICE CREAM
OKAY, HERE'S YOUR ICE CREAM. EAT UP.
EAT IT? NO WAY!
OUR FOUNDER 1823
WHY'D YOU WANT ME TO BUY IT FOR YOU, THEN?
SIMPLE! WHAT YOUNG GIRL'S HEART CAN RESIST A MONKEY WITH AN ICE CREAM CONE?

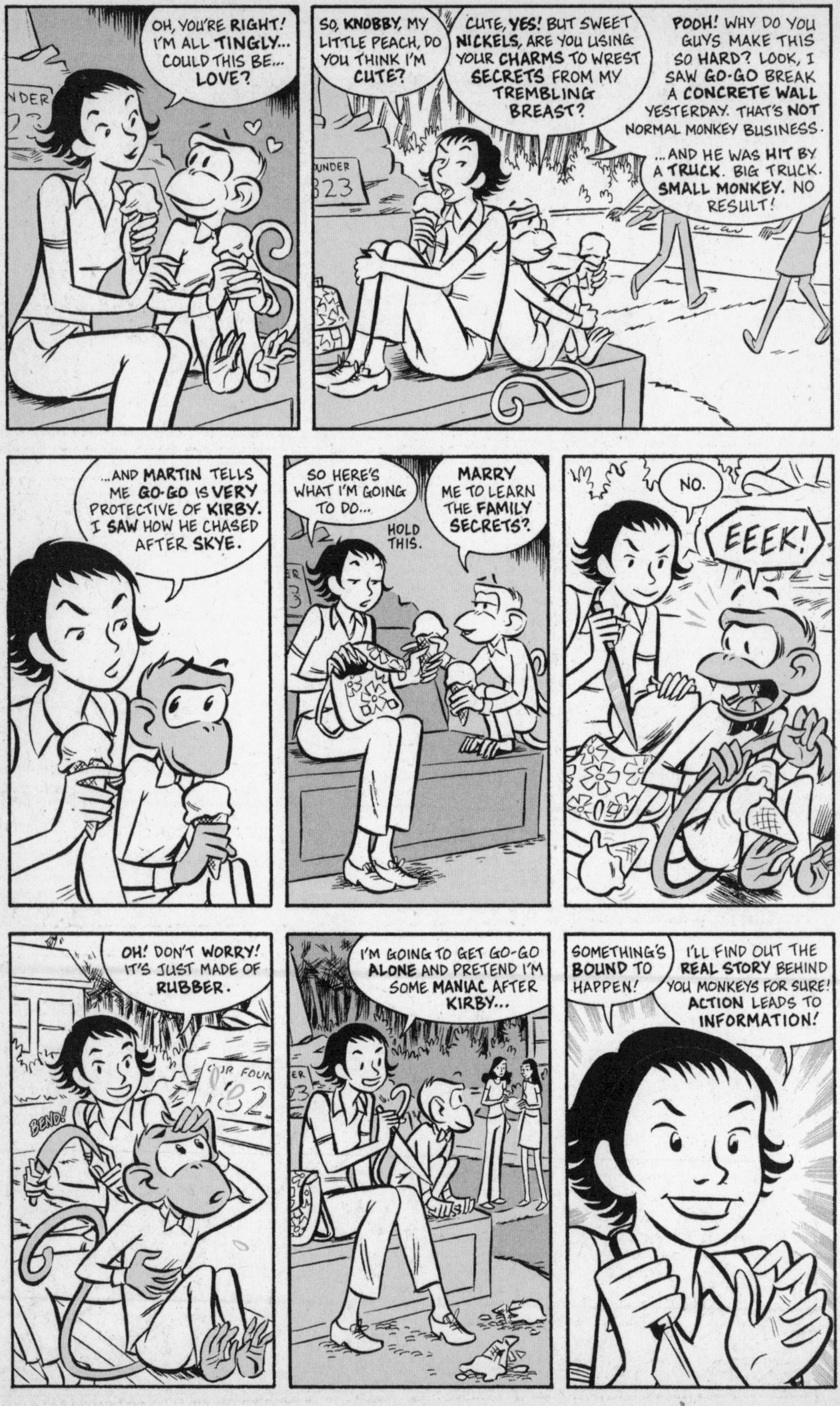
OH, YOU'RE RIGHT! I'M ALL TINGLY... COULD THIS BE... LOVE?
SO, KNOBBY, MY LITTLE PEACH, DO YOU THINK I'M CUTE?
CUTE, YES! BUT SWEET NICKELS, ARE YOU USING YOUR CHARMS TO WREST SECRETS FROM MY TREMBLING BREAST?
POOH! WHY DO YOU GUYS MAKE THIS SO HARD? LOOK, I SAW GO-GO BREAK A CONCRETE WALL YESTERDAY. THAT'S NOT NORMAL MONKEY BUSINESS.
...AND HE WAS HIT BY A TRUCK. BIG TRUCK. SMALL MONKEY. NO RESULT!
...AND MARTIN TELLS ME GO-GO IS VERY PROTECTIVE OF KIRBY. I SAW HOW HE CHASED AFTER SKYE.
SO HERE'S WHAT I'M GOING TO DO...
HOLD THIS.
MARRY ME TO LEARN THE FAMILY SECRETS?
NO.
EEEK!
OH! DON'T WORRY! IT'S JUST MADE OF RUBBER.
BEND!
I'M GOING TO GET GO-GO ALONE AND PRETEND I'M SOME MANIAC AFTER KIRBY...
SOMETHING'S BOUND TO HAPPEN!
I'LL FIND OUT THE REAL STORY BEHIND YOU MONKEYS FOR SURE! ACTION LEADS TO INFORMATION!

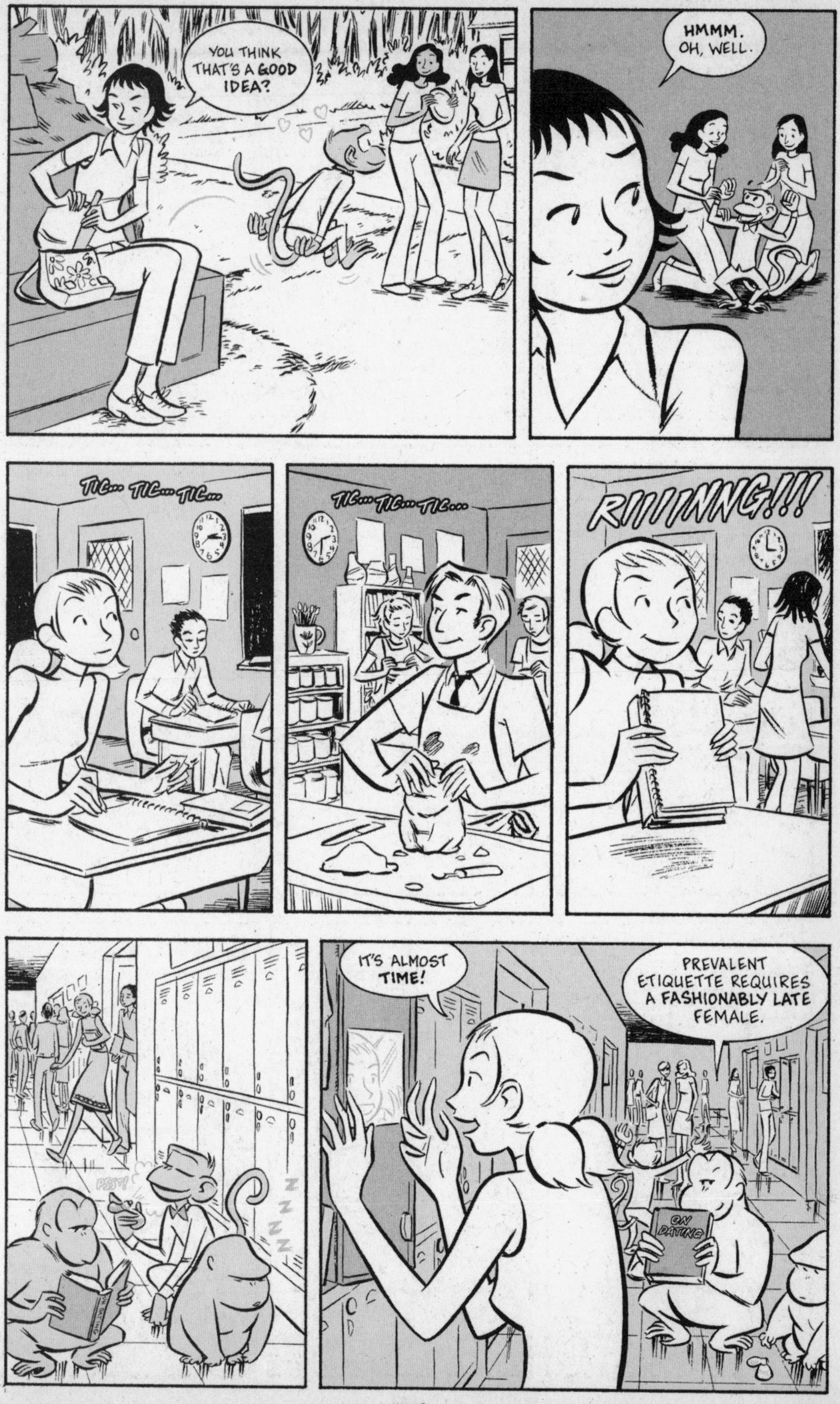

YOU THINK THAT'S A GOOD IDEA?
HMMM. OH, WELL.
TIC... TIC... TIC...
TIC... TIC... TIC...
RIIIINNG!!!
Z Z Z
IT'S ALMOST TIME!
PREVALENT ETIQUETTE REQUIRES A FASHIONABLY LATE FEMALE.
ON DATING

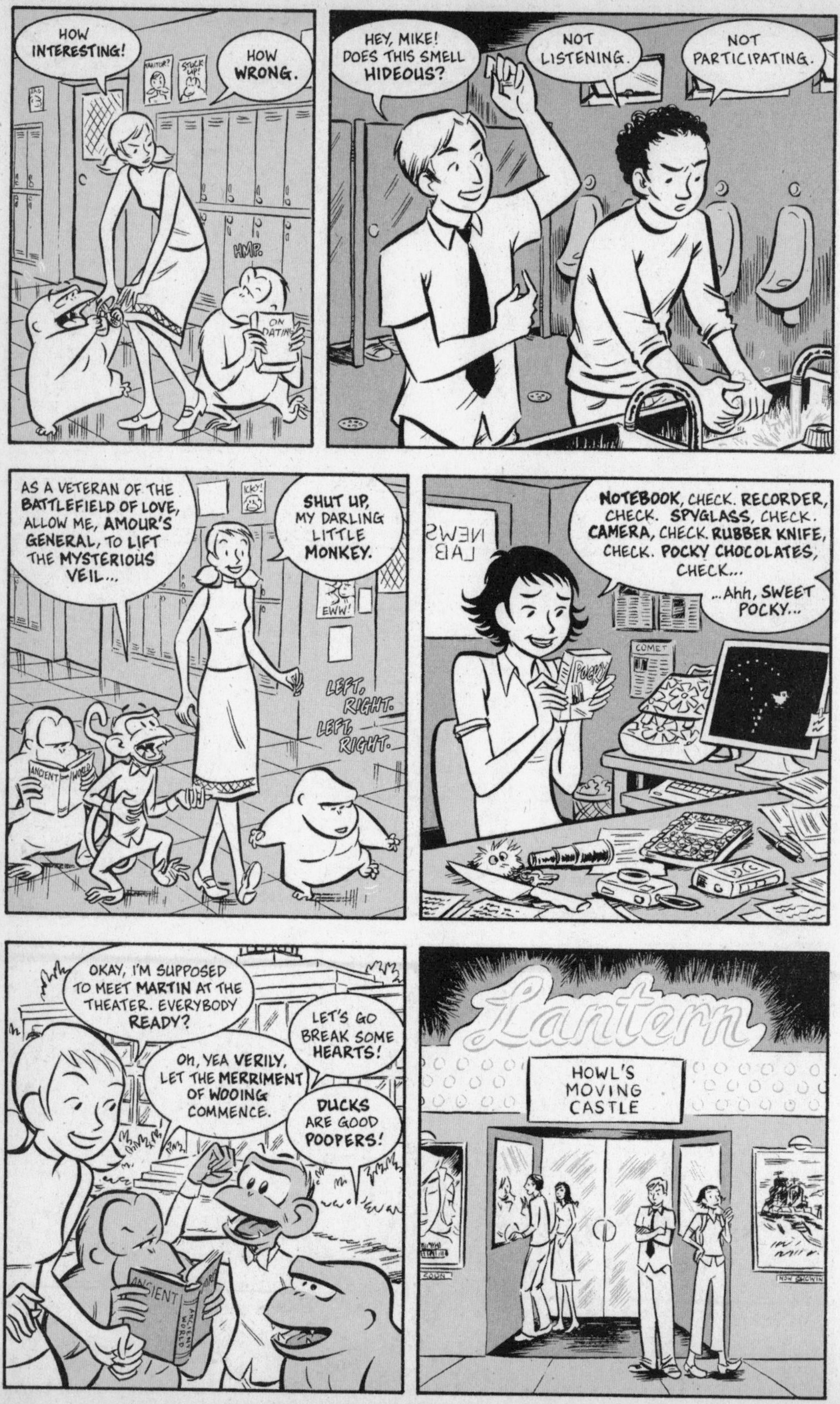
HOW INTERESTING!
HOW WRONG.
HMP.
ON DATING
HEY, MIKE! DOES THIS SMELL HIDEOUS?
NOT LISTENING.
NOT PARTICIPATING.
AS A VETERAN OF THE BATTLEFIELD OF LOVE, ALLOW ME, AMOUR'S GENERAL, TO LIFT THE MYSTERIOUS VEIL...
SHUT UP, MY DARLING LITTLE MONKEY.
ICKY!
EWW!
ANCIENT WORLD
LEFT. RIGHT. LEFT. RIGHT.
NEWS LAB
NOTEBOOK, CHECK. RECORDER, CHECK. SPYGLASS, CHECK. CAMERA, CHECK. RUBBER KNIFE, CHECK. POCKY CHOCOLATES, CHECK...
...Ahh, SWEET POCKY...
COMET
POCKY
OKAY, I'M SUPPOSED TO MEET MARTIN AT THE THEATER. EVERYBODY READY?
LET'S GO BREAK SOME HEARTS!
Oh, YEA VERILY, LET THE MERRIMENT OF WOOING COMMENCE.
DUCKS ARE GOOD POOPERS!
ANCIENT WORLD
Lantern
HOWL'S MOVING CASTLE

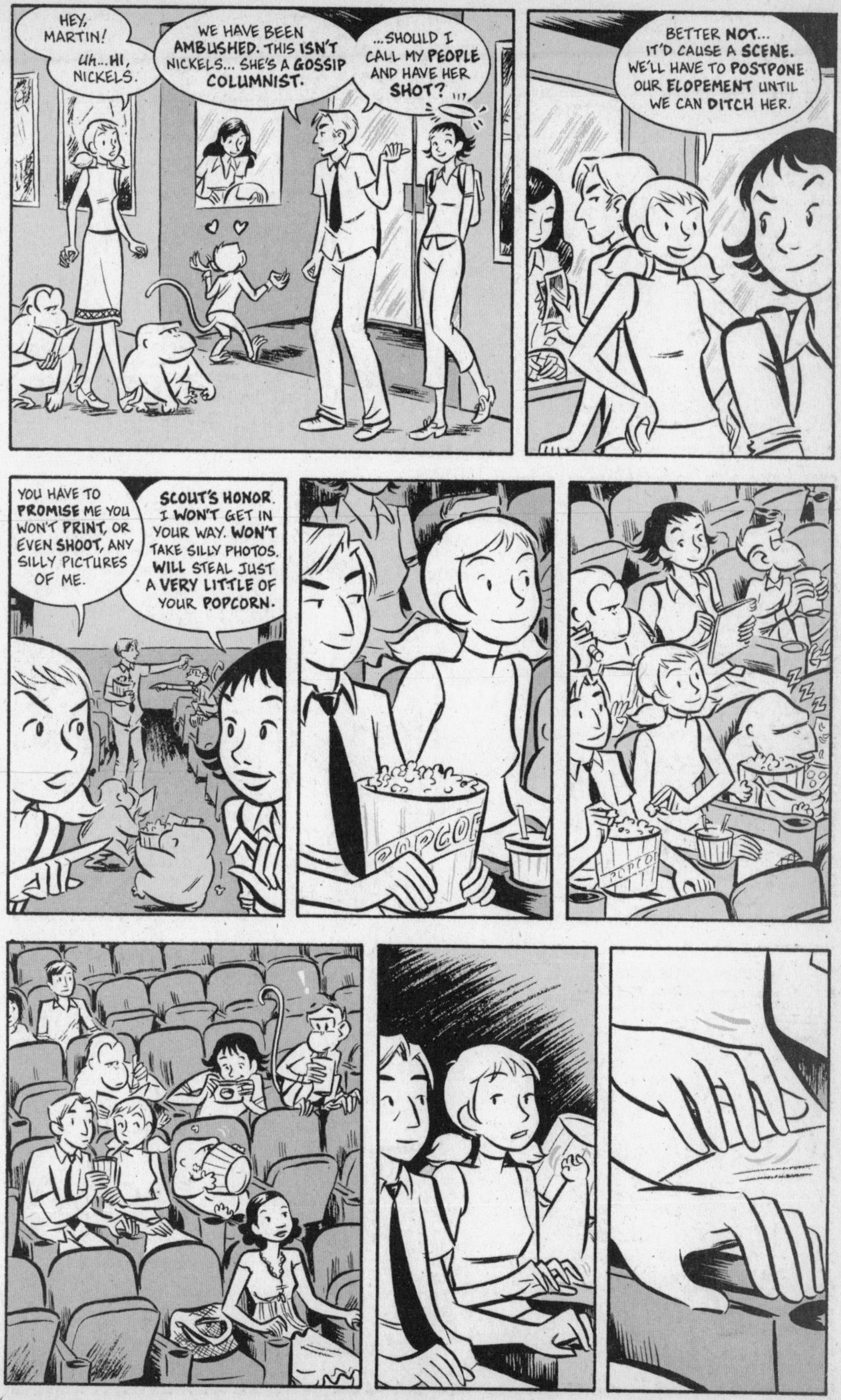
HEY, MARTIN!
Uh...HI, NICKELS.
WE HAVE BEEN AMBUSHED. THIS ISN'T NICKELS... SHE'S A GOSSIP COLUMNIST.
...SHOULD I CALL MY PEOPLE AND HAVE HER SHOT?
BETTER NOT... IT'D CAUSE A SCENE. WE'LL HAVE TO POSTPONE OUR ELOPEMENT UNTIL WE CAN DITCH HER.
YOU HAVE TO PROMISE ME YOU WON'T PRINT, OR EVEN SHOOT, ANY SILLY PICTURES OF ME.
SCOUT'S HONOR. I WON'T GET IN YOUR WAY. WON'T TAKE SILLY PHOTOS. WILL STEAL JUST A VERY LITTLE OF YOUR POPCORN.

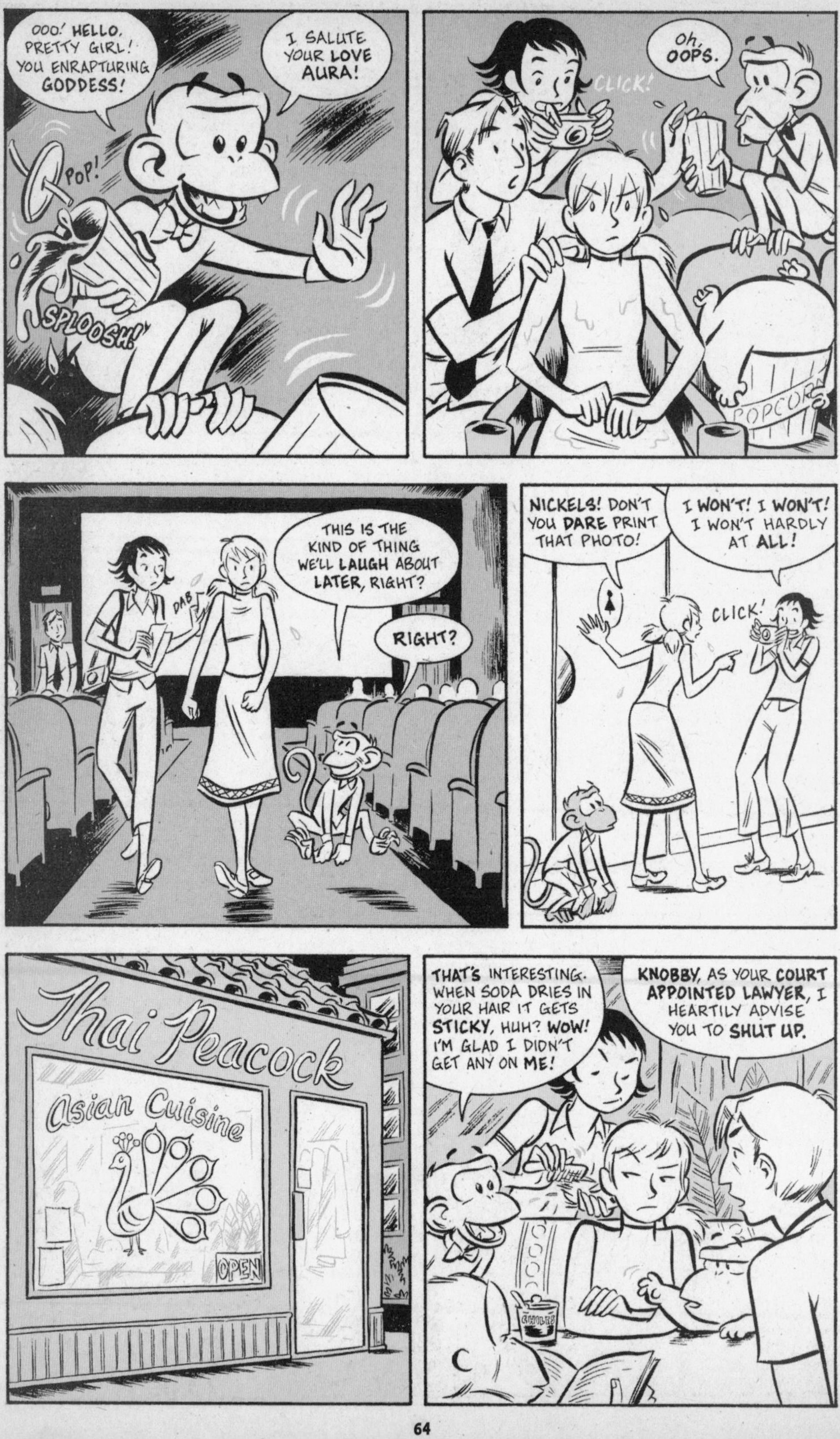
OOO! HELLO, PRETTY GIRL! YOU ENRAPTURING GODDESS!
I SALUTE YOUR LOVE AURA!
POP!
SPLOOSH!
Oh, OOPS.
CLICK!
POPCORN
THIS IS THE KIND OF THING WE'LL LAUGH ABOUT LATER, RIGHT?
RIGHT?
DAB
NICKELS! DON'T YOU DARE PRINT THAT PHOTO!
I WON'T! I WON'T! I WON'T HARDLY AT ALL!
CLICK!
Thai Peacock
Asian Cuisine
OPEN
THAT'S INTERESTING. WHEN SODA DRIES IN YOUR HAIR IT GETS STICKY, HUH? WOW! I'M GLAD I DIDN'T GET ANY ON ME!
KNOBBY, AS YOUR COURT APPOINTED LAWYER, I HEARTILY ADVISE YOU TO SHUT UP.

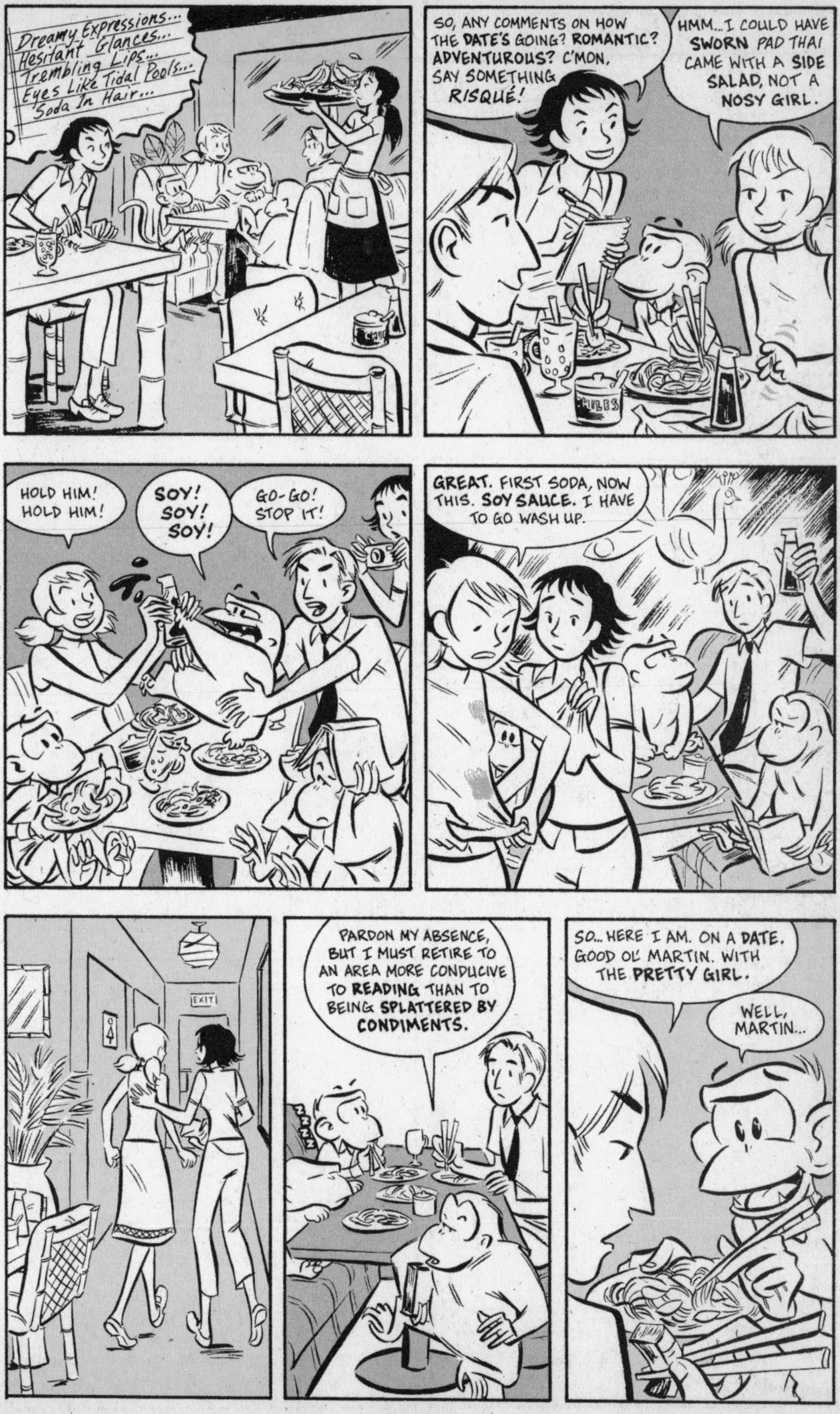
Dreamy Expressions...
Hesitant Glances...
Trembling Lips...
Eyes Like Tidal Pools...
Soda In Hair...
SO, ANY COMMENTS ON HOW THE DATE'S GOING? ROMANTIC? ADVENTUROUS? C'MON, SAY SOMETHING RISQUÉ!
HMM... I COULD HAVE SWORN PAD THAI CAME WITH A SIDE SALAD, NOT A NOSY GIRL.
CHILES
HOLD HIM! HOLD HIM!
SOY! SOY! SOY!
GO-GO! STOP IT!
GREAT. FIRST SODA, NOW THIS. SOY SAUCE. I HAVE TO GO WASH UP.
EXIT
PARDON MY ABSENCE, BUT I MUST RETIRE TO AN AREA MORE CONDUCIVE TO READING THAN TO BEING SPLATTERED BY CONDIMENTS.
SO... HERE I AM. ON A DATE. GOOD OL' MARTIN. WITH THE PRETTY GIRL.
WELL, MARTIN...

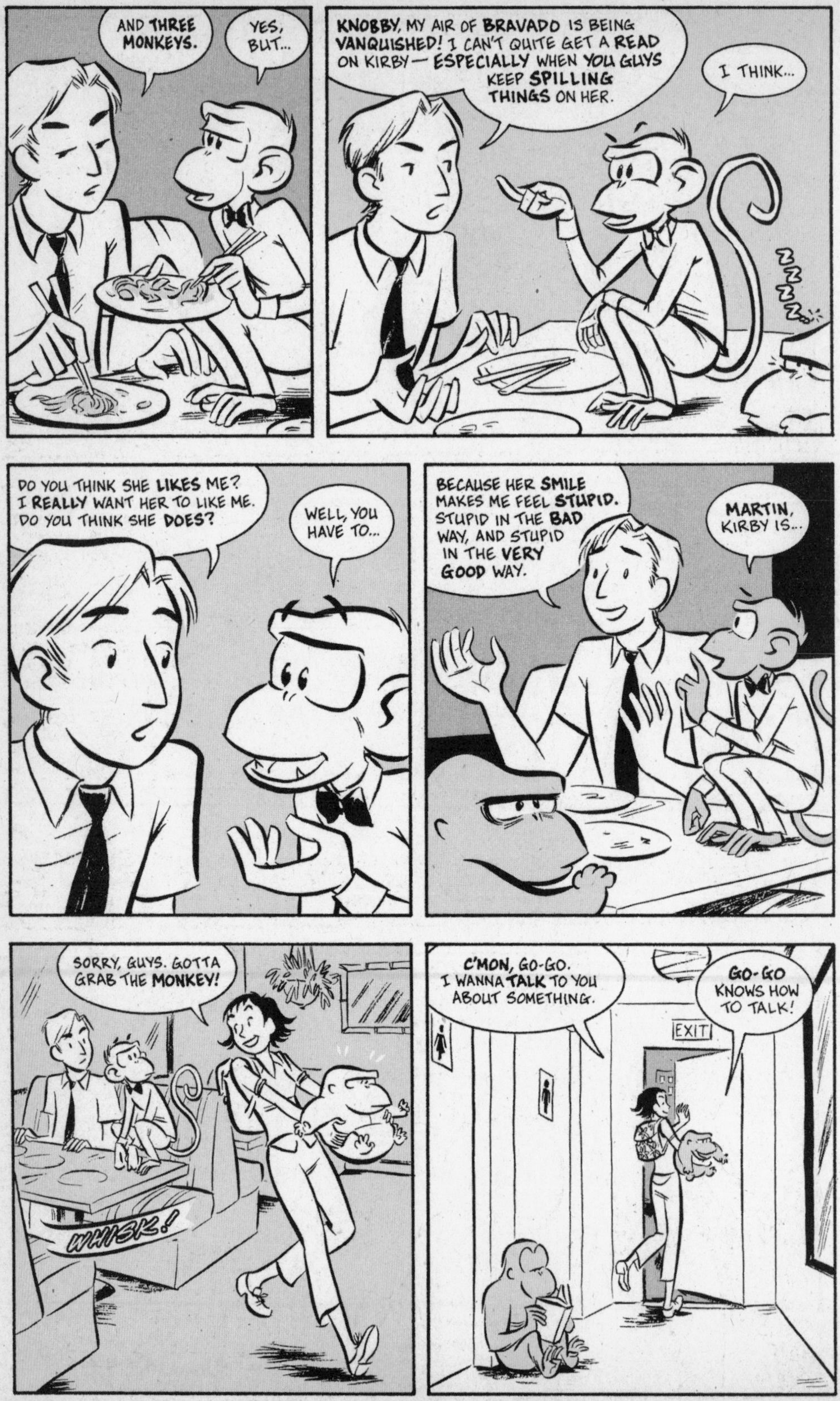
AND THREE MONKEYS.
YES, BUT...
KNOBBY, MY AIR OF BRAVADO IS BEING VANQUISHED! I CAN'T QUITE GET A READ ON KIRBY— ESPECIALLY WHEN YOU GUYS KEEP SPILLING THINGS ON HER.
I THINK...
ZZZZ
DO YOU THINK SHE LIKES ME? I REALLY WANT HER TO LIKE ME. DO YOU THINK SHE DOES?
WELL, YOU HAVE TO...
BECAUSE HER SMILE MAKES ME FEEL STUPID. STUPID IN THE BAD WAY, AND STUPID IN THE VERY GOOD WAY.
MARTIN, KIRBY IS...
SORRY, GUYS. GOTTA GRAB THE MONKEY!
WHISK!
C'MON, GO-GO. I WANNA TALK TO YOU ABOUT SOMETHING.
GO-GO KNOWS HOW TO TALK!
EXIT

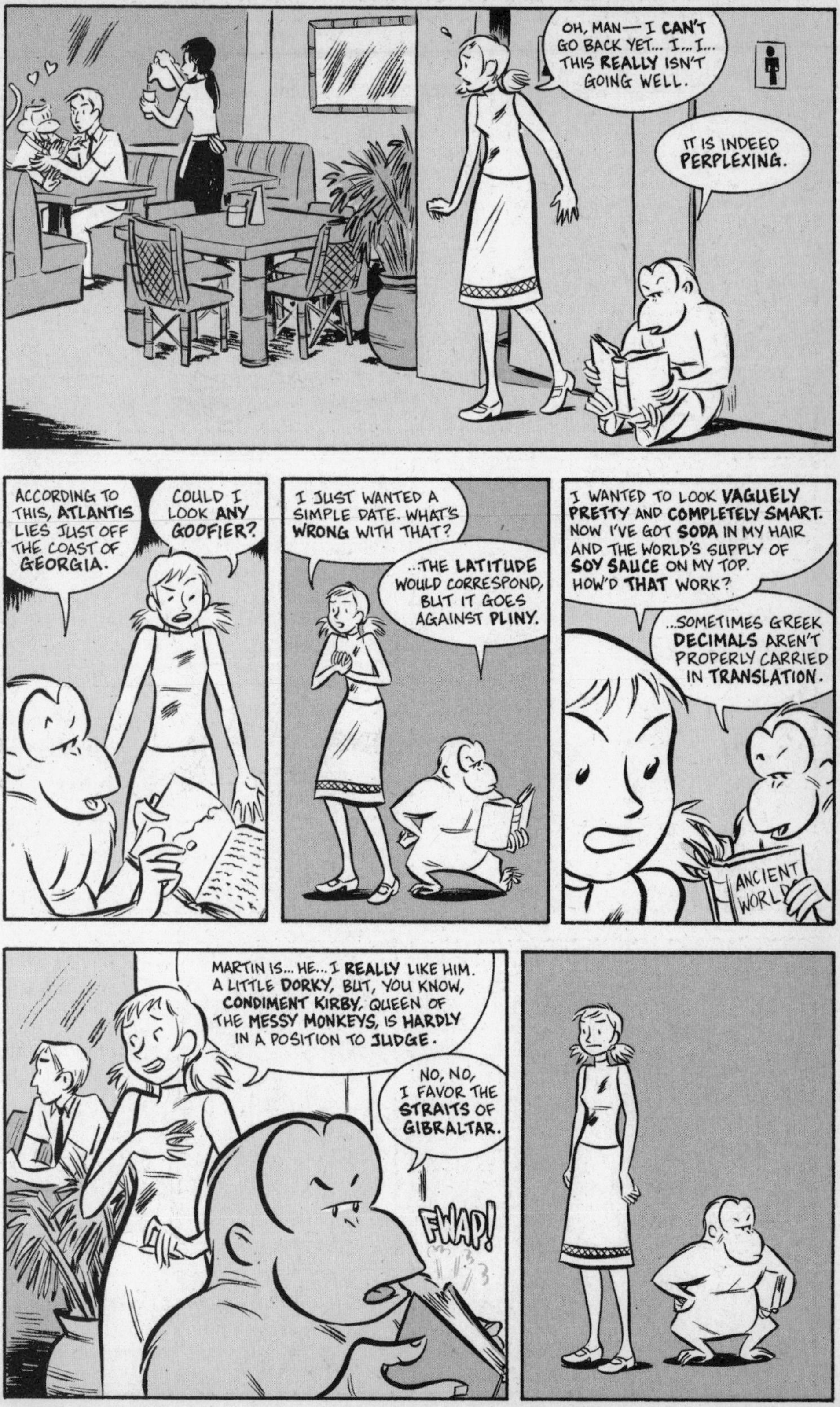
OH, MAN— I CAN'T GO BACK YET... I... I... THIS REALLY ISN'T GOING WELL.
IT IS INDEED PERPLEXING.
ACCORDING TO THIS, ATLANTIS LIES JUST OFF THE COAST OF GEORGIA.
COULD I LOOK ANY GOOFIER?
I JUST WANTED A SIMPLE DATE. WHAT'S WRONG WITH THAT?
...THE LATITUDE WOULD CORRESPOND, BUT IT GOES AGAINST PLINY.
I WANTED TO LOOK VAGUELY PRETTY AND COMPLETELY SMART. NOW I'VE GOT SODA IN MY HAIR AND THE WORLD'S SUPPLY OF SOY SAUCE ON MY TOP. HOW'D THAT WORK?
...SOMETIMES GREEK DECIMALS AREN'T PROPERLY CARRIED IN TRANSLATION.
ANCIENT WORLD
MARTIN IS... HE... I REALLY LIKE HIM. A LITTLE DORKY, BUT, YOU KNOW, CONDIMENT KIRBY, QUEEN OF THE MESSY MONKEYS, IS HARDLY IN A POSITION TO JUDGE.
NO, NO, I FAVOR THE STRAITS OF GIBRALTAR.
FWAP!

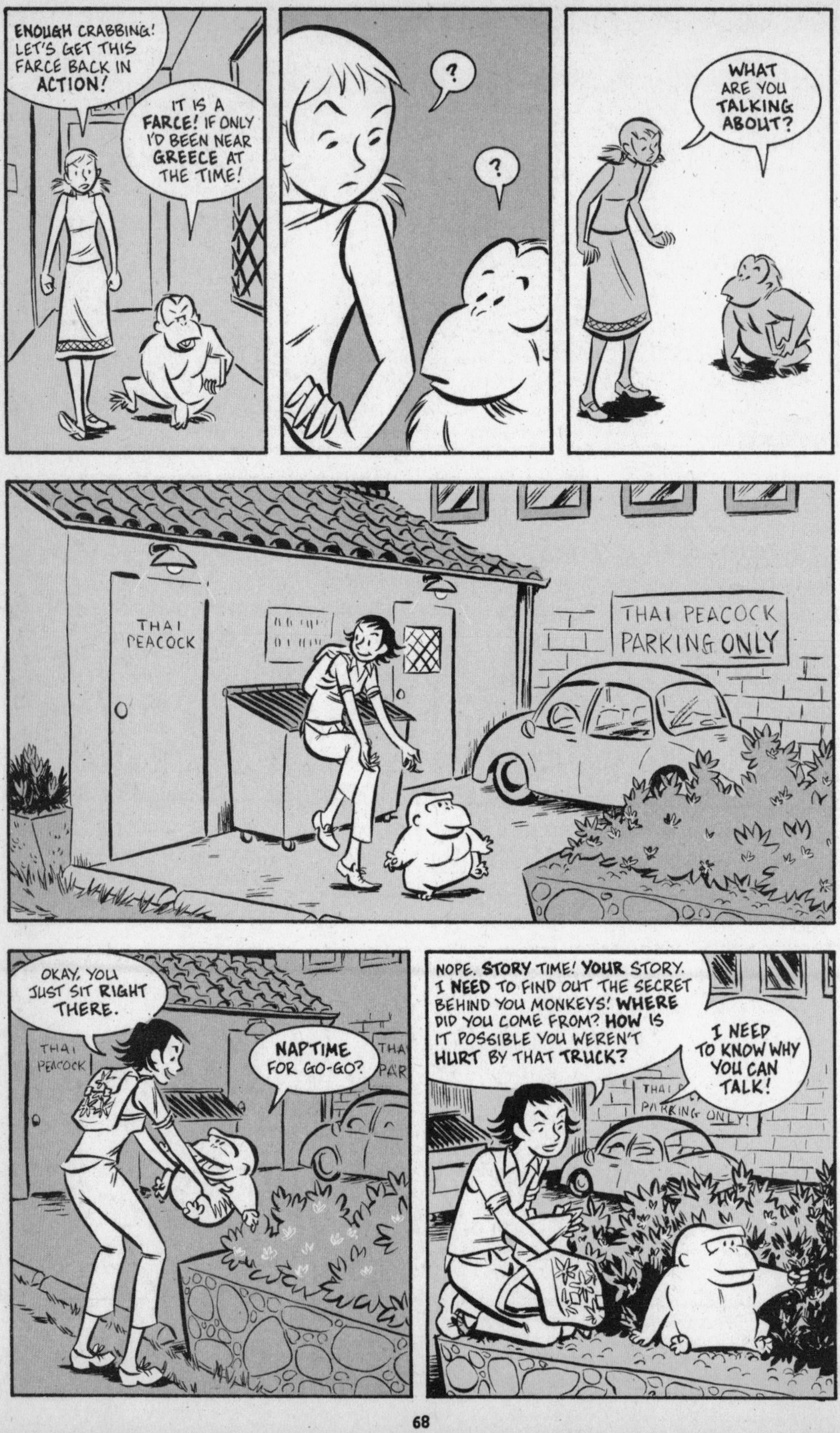
ENOUGH CRABBING! LET'S GET THIS FARCE BACK IN ACTION!
IT IS A FARCE! IF ONLY I'D BEEN NEAR GREECE AT THE TIME!
?
?
WHAT ARE YOU TALKING ABOUT?
THAI PEACOCK
THAI PEACOCK PARKING ONLY
OKAY, YOU JUST SIT RIGHT THERE.
THAI PEACOCK
NAPTIME FOR GO-GO?
NOPE. STORY TIME! YOUR STORY. I NEED TO FIND OUT THE SECRET BEHIND YOU MONKEYS! WHERE DID YOU COME FROM? HOW IS IT POSSIBLE YOU WEREN'T HURT BY THAT TRUCK?
I NEED TO KNOW WHY YOU CAN TALK!
THAI PARKING ONLY

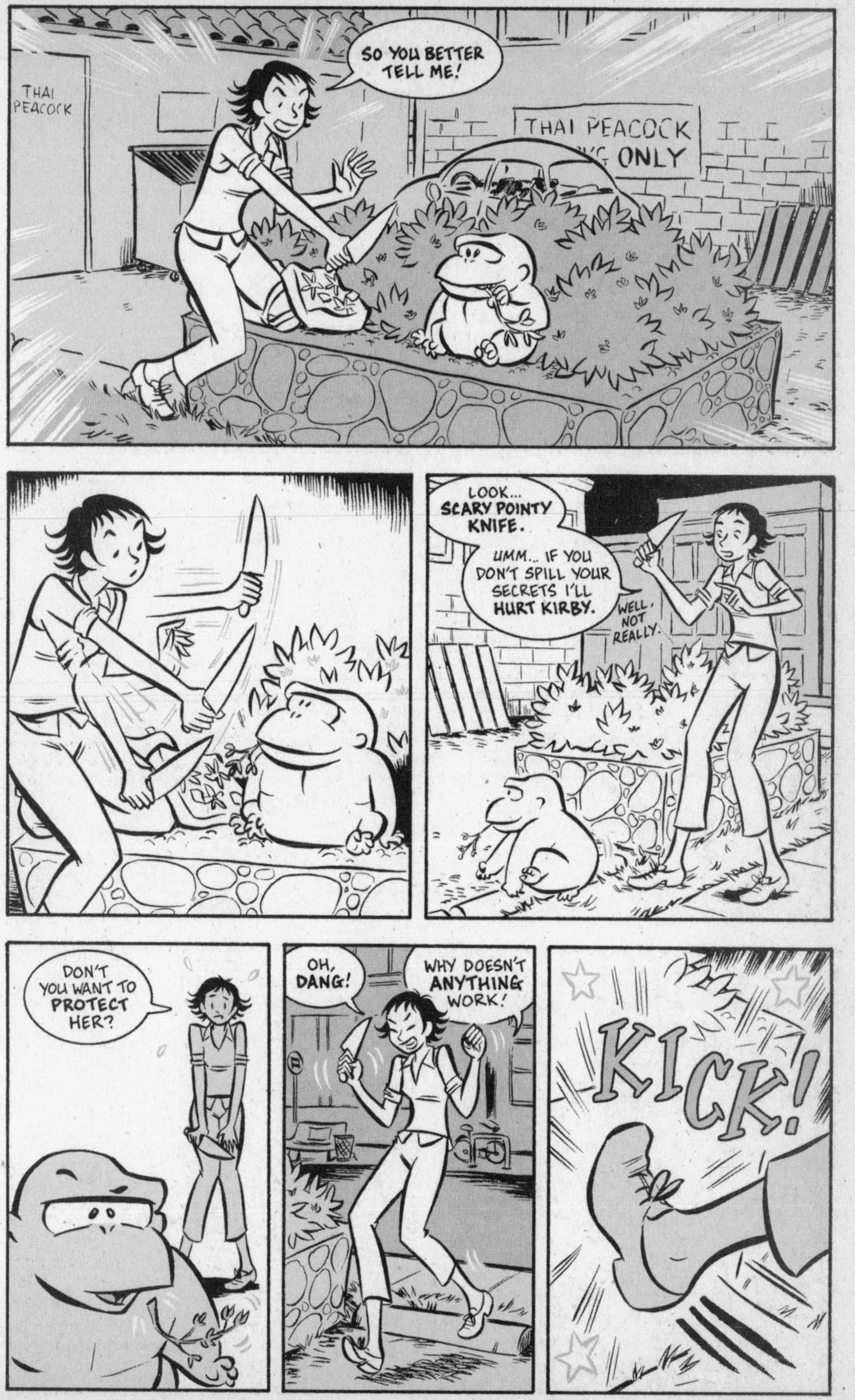

SO YOU BETTER TELL ME!
THAI PEACOCK
THAI PEACOCK
ONLY
LOOK... SCARY POINTY KNIFE.
UMM... IF YOU DON'T SPILL YOUR SECRETS I'LL HURT KIRBY.
WELL, NOT REALLY.
DON'T YOU WANT TO PROTECT HER?
OH, DANG!
WHY DOESN'T ANYTHING WORK!
KICK!

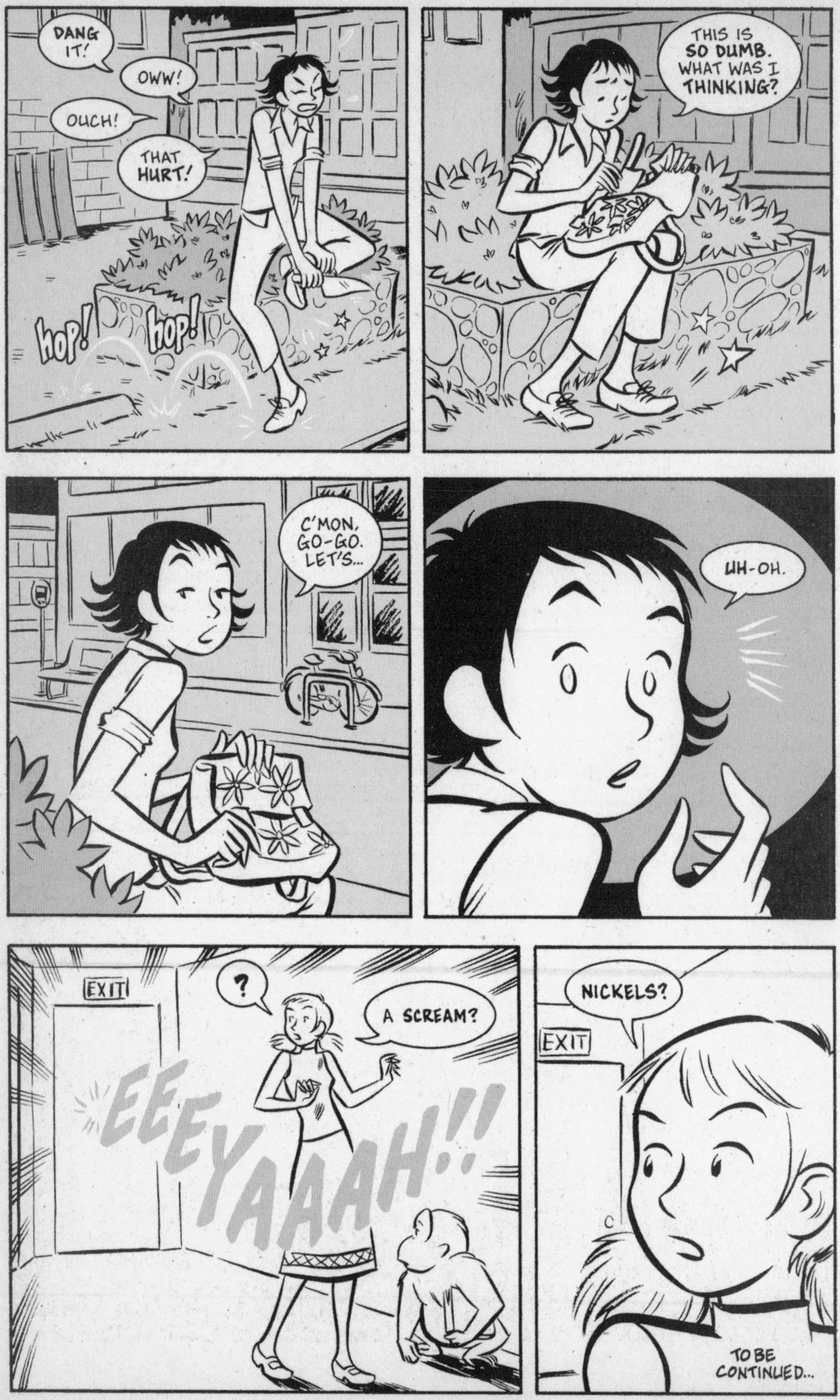
DANG IT!
OWW!
OUCH!
THAT HURT!
hop! hop!
THIS IS SO DUMB. WHAT WAS I THINKING?
C'MON, GO-GO. LET'S...
UH-OH.
?
A SCREAM?
EEEYAAAH!!
NICKELS?
EXIT
TO BE CONTINUED...

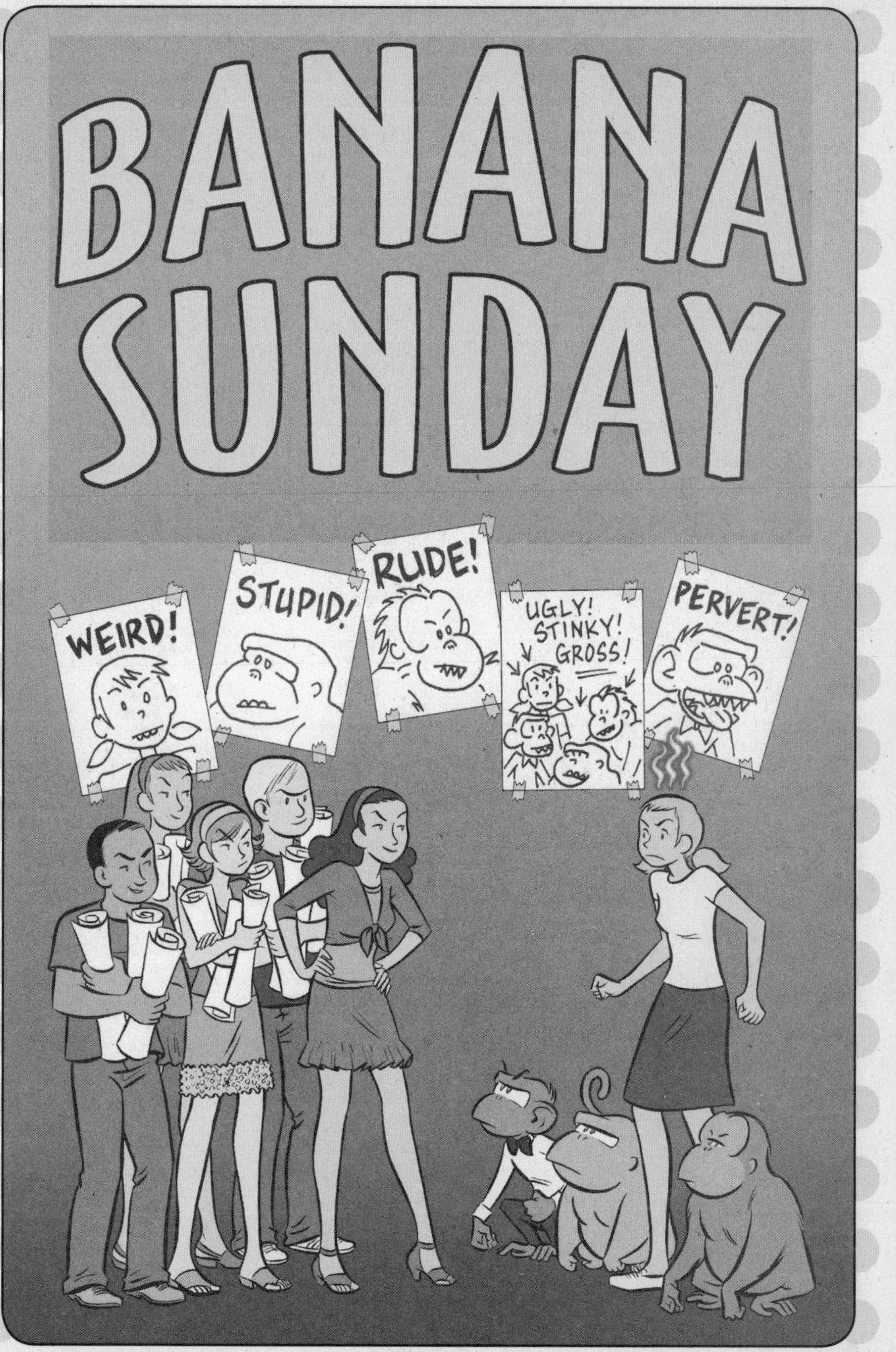
BANANA
SUNDAY
WEIRD!
STUPID!
RUDE!
UGLY!
STINKY!
GROSS!
PERVERT!

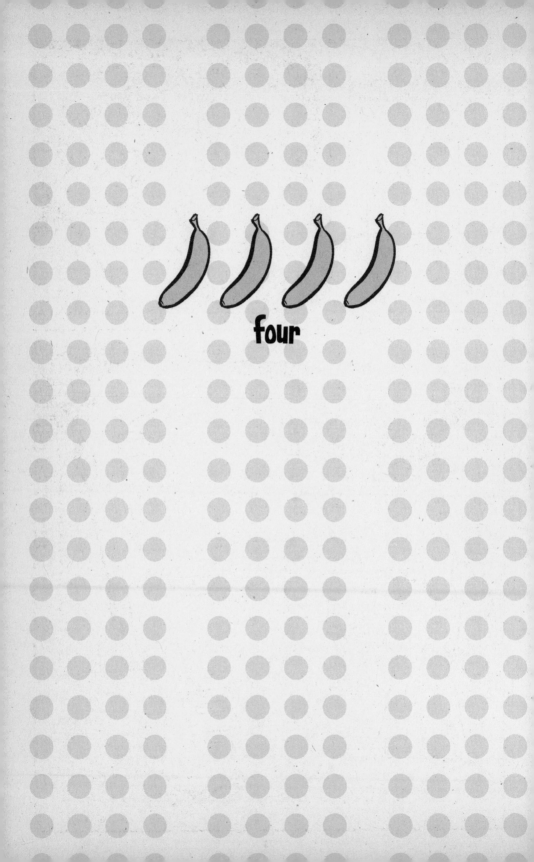

four

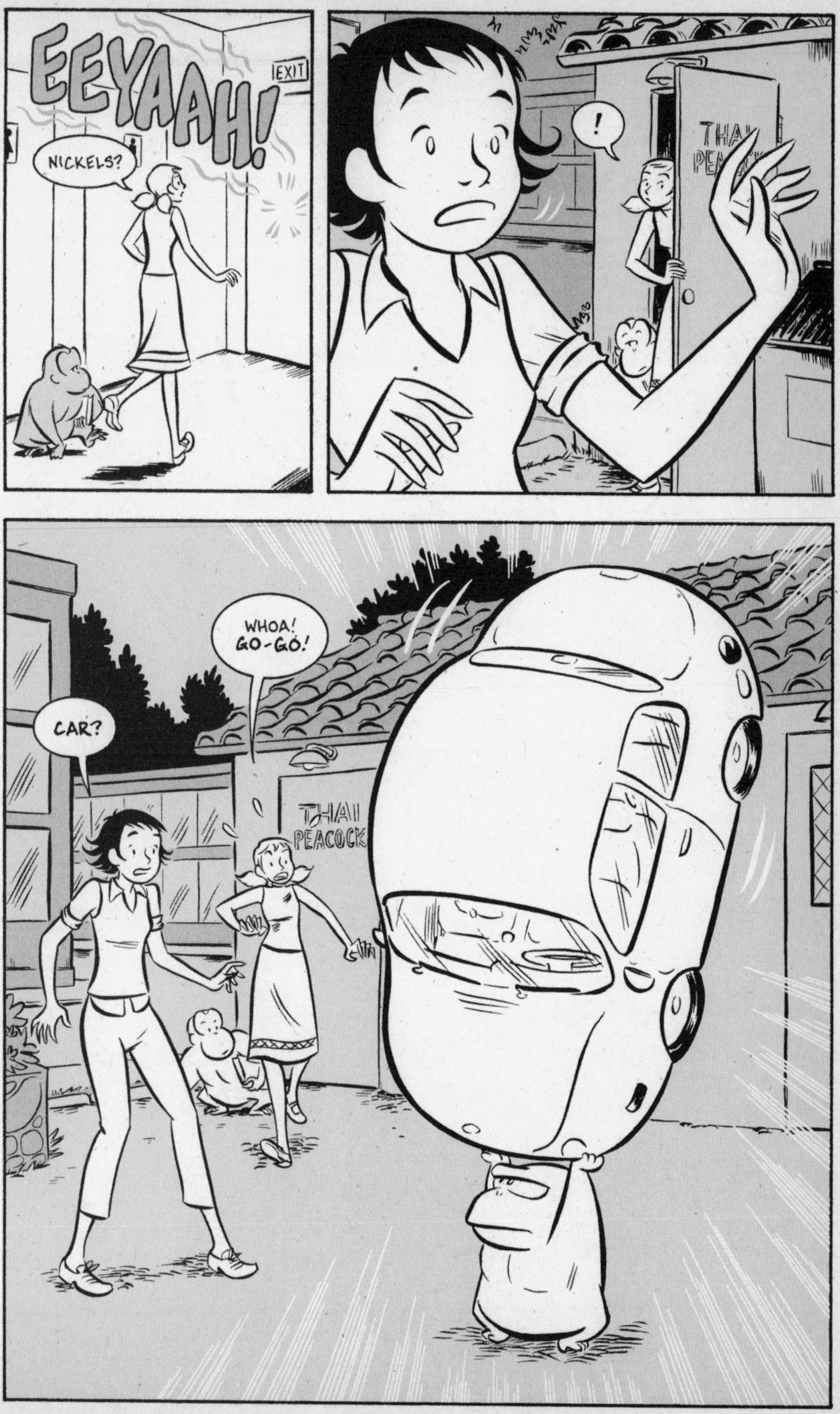
EEYAAH!
EXIT
NICKELS?
!
THAI PEA
WHOA! GO-GO!
CAR?
THAI PEACOCK

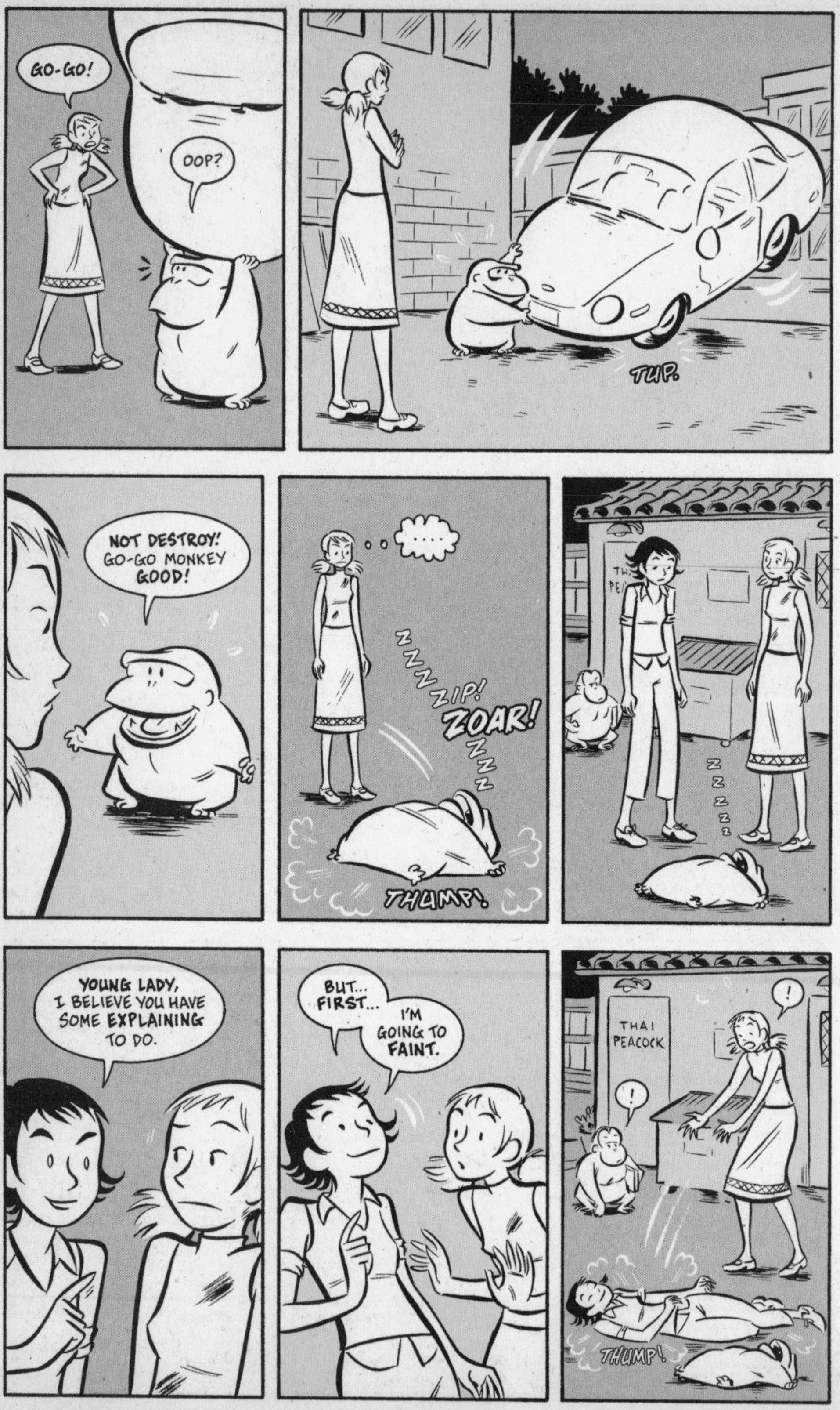
GO-GO!
OOP?
TUP.
NOT DESTROY! GO-GO MONKEY GOOD!
.....
ZZZZZIP!
ZOAR!
ZZZZ
THUMP!
ZZZZZ
YOUNG LADY, I BELIEVE YOU HAVE SOME EXPLAINING TO DO.
BUT... FIRST...
I'M GOING TO FAINT.
THAI PEACOCK
!
!
THUMP!

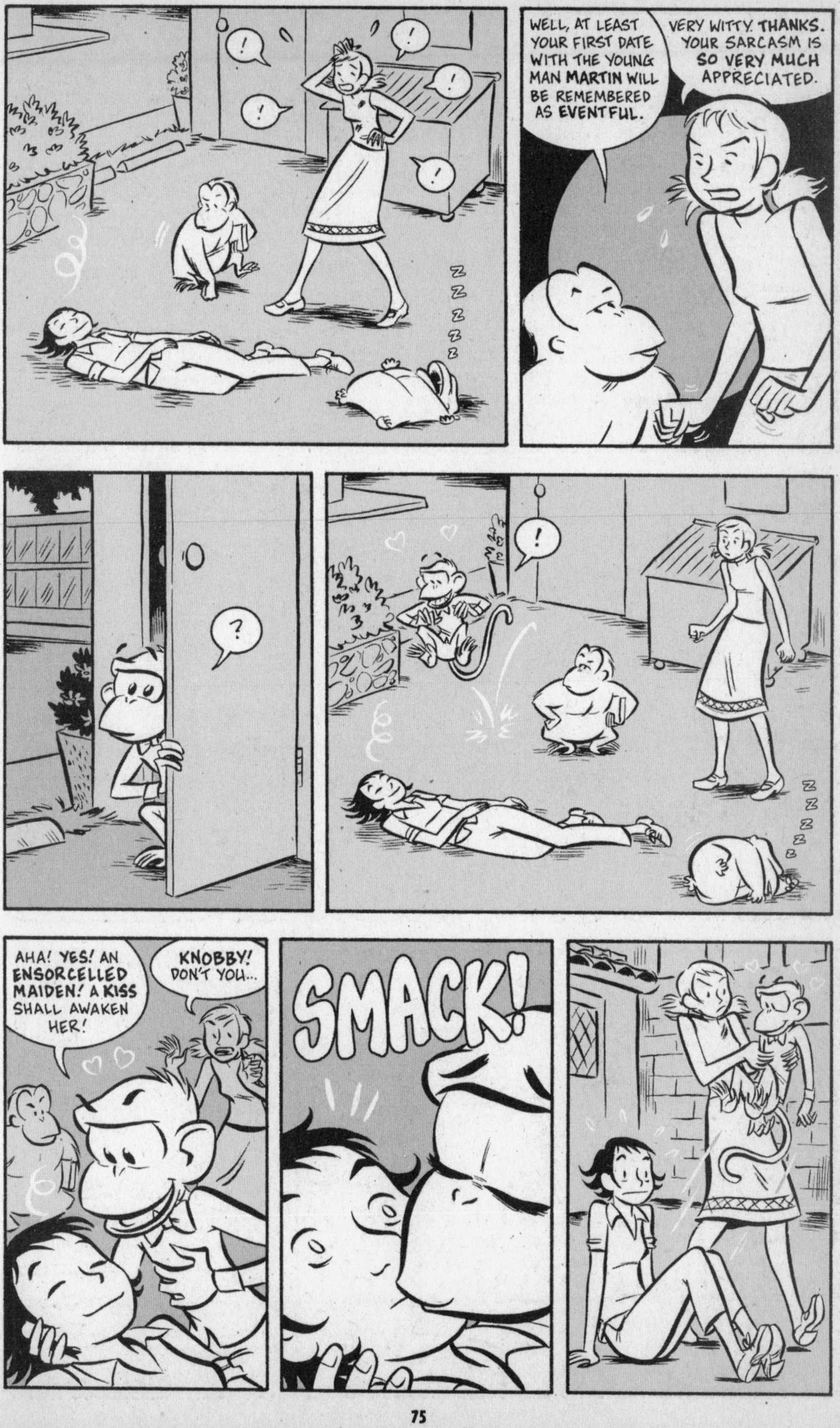
!
!
!
!
!
WELL, AT LEAST YOUR FIRST DATE WITH THE YOUNG MAN MARTIN WILL BE REMEMBERED AS EVENTFUL.
VERY WITTY. THANKS. YOUR SARCASM IS SO VERY MUCH APPRECIATED.
?
!
AHA! YES! AN ENSORCELLED MAIDEN! A KISS SHALL AWAKEN HER!
KNOBBY! DON'T YOU...
SMACK!

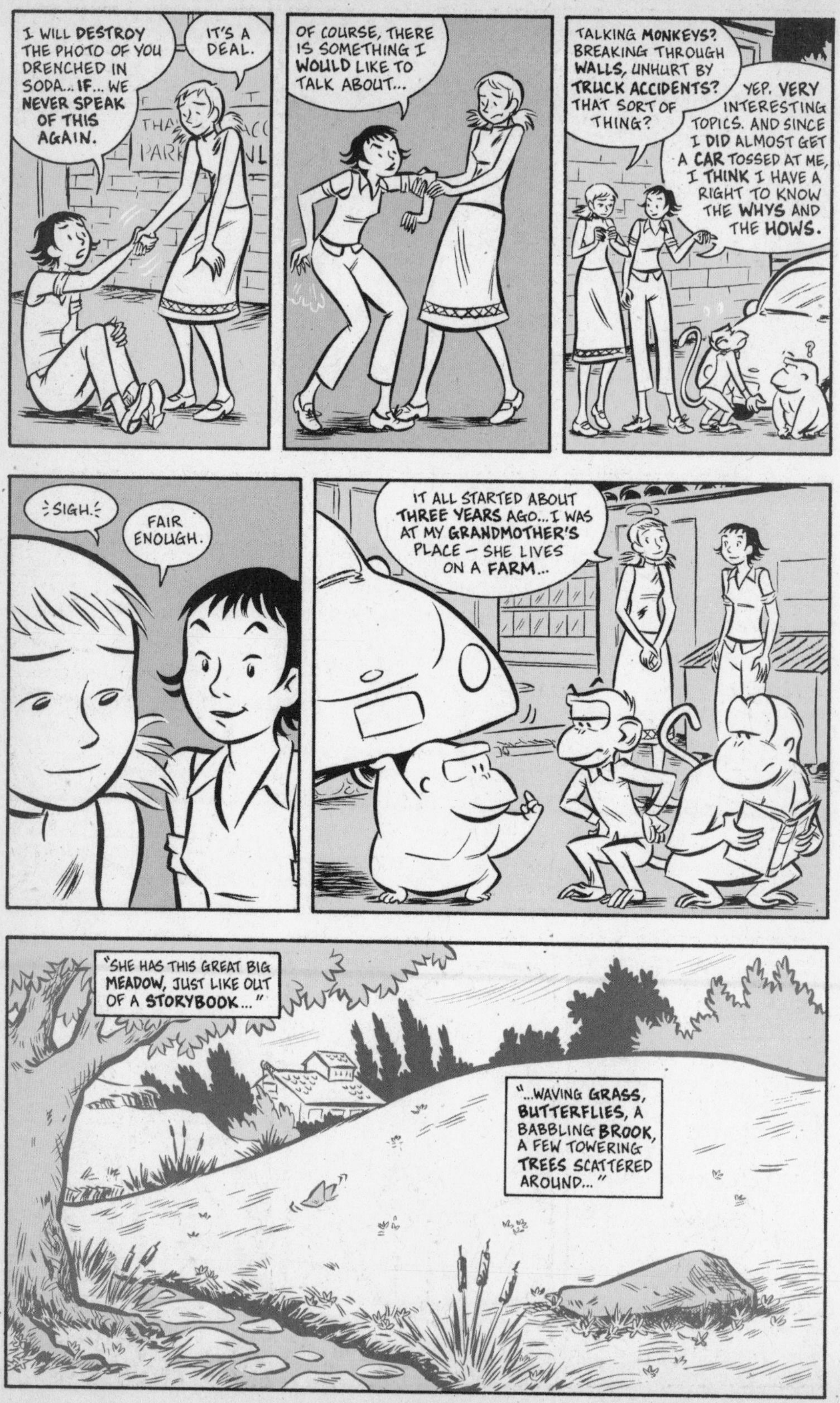
I WILL DESTROY THE PHOTO OF YOU DRENCHED IN SODA... IF... WE NEVER SPEAK OF THIS AGAIN.
IT'S A DEAL.
OF COURSE, THERE IS SOMETHING I WOULD LIKE TO TALK ABOUT...
TALKING MONKEYS? BREAKING THROUGH WALLS, UNHURT BY TRUCK ACCIDENTS? THAT SORT OF THING?
YEP. VERY INTERESTING TOPICS. AND SINCE I DID ALMOST GET A CAR TOSSED AT ME, I THINK I HAVE A RIGHT TO KNOW THE WHYS AND THE HOWS.
?
SIGH.
FAIR ENOUGH.
IT ALL STARTED ABOUT THREE YEARS AGO... I WAS AT MY GRANDMOTHER'S PLACE — SHE LIVES ON A FARM...
"SHE HAS THIS GREAT BIG MEADOW, JUST LIKE OUT OF A STORYBOOK..."
"...WAVING GRASS, BUTTERFLIES, A BABBLING BROOK, A FEW TOWERING TREES SCATTERED AROUND..."

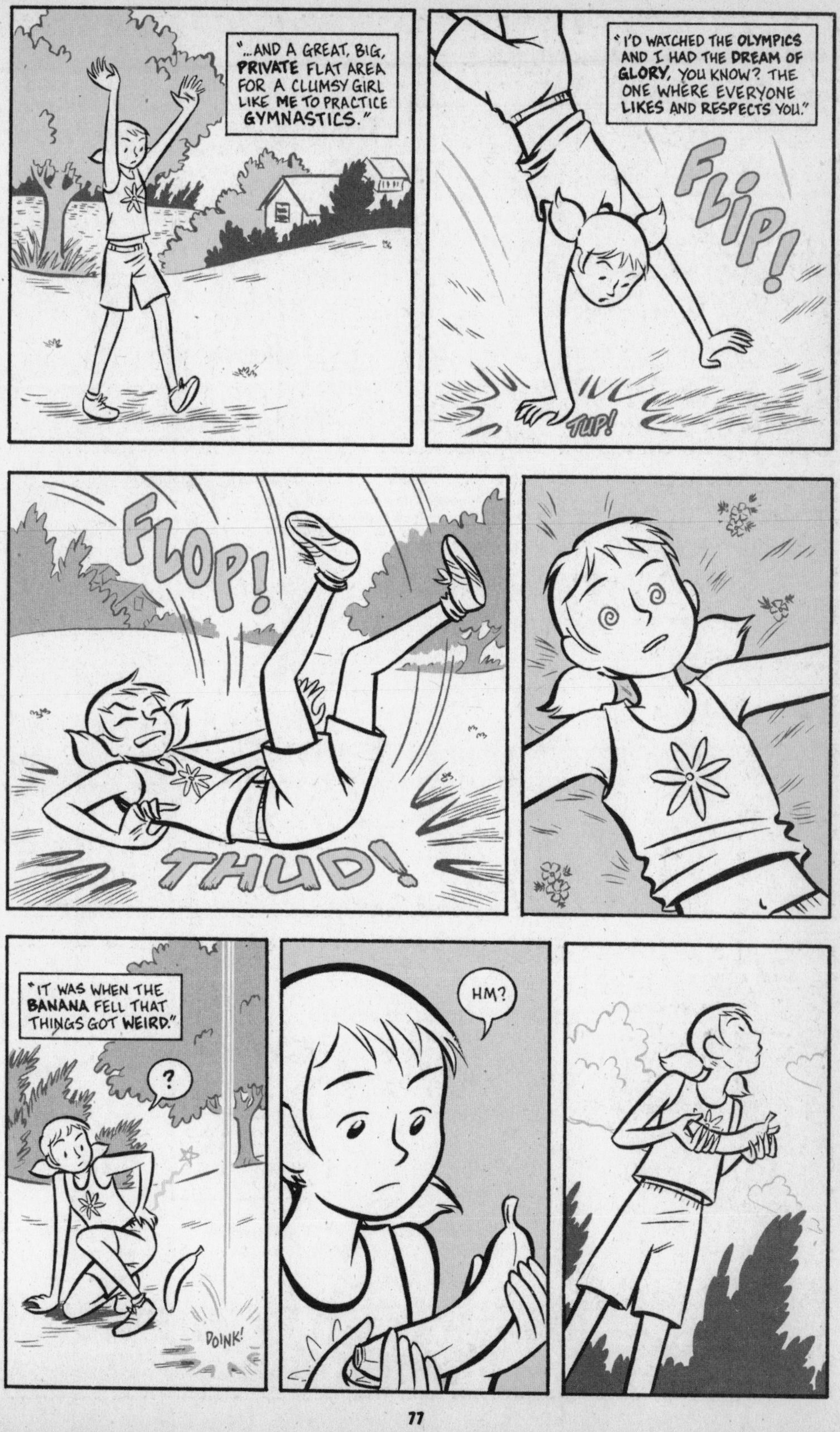
"...AND A GREAT, BIG, PRIVATE FLAT AREA FOR A CLUMSY GIRL LIKE ME TO PRACTICE GYMNASTICS."
"I'D WATCHED THE OLYMPICS AND I HAD THE DREAM OF GLORY, YOU KNOW? THE ONE WHERE EVERYONE LIKES AND RESPECTS YOU."
FLIP!
TUP!
FLOP!
THUD!
"IT WAS WHEN THE BANANA FELL THAT THINGS GOT WEIRD."
?
DOINK!
HM?

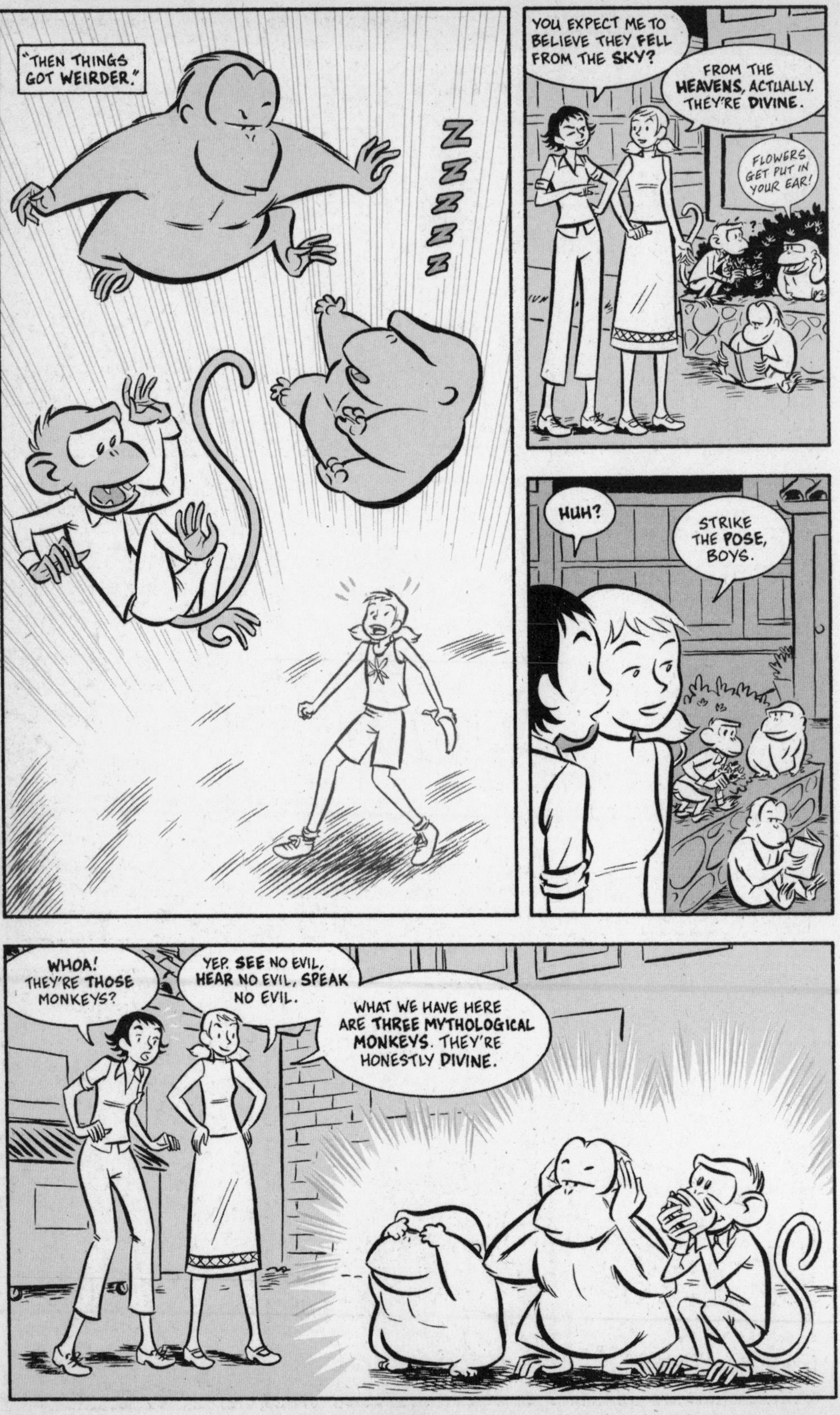
"THEN THINGS GOT WEIRDER."
ZZZZZZ
YOU EXPECT ME TO BELIEVE THEY FELL FROM THE SKY?
FROM THE HEAVENS, ACTUALLY. THEY'RE DIVINE.
FLOWERS GET PUT IN YOUR EAR!
HUH?
STRIKE THE POSE, BOYS.
WHOA! THEY'RE THOSE MONKEYS?
YEP. SEE NO EVIL, HEAR NO EVIL, SPEAK NO EVIL.
WHAT WE HAVE HERE ARE THREE MYTHOLOGICAL MONKEYS. THEY'RE HONESTLY DIVINE.

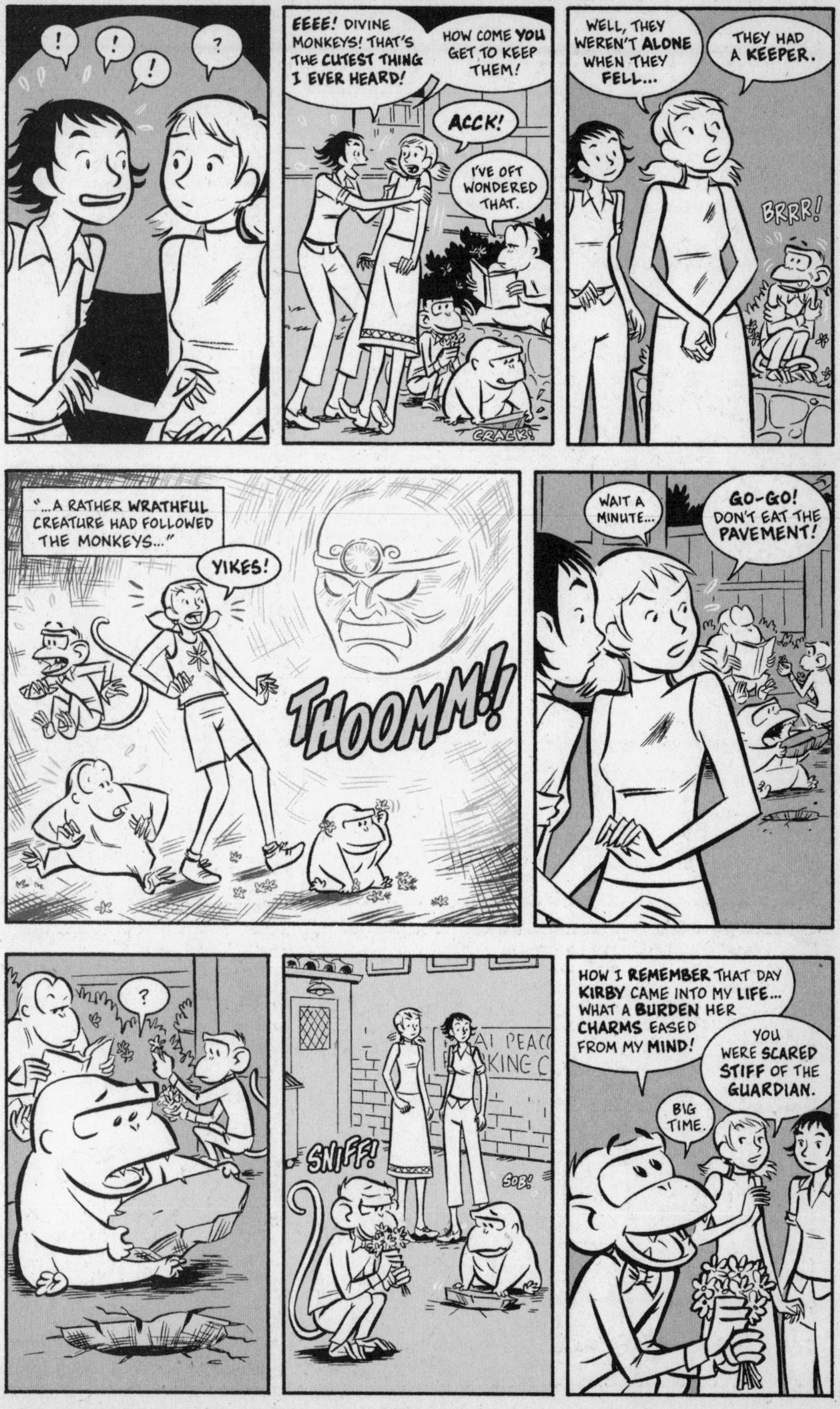
!
!
!
?
EEEE! DIVINE MONKEYS! THAT'S THE CUTEST THING I EVER HEARD!
HOW COME YOU GET TO KEEP THEM!
ACCK!
I'VE OFT WONDERED THAT.
CRACK!
WELL, THEY WEREN'T ALONE WHEN THEY FELL...
THEY HAD A KEEPER.
BRRR!
"...A RATHER WRATHFUL CREATURE HAD FOLLOWED THE MONKEYS..."
YIKES!
THOOMM!!
WAIT A MINUTE...
GO-GO! DON'T EAT THE PAVEMENT!
?
SNIFF!
SOB!
HOW I REMEMBER THAT DAY KIRBY CAME INTO MY LIFE... WHAT A BURDEN HER CHARMS EASED FROM MY MIND!
YOU WERE SCARED STIFF OF THE GUARDIAN.
BIG TIME.

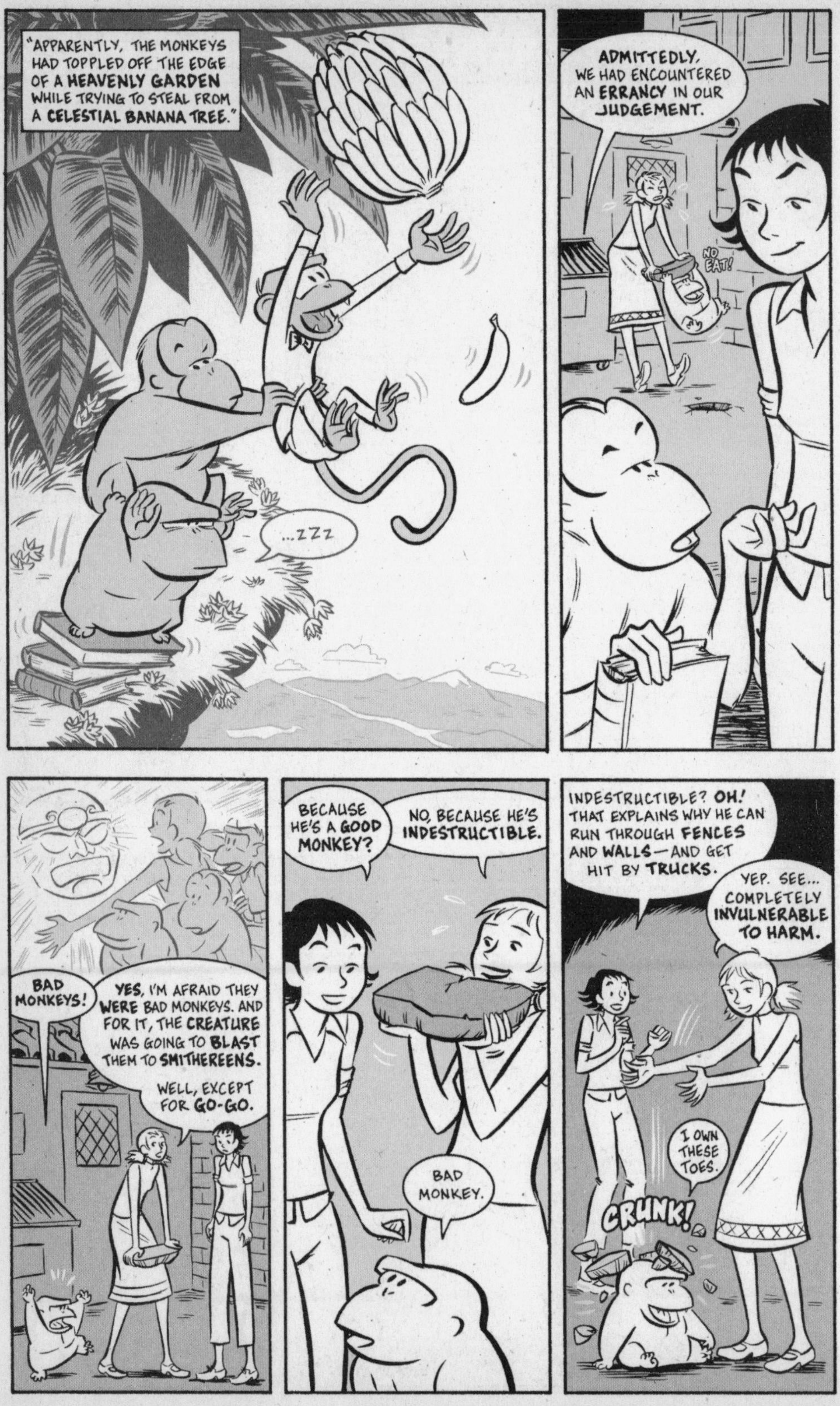
"APPARENTLY, THE MONKEYS HAD TOPPLED OFF THE EDGE OF A HEAVENLY GARDEN WHILE TRYING TO STEAL FROM A CELESTIAL BANANA TREE."
...ZZZ
ADMITTEDLY, WE HAD ENCOUNTERED AN ERRANCY IN OUR JUDGEMENT.
NO EAT!
BAD MONKEYS!
YES, I'M AFRAID THEY WERE BAD MONKEYS. AND FOR IT, THE CREATURE WAS GOING TO BLAST THEM TO SMITHEREENS.
WELL, EXCEPT FOR GO-GO.
BECAUSE HE'S A GOOD MONKEY?
NO, BECAUSE HE'S INDESTRUCTIBLE.
BAD MONKEY.
INDESTRUCTIBLE? OH! THAT EXPLAINS WHY HE CAN RUN THROUGH FENCES AND WALLS—AND GET HIT BY TRUCKS.
YEP. SEE... COMPLETELY INVULNERABLE TO HARM.
I OWN THESE TOES.
CRUNK!

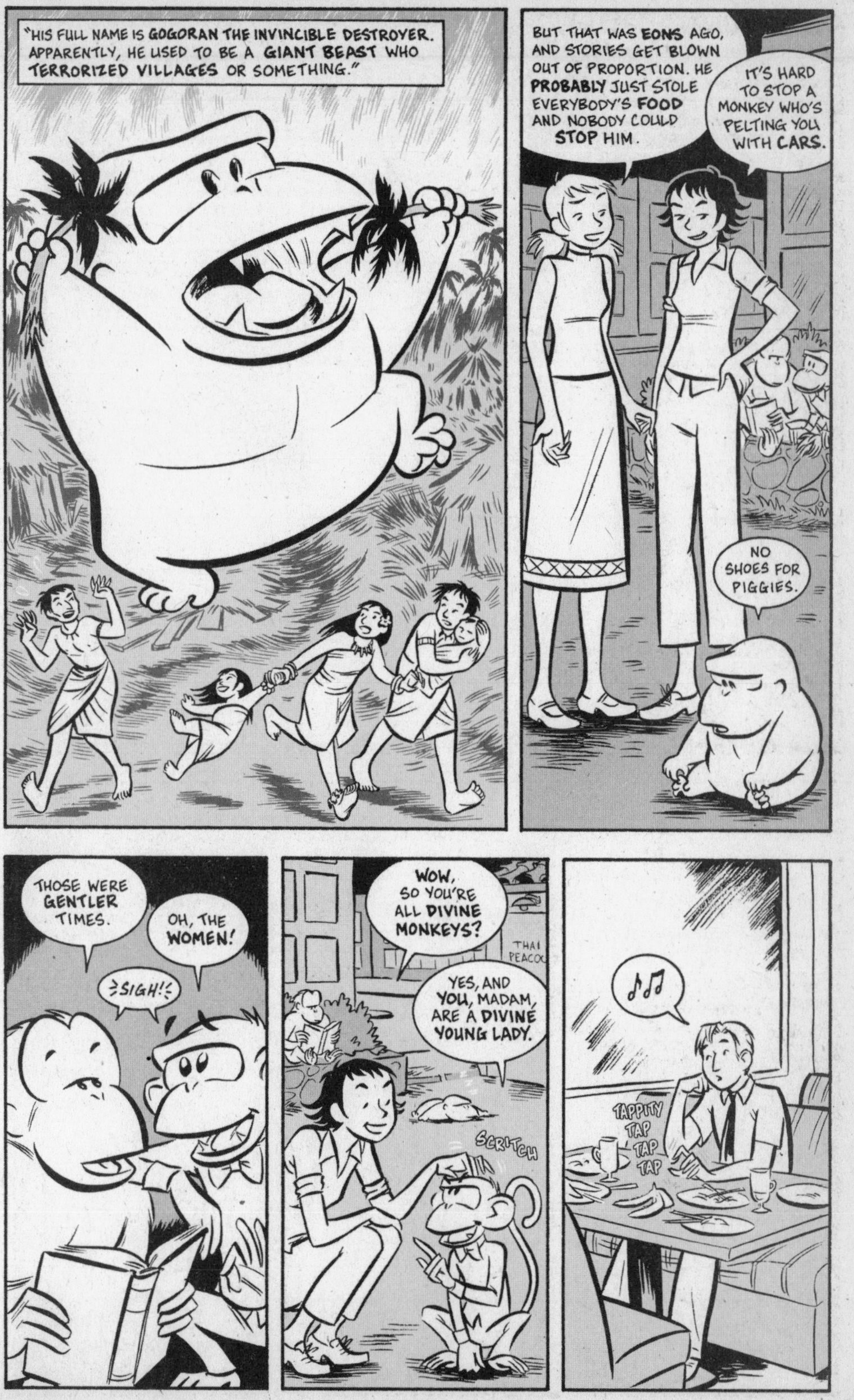
"HIS FULL NAME IS GOGORAN THE INVINCIBLE DESTROYER. APPARENTLY, HE USED TO BE A GIANT BEAST WHO TERRORIZED VILLAGES OR SOMETHING."
BUT THAT WAS EONS AGO, AND STORIES GET BLOWN OUT OF PROPORTION. HE PROBABLY JUST STOLE EVERYBODY'S FOOD AND NOBODY COULD STOP HIM.
IT'S HARD TO STOP A MONKEY WHO'S PELTING YOU WITH CARS.
NO SHOES FOR PIGGIES.
THOSE WERE GENTLER TIMES.
OH, THE WOMEN!
SIGH!
WOW, SO YOU'RE ALL DIVINE MONKEYS?
THAI PEACO
YES, AND YOU, MADAM, ARE A DIVINE YOUNG LADY.
SCRITCH
TAPPITY TAP TAP TAP

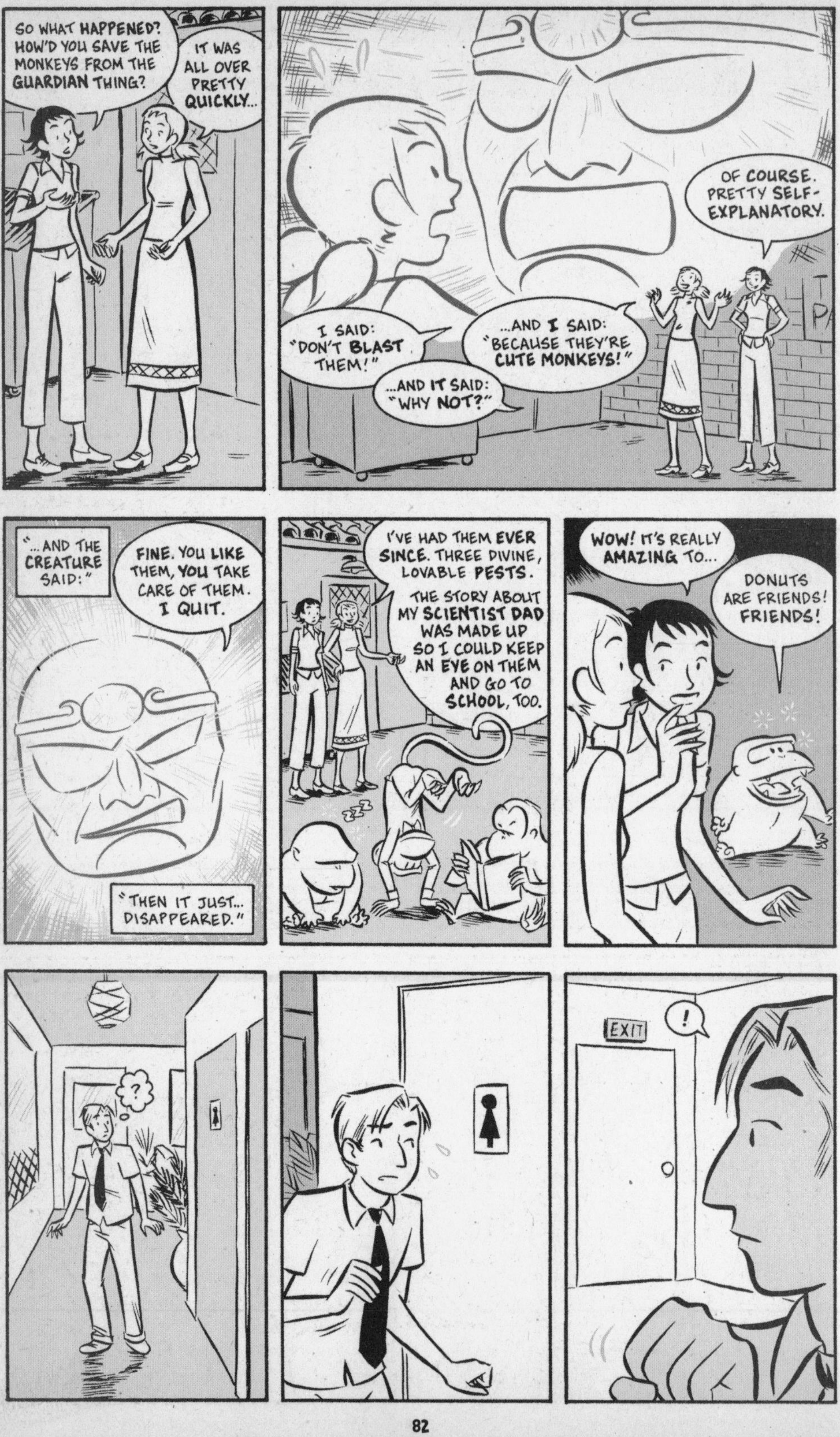
SO WHAT HAPPENED? HOW'D YOU SAVE THE MONKEYS FROM THE GUARDIAN THING?
IT WAS ALL OVER PRETTY QUICKLY...
I SAID: "DON'T BLAST THEM!"
...AND IT SAID: "WHY NOT?"
...AND I SAID: "BECAUSE THEY'RE CUTE MONKEYS!"
OF COURSE. PRETTY SELF-EXPLANATORY.
"...AND THE CREATURE SAID:"
FINE. YOU LIKE THEM, YOU TAKE CARE OF THEM. I QUIT.
"THEN IT JUST... DISAPPEARED."
I'VE HAD THEM EVER SINCE. THREE DIVINE, LOVABLE PESTS.
THE STORY ABOUT MY SCIENTIST DAD WAS MADE UP SO I COULD KEEP AN EYE ON THEM AND GO TO SCHOOL, TOO.
ZZZ
WOW! IT'S REALLY AMAZING TO...
DONUTS ARE FRIENDS! FRIENDS!
?
EXIT
!

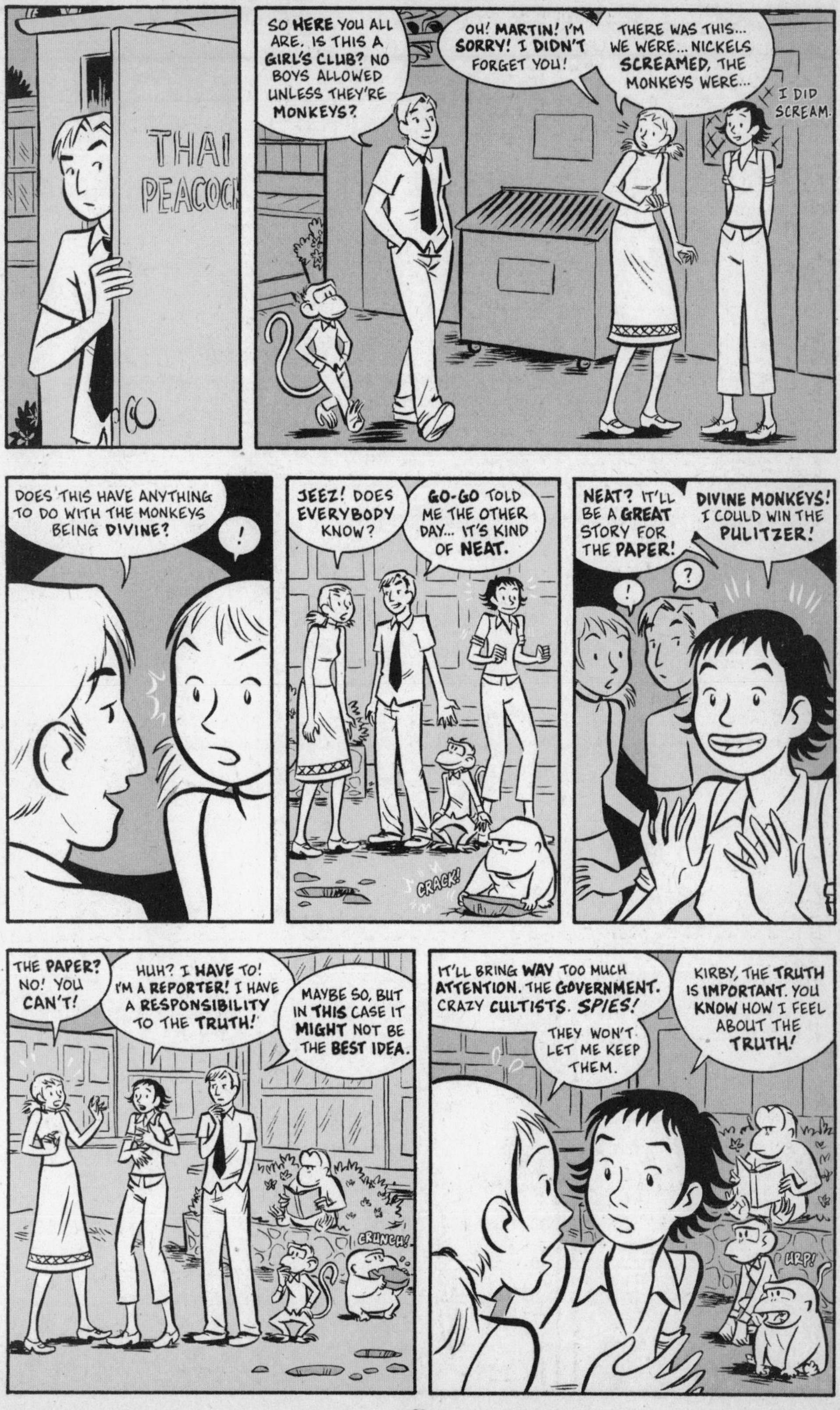
THAI PEACOCK
SO HERE YOU ALL ARE. IS THIS A GIRL'S CLUB? NO BOYS ALLOWED UNLESS THEY'RE MONKEYS?
OH! MARTIN! I'M SORRY! I DIDN'T FORGET YOU!
THERE WAS THIS... WE WERE... NICKELS SCREAMED, THE MONKEYS WERE...
I DID SCREAM.
DOES THIS HAVE ANYTHING TO DO WITH THE MONKEYS BEING DIVINE?
!
JEEZ! DOES EVERYBODY KNOW?
GO-GO TOLD ME THE OTHER DAY... IT'S KIND OF NEAT.
CRACK!
NEAT? IT'LL BE A GREAT STORY FOR THE PAPER!
DIVINE MONKEYS! I COULD WIN THE PULITZER!
!
?
THE PAPER? NO! YOU CAN'T!
HUH? I HAVE TO! I'M A REPORTER! I HAVE A RESPONSIBILITY TO THE TRUTH!
MAYBE SO, BUT IN THIS CASE IT MIGHT NOT BE THE BEST IDEA.
CRUNCH!
IT'LL BRING WAY TOO MUCH ATTENTION. THE GOVERNMENT. CRAZY CULTISTS. SPIES!
THEY WON'T LET ME KEEP THEM.
KIRBY, THE TRUTH IS IMPORTANT. YOU KNOW HOW I FEEL ABOUT THE TRUTH!
HRP!

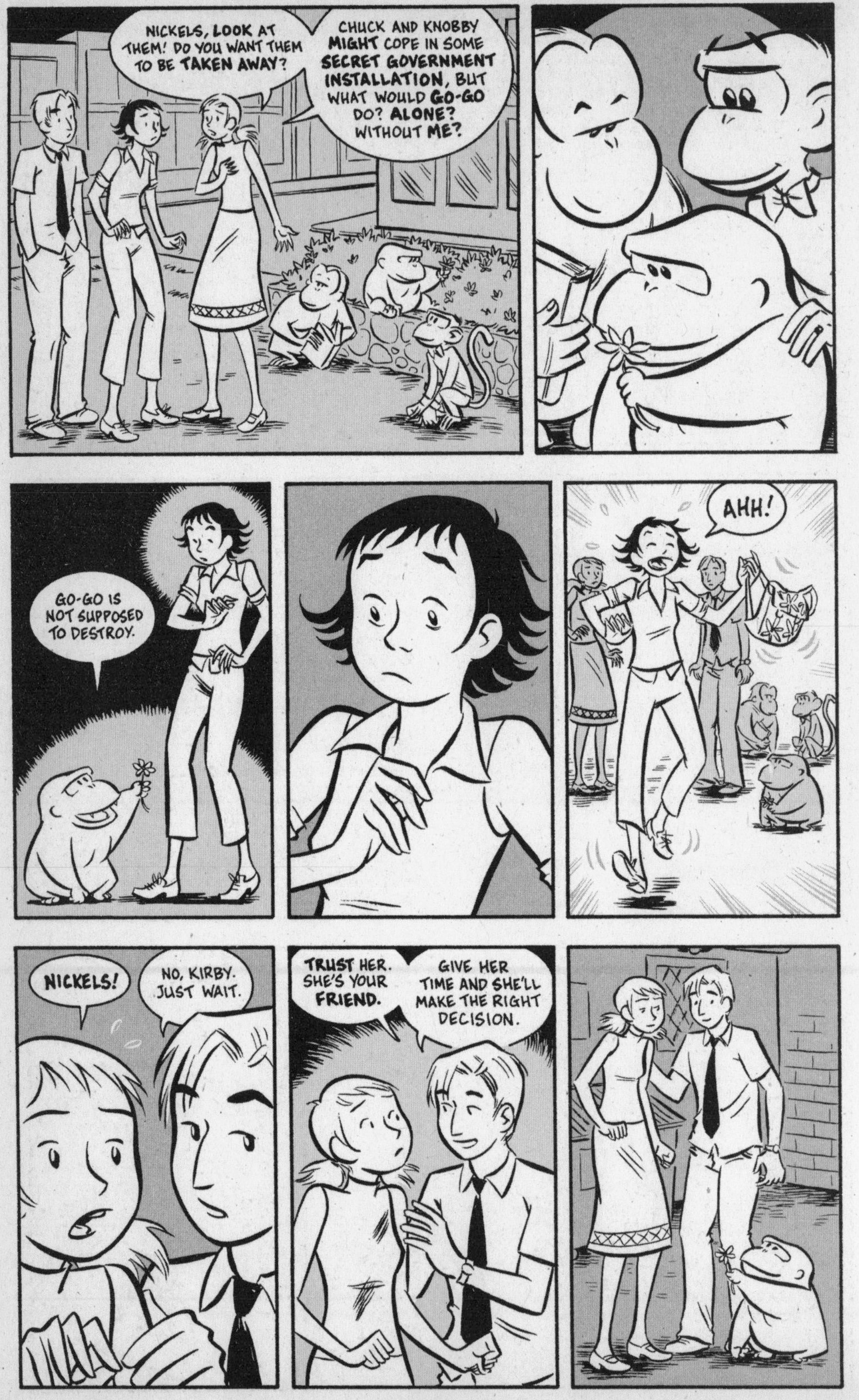
NICKELS, LOOK AT THEM! DO YOU WANT THEM TO BE TAKEN AWAY?
CHUCK AND KNOBBY MIGHT COPE IN SOME SECRET GOVERNMENT INSTALLATION, BUT WHAT WOULD GO-GO DO? ALONE? WITHOUT ME?
GO-GO IS NOT SUPPOSED TO DESTROY.
AHH!
NICKELS!
NO, KIRBY. JUST WAIT.
TRUST HER. SHE'S YOUR FRIEND.
GIVE HER TIME AND SHE'LL MAKE THE RIGHT DECISION.

OKAY. SHE'S MY FRIEND AND I'LL TRUST HER.

OH, MARTIN! I'M SO SORRY ABOUT OUR DATE!

I'D SAY **SHUT UP** AND KISS YOU MANFULLY, BUT I'VE ALREADY STOLEN **ONE** KISS.

...IF I TRIED IT **AGAIN**, YOU MIGHT **SLAP ME.**

THURSDAY. THE 5th.

FRIDAY. THE 6th.

NEWS LAB.

...SO, WAIT. IF A SPACESHIP TRAVELS AT **LIGHT SPEED** FOR FIVE YEARS, THE **TIME DISPLACEMENT FACTOR** WOULD BE... IT'D BE...

KNOBBY, HOW ARE THOSE **FIGURES** COMING ALONG?

WORKING! **WORKING!** WHAT ARE THE ASTRONAUTS' **NAMES** AGAIN?

BOOP BOOP

THE ASTRONAUTS' **NAMES?** WHAT'S THAT GOT TO DO WITH...

OH, **CRAP!**

SMELLS!

NASTY!

DIRTY!

!

DOR

NA

DIR

DAY AFTER **DAY** I PUT UP WITH...

WAAGH!

SHOVE!

DOR

NHAM

SMELLS

ME!

N

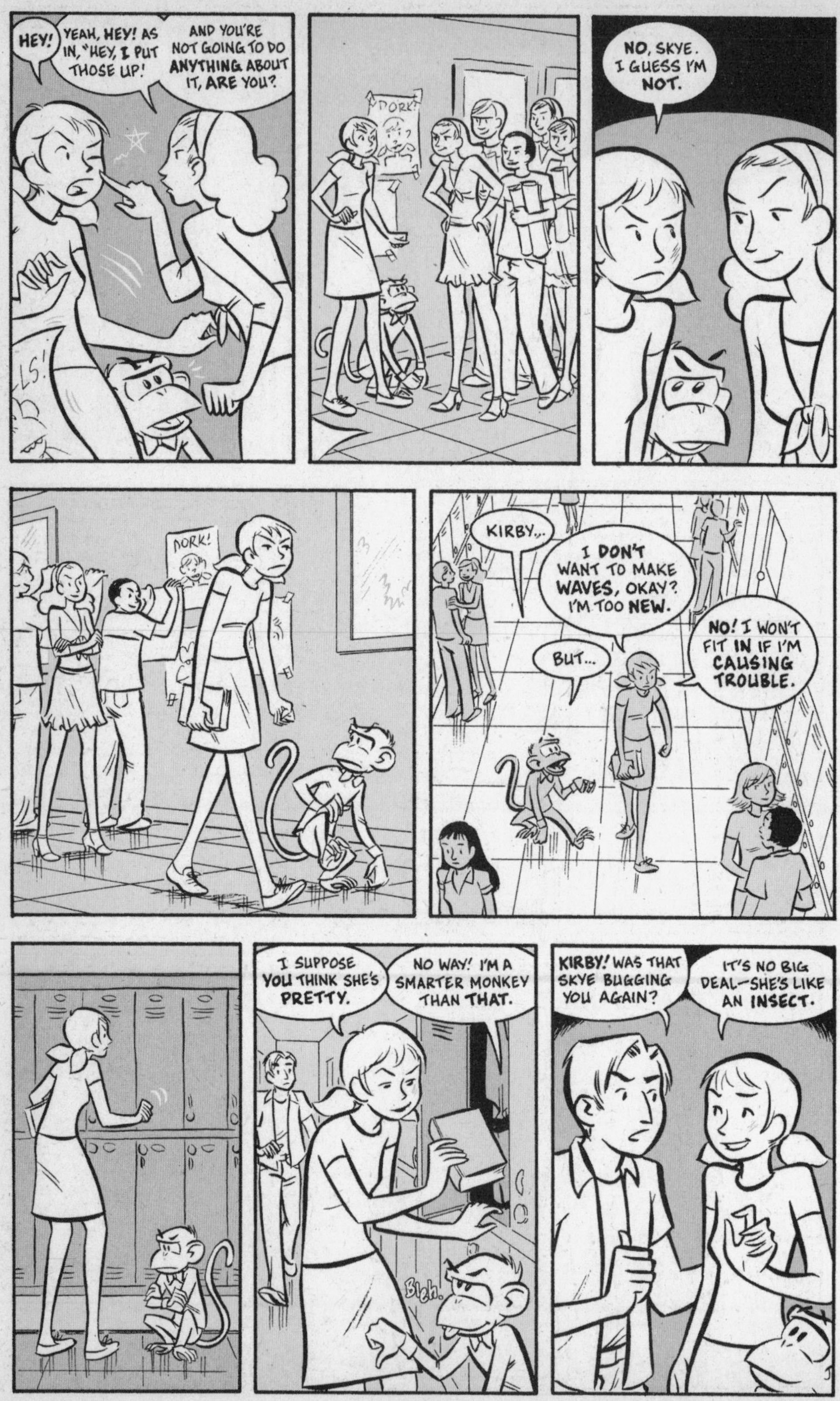
HEY!
YEAH, HEY! AS IN, "HEY, I PUT THOSE UP!
AND YOU'RE NOT GOING TO DO ANYTHING ABOUT IT, ARE YOU?
DORK!
NO, SKYE. I GUESS I'M NOT.
DORK!
KIRBY...
I DON'T WANT TO MAKE WAVES, OKAY? I'M TOO NEW.
BUT...
NO! I WON'T FIT IN IF I'M CAUSING TROUBLE.
I SUPPOSE YOU THINK SHE'S PRETTY.
NO WAY! I'M A SMARTER MONKEY THAN THAT.
Bleh.
KIRBY! WAS THAT SKYE BUGGING YOU AGAIN?
IT'S NO BIG DEAL—SHE'S LIKE AN INSECT.

YEAH, WELL, INSECT BITES HURT, TOO.

THANK YOU FOR CARING, MARTIN. IT HELPS A LOT.

COULD WE HOLD HANDS?

SURE! MY ARMS SWING FUNNY WHEN I WALK ANYWAY, SO IT'S BEST TO KEEP THEM OCCUPIED.

!

THANKS. I JUST... I JUST REALLY WANT SOMEONE TO HOLD MY HAND RIGHT NOW.

WELL, TELL ME WHEN TO LET GO, BECAUSE IF YOU DON'T, I'LL HOLD YOUR HAND FOREVER.

HOLD YOUR HAND FOREVER? WOW, THAT WAS CHEESY!

CHEESY ENOUGH THAT I SHOULD LET YOUR HAND GO?

HM... I'LL LET YOU KNOW IN A FEW HOURS.

JERK!

GO CAMELS!

DOOFUS!

NAST

...ALL THIS CRAP WITH SKYE, AND NICKELS WON'T TALK TO ME SINCE I ASKED HER NOT TO PRINT THE STORY!

SHE CAN'T PRINT IT! HOW MANY WAYS CAN I POSSIBLY ASK?

ACTUALLY, THE POTENTIALITY IS INFINITE WHEN FACTORING DIALECTS, PHRASING, NON-VERBAL COMMUNICA-TION, AND...

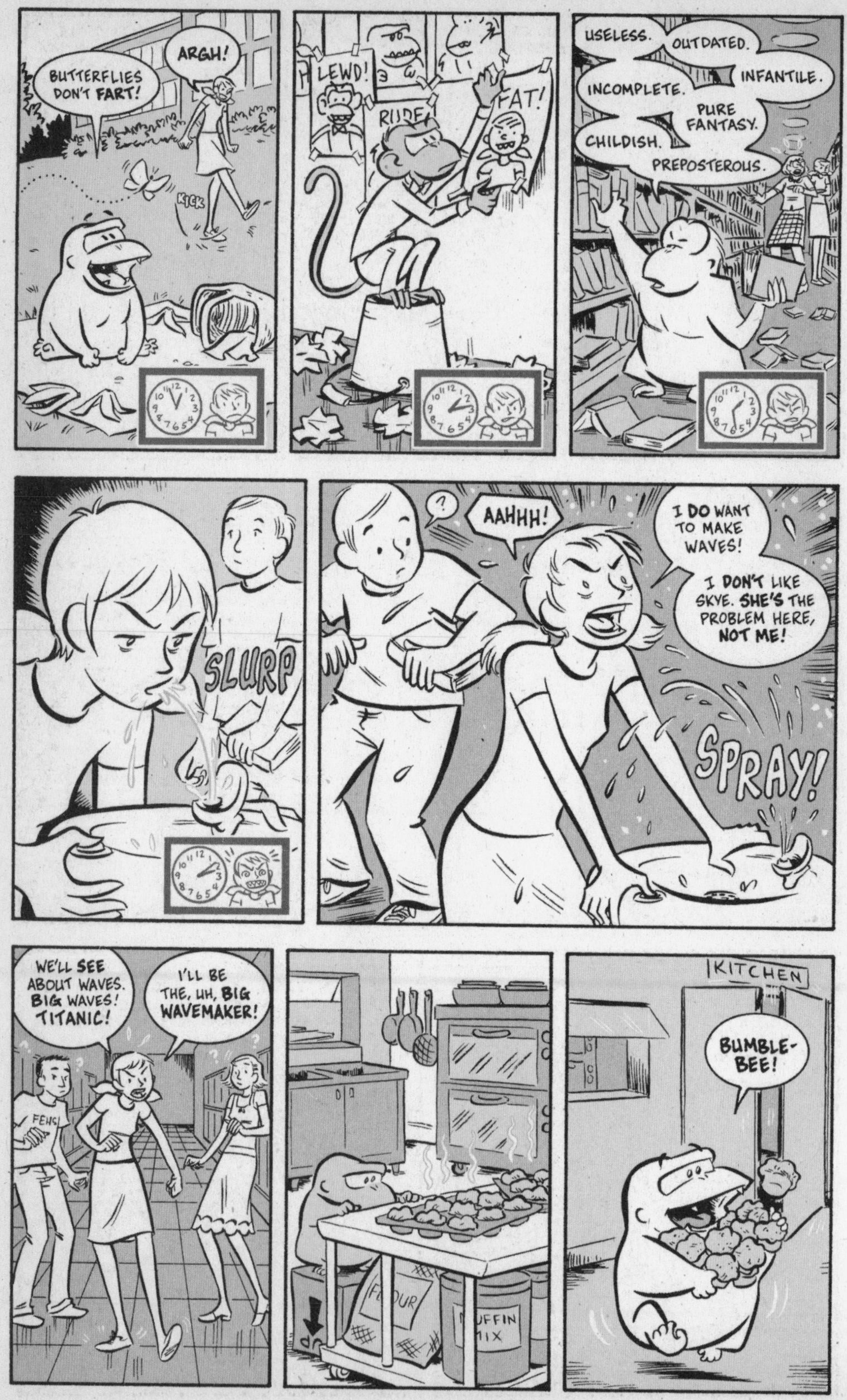
BUTTERFLIES DON'T FART!
ARGH!
KICK
LEWD!
RUDE
FAT!
USELESS.
OUTDATED.
INFANTILE.
INCOMPLETE.
PURE FANTASY.
CHILDISH.
PREPOSTEROUS.
SLURP
?
AAHHH!
I DO WANT TO MAKE WAVES!
I DON'T LIKE SKYE. SHE'S THE PROBLEM HERE, NOT ME!
SPRAY!
WE'LL SEE ABOUT WAVES. BIG WAVES! TITANIC!
I'LL BE THE, UH, BIG WAVEMAKER!
FENS
FLOUR
MUFFIN MIX
KITCHEN
BUMBLE-BEE!

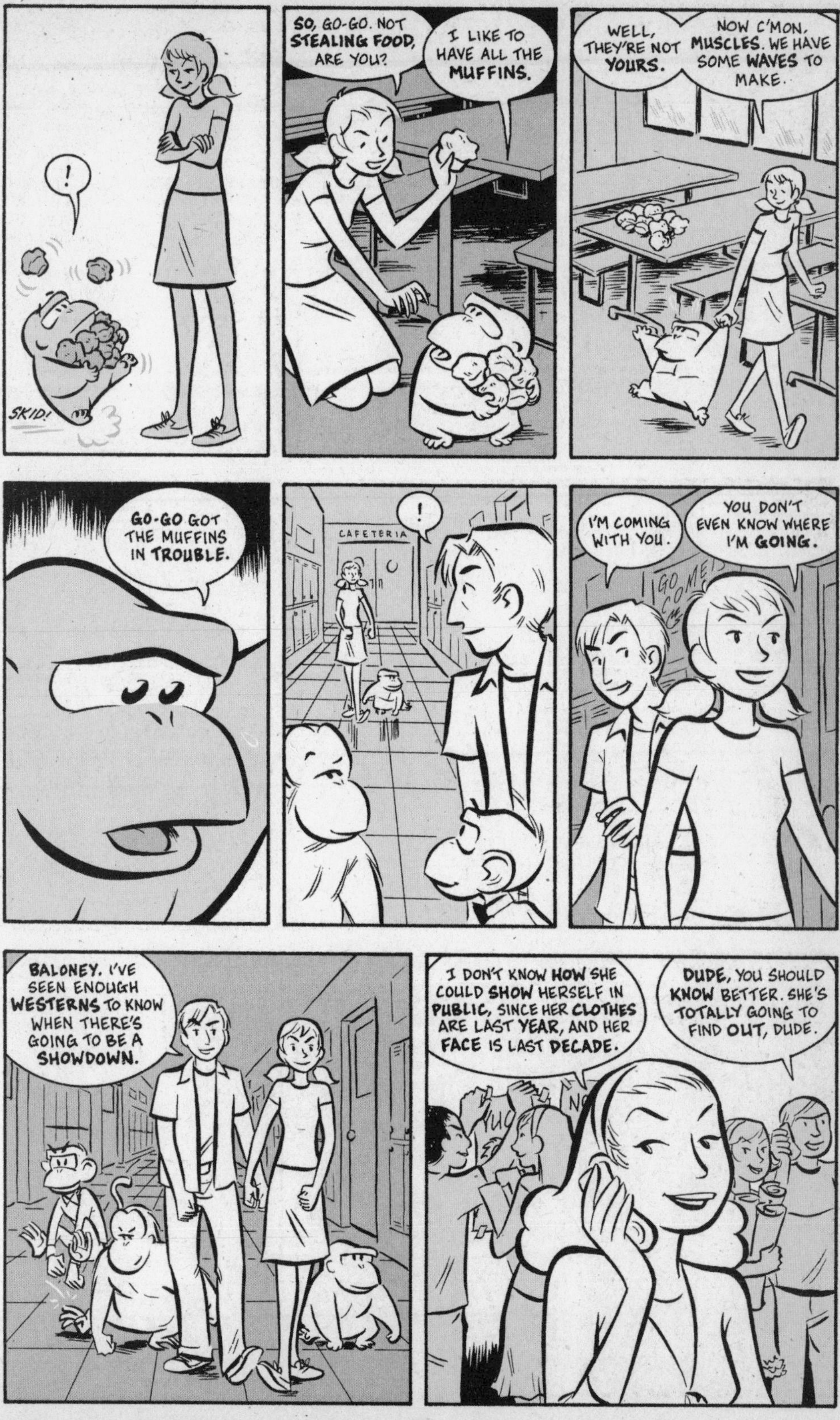
!
SKID!
SO, GO-GO. NOT STEALING FOOD, ARE YOU?
I LIKE TO HAVE ALL THE MUFFINS.
WELL, THEY'RE NOT YOURS.
NOW C'MON, MUSCLES. WE HAVE SOME WAVES TO MAKE.
GO-GO GOT THE MUFFINS IN TROUBLE.
!
CAFETERIA
I'M COMING WITH YOU.
YOU DON'T EVEN KNOW WHERE I'M GOING.
BALONEY. I'VE SEEN ENOUGH WESTERNS TO KNOW WHEN THERE'S GOING TO BE A SHOWDOWN.
I DON'T KNOW HOW SHE COULD SHOW HERSELF IN PUBLIC, SINCE HER CLOTHES ARE LAST YEAR, AND HER FACE IS LAST DECADE.
DUDE, YOU SHOULD KNOW BETTER. SHE'S TOTALLY GOING TO FIND OUT, DUDE.

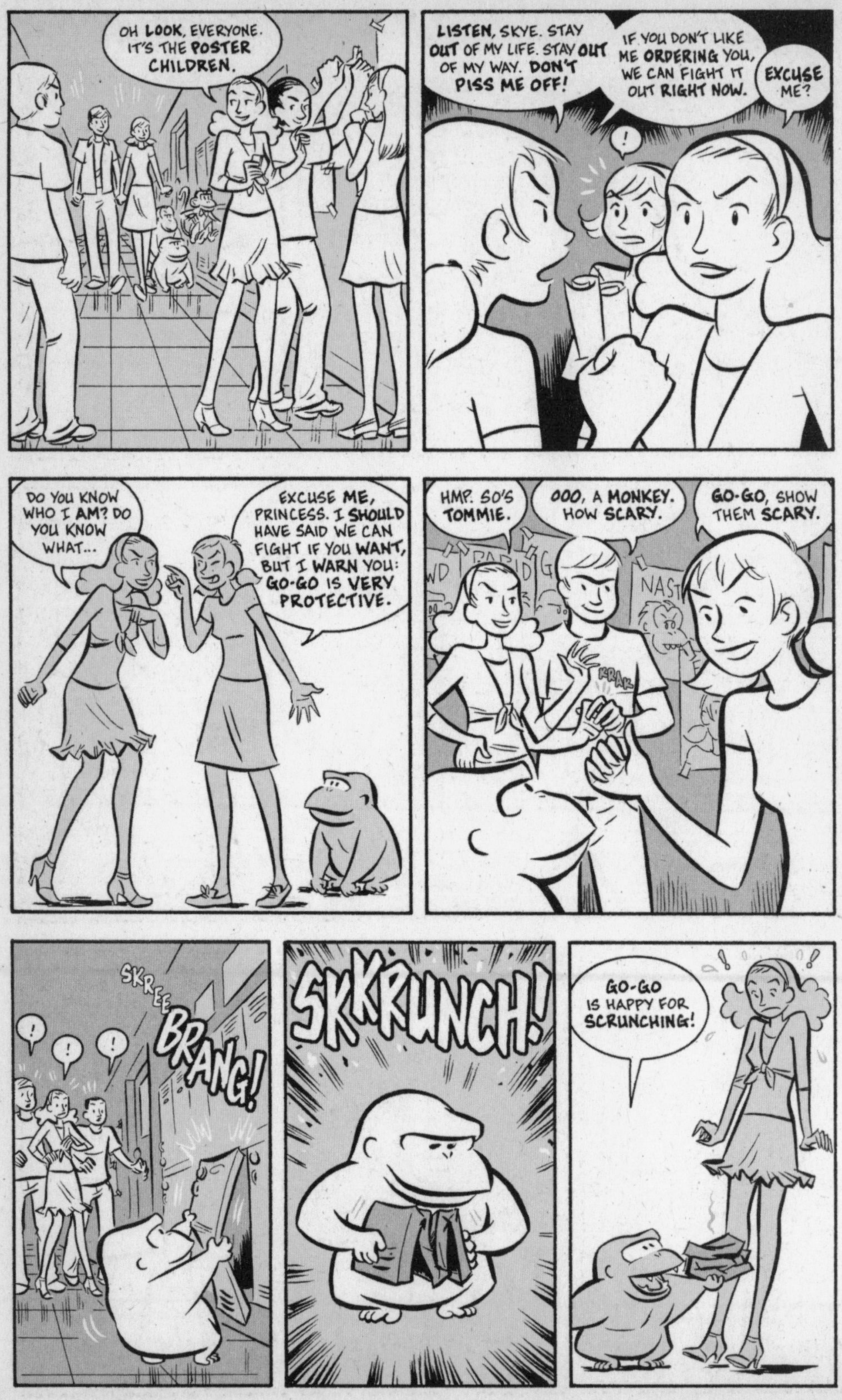
OH LOOK, EVERYONE. IT'S THE POSTER CHILDREN.
LISTEN, SKYE. STAY OUT OF MY LIFE. STAY OUT OF MY WAY. DON'T PISS ME OFF!
IF YOU DON'T LIKE ME ORDERING YOU, WE CAN FIGHT IT OUT RIGHT NOW.
EXCUSE ME?
!
DO YOU KNOW WHO I AM? DO YOU KNOW WHAT...
EXCUSE ME, PRINCESS. I SHOULD HAVE SAID WE CAN FIGHT IF YOU WANT, BUT I WARN YOU: GO-GO IS VERY PROTECTIVE.
HMP. SO'S TOMMIE.
OOO, A MONKEY. HOW SCARY.
GO-GO, SHOW THEM SCARY.
SKREE
BRANG!
! ! !
SKKRUNCH!
GO-GO IS HAPPY FOR SCRUNCHING!
! !

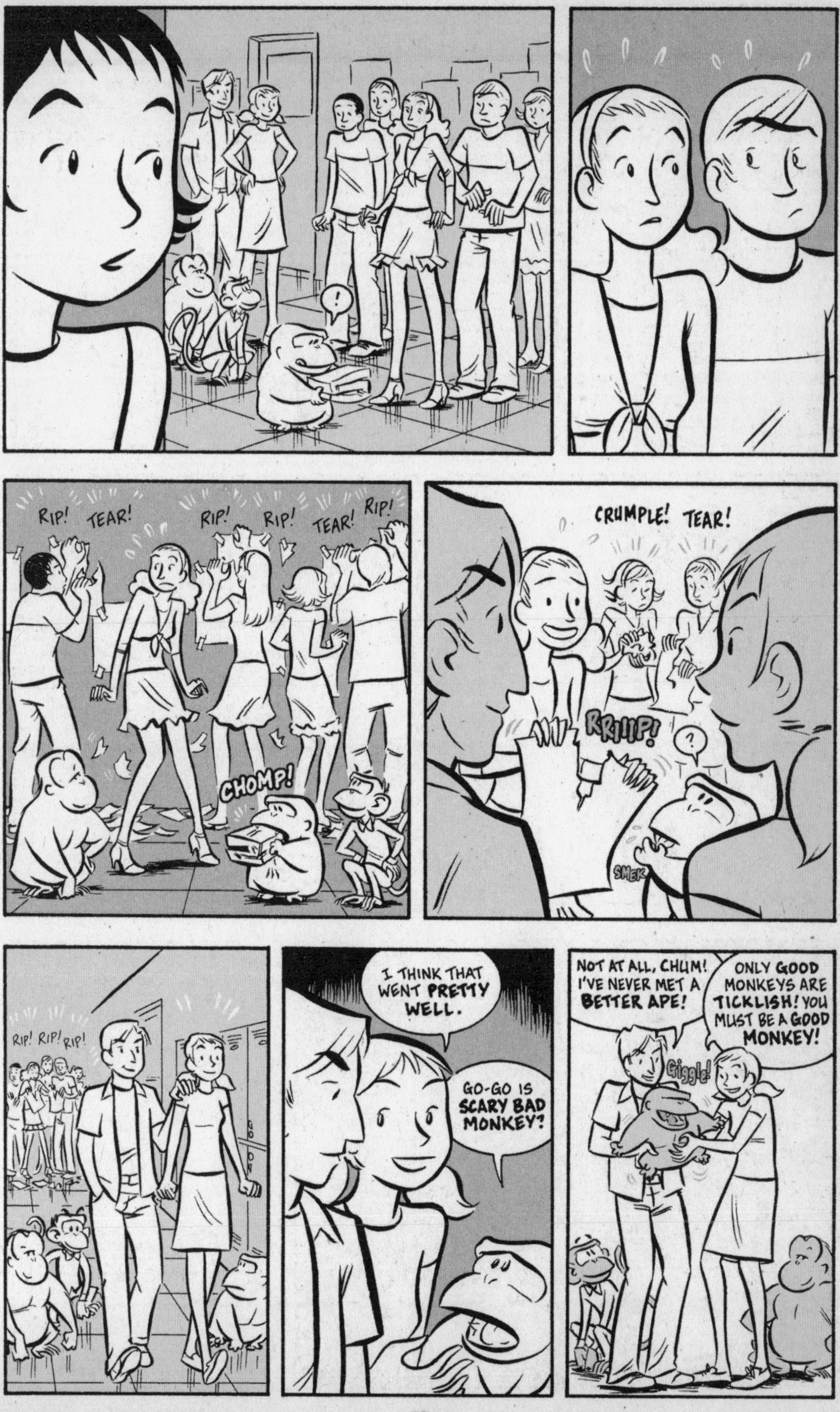

!
RIP! TEAR! RIP! RIP! TEAR! RIP!
CHOMP!
CRUMPLE! TEAR!
KRIIIP!
?
SMEK
RIP! RIP! RIP!
I THINK THAT WENT PRETTY WELL.
GO-GO IS SCARY BAD MONKEY?
NOT AT ALL, CHUM! I'VE NEVER MET A BETTER APE!
ONLY GOOD MONKEYS ARE TICKLISH! YOU MUST BE A GOOD MONKEY!
Giggle!

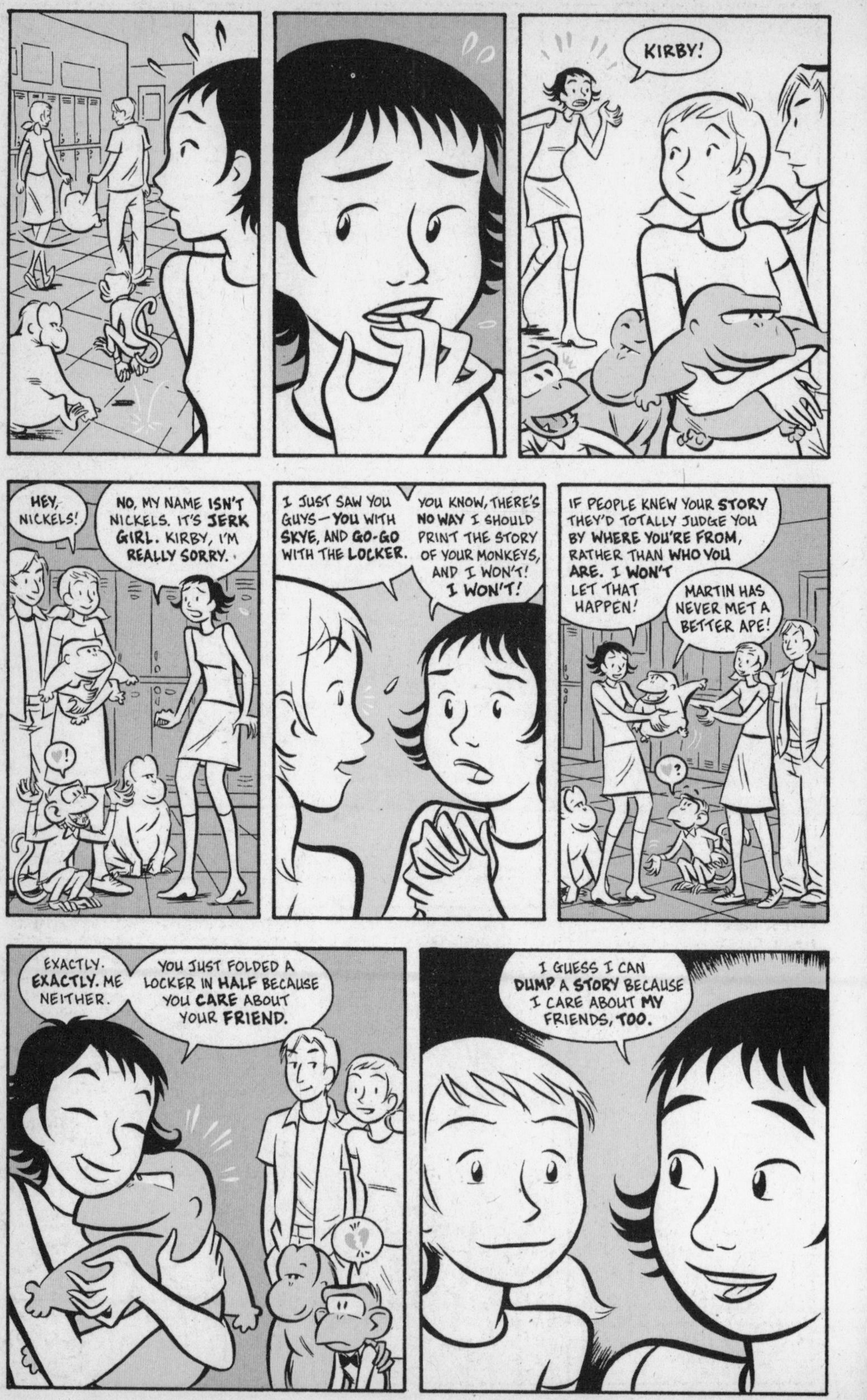
KIRBY!
HEY, NICKELS!
NO, MY NAME ISN'T NICKELS. IT'S JERK GIRL. KIRBY, I'M REALLY SORRY.
I JUST SAW YOU GUYS—YOU WITH SKYE, AND GO-GO WITH THE LOCKER.
YOU KNOW, THERE'S NO WAY I SHOULD PRINT THE STORY OF YOUR MONKEYS, AND I WON'T! I WON'T!
IF PEOPLE KNEW YOUR STORY THEY'D TOTALLY JUDGE YOU BY WHERE YOU'RE FROM, RATHER THAN WHO YOU ARE. I WON'T LET THAT HAPPEN!
MARTIN HAS NEVER MET A BETTER APE!
EXACTLY. EXACTLY. ME NEITHER.
YOU JUST FOLDED A LOCKER IN HALF BECAUSE YOU CARE ABOUT YOUR FRIEND.
I GUESS I CAN DUMP A STORY BECAUSE I CARE ABOUT MY FRIENDS, TOO.

THANK YOU!

HEY, IT'S THE LEAST THE ENIGMATIC HERO KNOWN AS **TRUTH GIRL** COULD DO.

SLAP!

SATURDAY. THE 7th.

Z Z Z

SUNDAY. THE 8th.

I CAN'T BELIEVE WE'VE ONLY BEEN FRIENDS A **WEEK!**

MAYBE WE WERE **SISTERS** IN A PAST LIFE.

I CAN'T BELIEVE YOUR **EYES** — SUCH **LUSTROUS** POOLS!

I CAN'T BELIEVE THIS **ICE CREAM** IS SO **GOOD.**

ICE CREAM

PSST

THE **SPOON** IS NOT TO **EAT** OR PUT IN YOUR EAR.

SLOW. SLOW. YOUR **BOUNTY** OF INFORMATION OVERWHELMS ME.

SUPER SPLIT

THANKS FOR TREATING US ALL TO YUMMY ICE CREAM!

OF COURSE! IN FACT... I, **NOBLE MARTIN THE FIRST,** DECLARE EVERY SUNDAY TO BE **BANANA SUNDAY...** A DAY OF FREE BANANAS AND ICE CREAM!

IN **RETURN**, YOU MUST CONSTANTLY TALK ABOUT HOW **HANDSOME** I AM.

WHAT HAPPENS IF I MENTION YOUR **CHICKEN LEGS?**

ICE CREAM EVERY SUNDAY? COUNT ME IN! **BANANA SUNDAY** IT SHALL HENCEFORTH BE! DELICIOUS **DESSERT** AND FINE **COMPANION-SHIP** WITH MY BEST FRIEND, HER **STUN-NINGLY HANDSOME** BOYFRIEND...

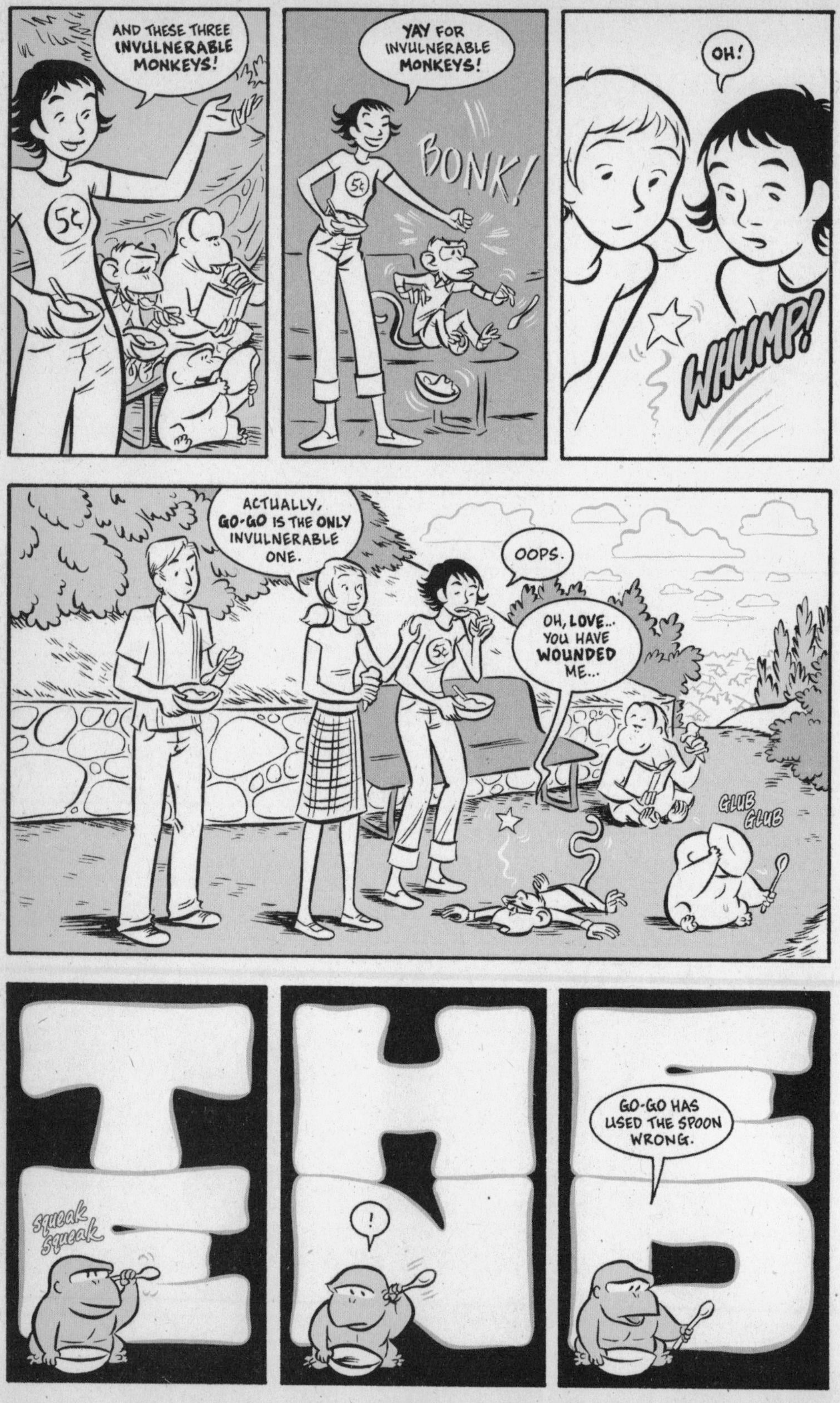
AND THESE THREE INVULNERABLE MONKEYS!
YAY FOR INVULNERABLE MONKEYS!
BONK!
OH!
WHUMP!
ACTUALLY, GO-GO IS THE ONLY INVULNERABLE ONE.
OOPS.
OH, LOVE... YOU HAVE WOUNDED ME...
GLUB GLUB
THE END
squeak squeak
!
GO-GO HAS USED THE SPOON WRONG.

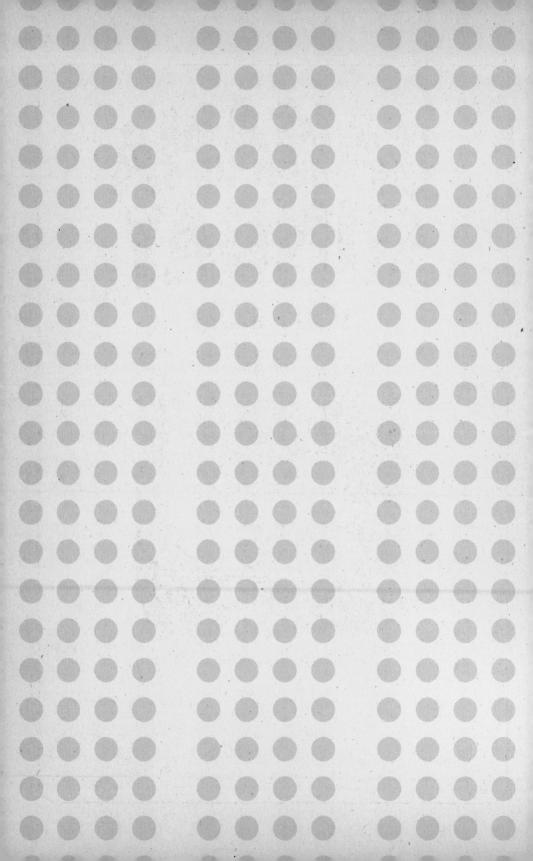

BANANA SUNDAY

Sketch Gallery

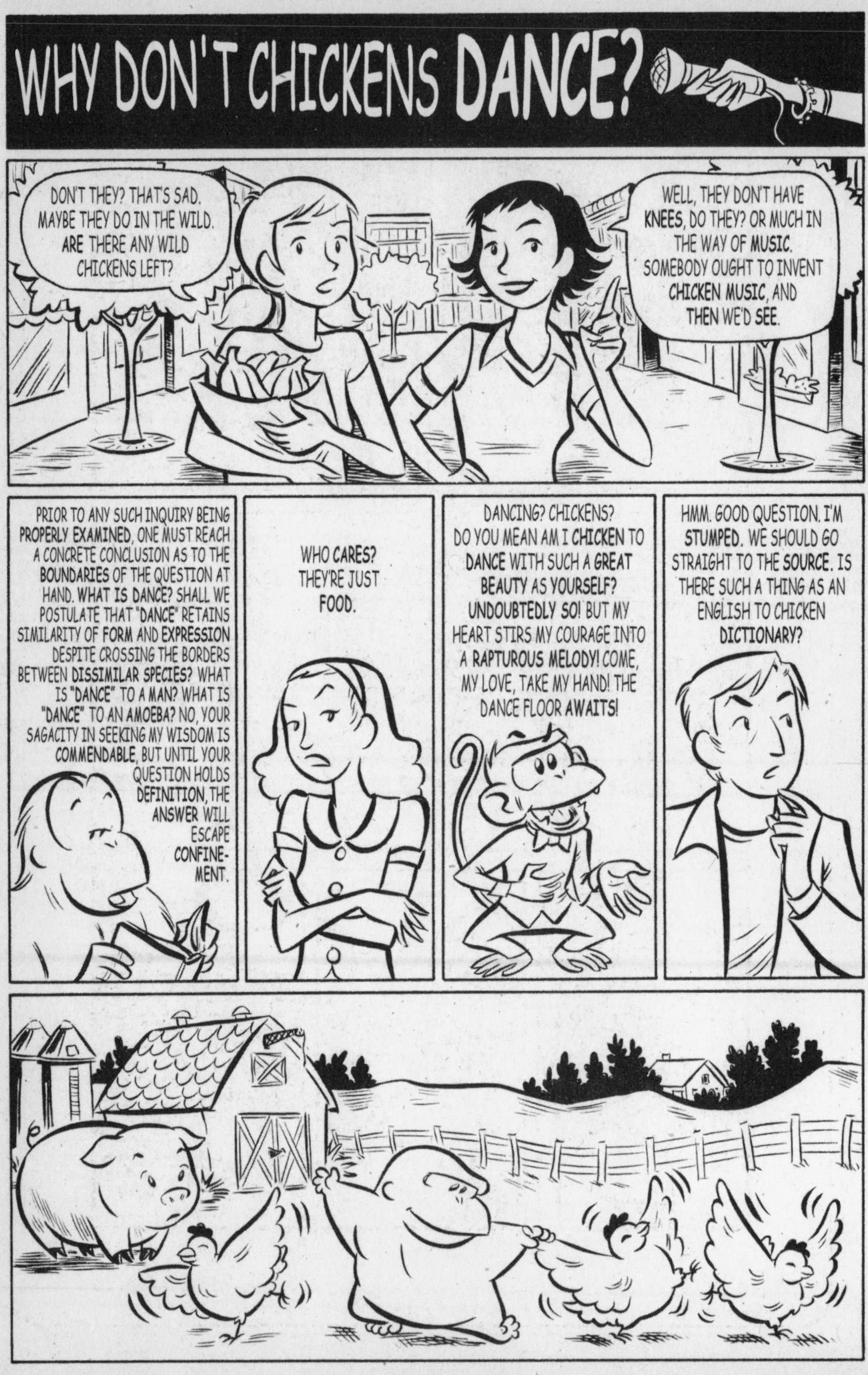
WHY DON'T CHICKENS DANCE?
DON'T THEY? THAT'S SAD. MAYBE THEY DO IN THE WILD. ARE THERE ANY WILD CHICKENS LEFT?
WELL, THEY DON'T HAVE KNEES, DO THEY? OR MUCH IN THE WAY OF MUSIC. SOMEBODY OUGHT TO INVENT CHICKEN MUSIC, AND THEN WE'D SEE.
PRIOR TO ANY SUCH INQUIRY BEING PROPERLY EXAMINED, ONE MUST REACH A CONCRETE CONCLUSION AS TO THE BOUNDARIES OF THE QUESTION AT HAND. WHAT IS DANCE? SHALL WE POSTULATE THAT "DANCE" RETAINS SIMILARITY OF FORM AND EXPRESSION DESPITE CROSSING THE BORDERS BETWEEN DISSIMILAR SPECIES? WHAT IS "DANCE" TO A MAN? WHAT IS "DANCE" TO AN AMOEBA? NO, YOUR SAGACITY IN SEEKING MY WISDOM IS COMMENDABLE, BUT UNTIL YOUR QUESTION HOLDS DEFINITION, THE ANSWER WILL ESCAPE CONFINE-MENT.
WHO CARES? THEY'RE JUST FOOD.
DANCING? CHICKENS? DO YOU MEAN AM I CHICKEN TO DANCE WITH SUCH A GREAT BEAUTY AS YOURSELF? UNDOUBTEDLY SO! BUT MY HEART STIRS MY COURAGE INTO A RAPTUROUS MELODY! COME, MY LOVE, TAKE MY HAND! THE DANCE FLOOR AWAITS!
HMM. GOOD QUESTION. I'M STUMPED. WE SHOULD GO STRAIGHT TO THE SOURCE. IS THERE SUCH A THING AS AN ENGLISH TO CHICKEN DICTIONARY?

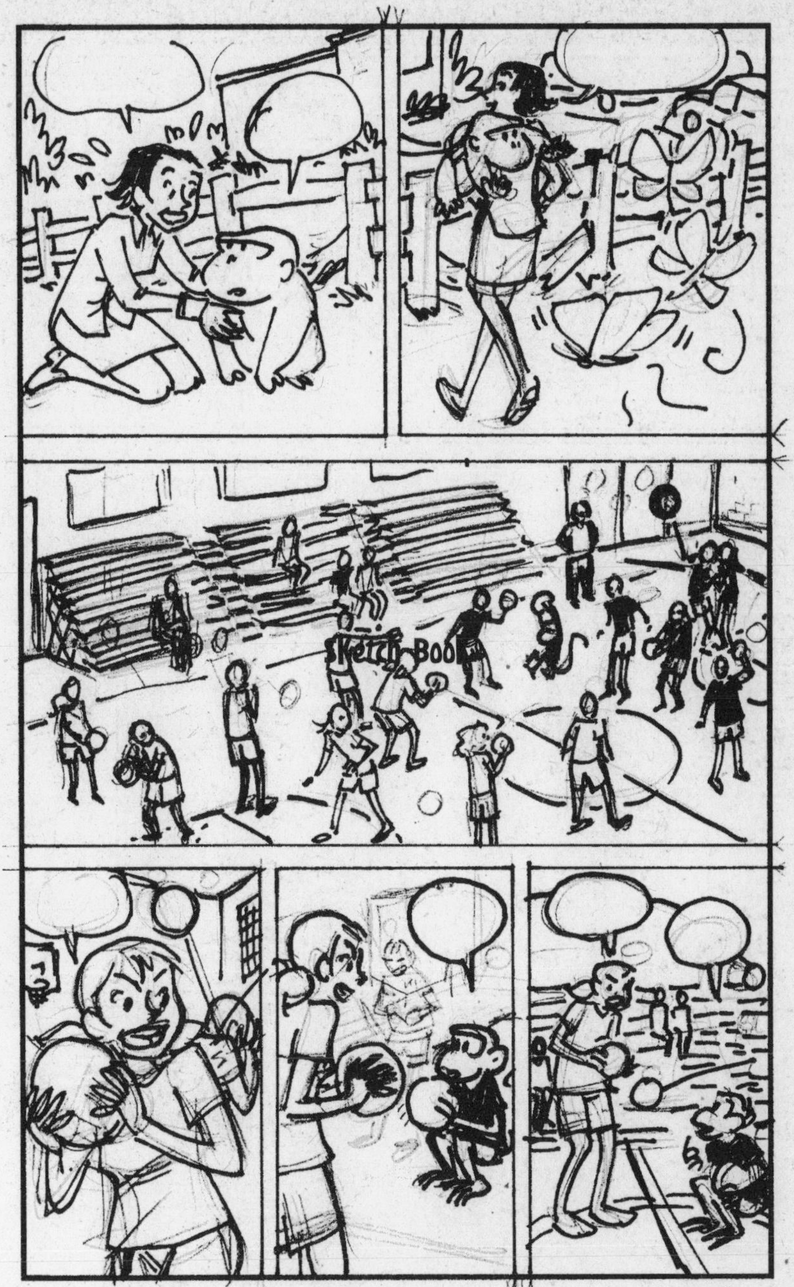
Sketch Boo

HEY, MONKEY!
TOOM TOOM TOOM
TOOM TOOM TOOM
BAD MONKEY!
OOF!

HEY, MONKEY!
TOOM TOOM TOOM
TOOM TOOM TOOM
BAD MONKEY!
OOF!

ACCK!
NOTHING!
...GOTTA GO!

ACCK!
NOTHING!
...GOTTA GO!

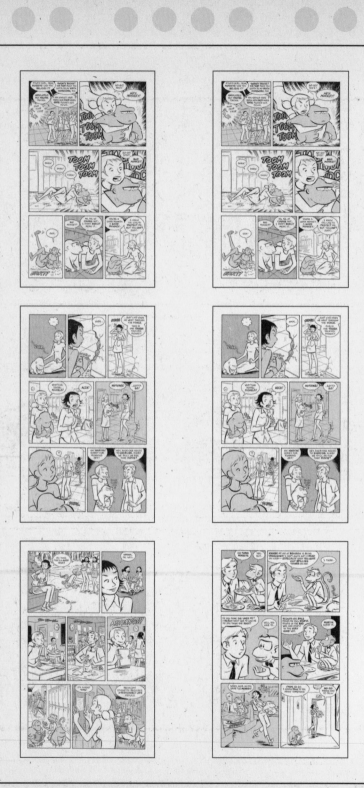

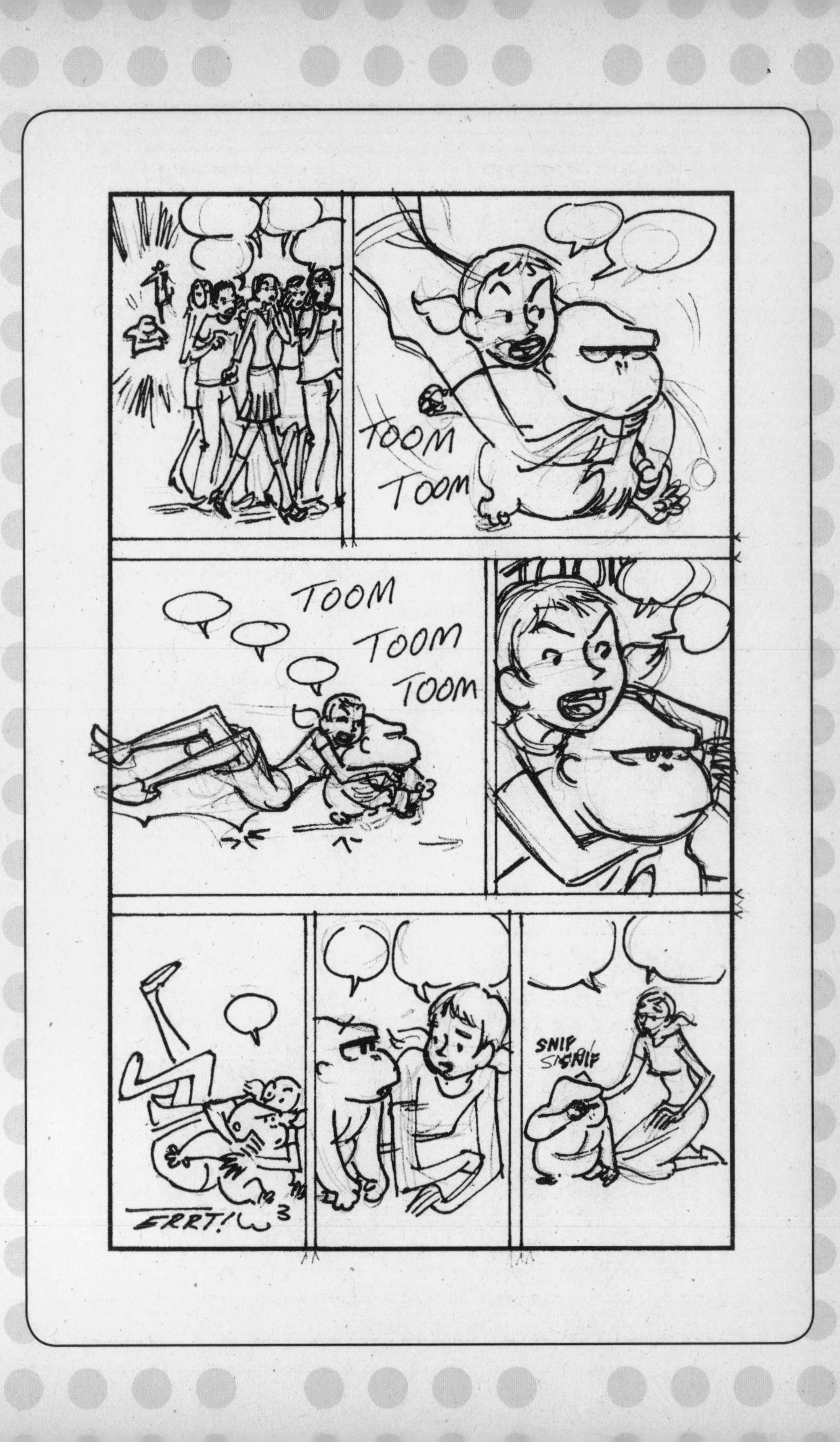
TOOM
TOOM
TOOM
TOOM
TOOM
ERRT!
SNIF
SNIF

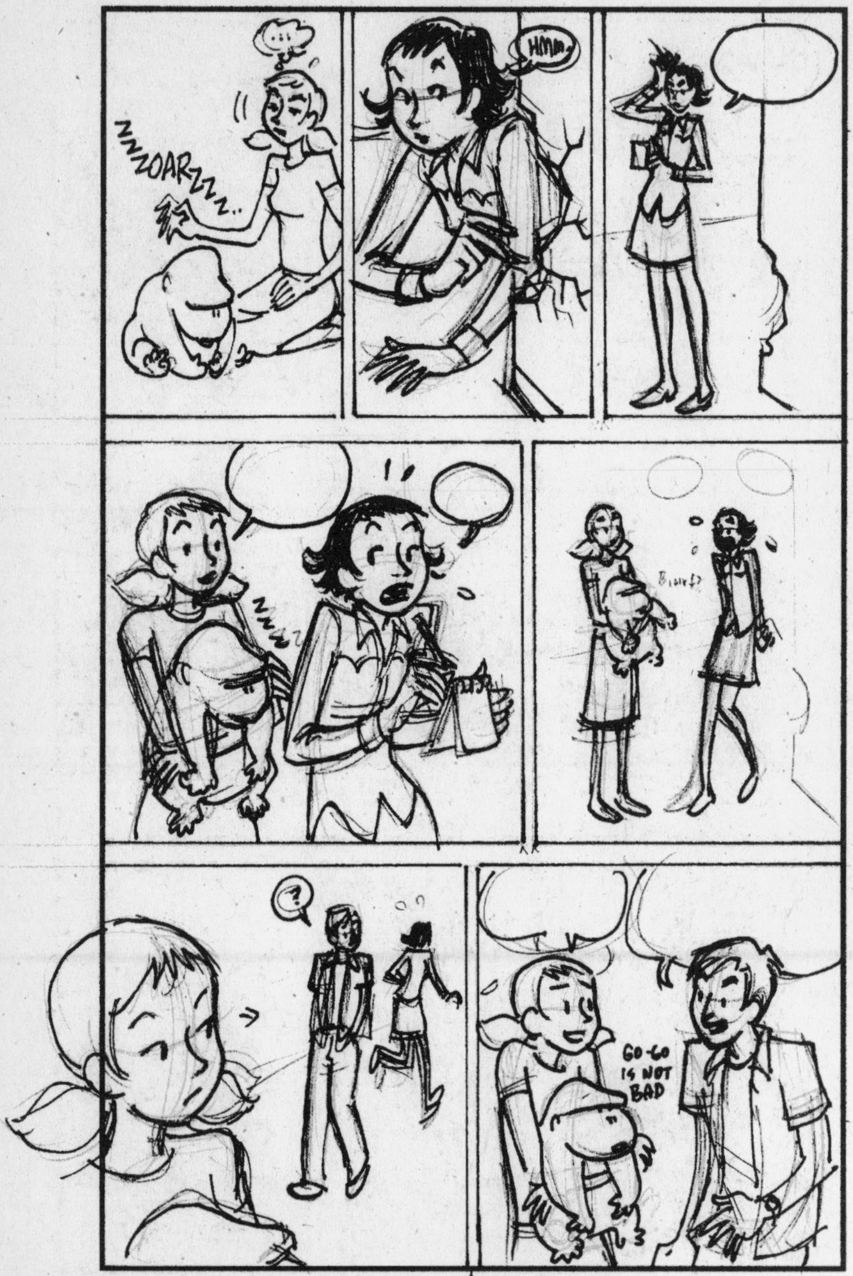
NNZOARZZZZ..
HMM
GO-GO
IS NOT
BAD

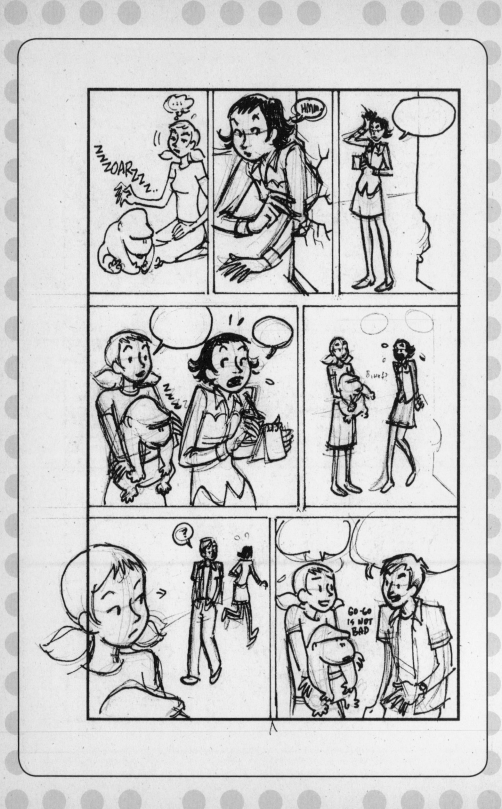

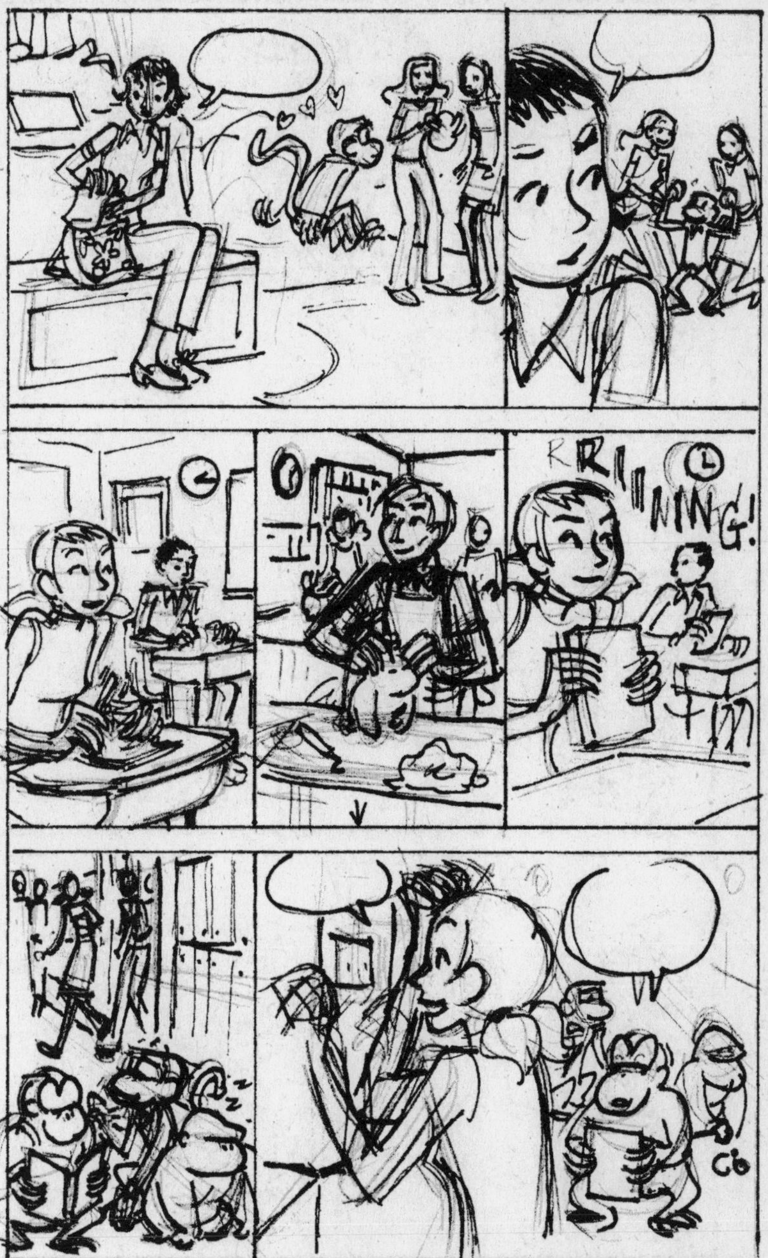
RIIIING!

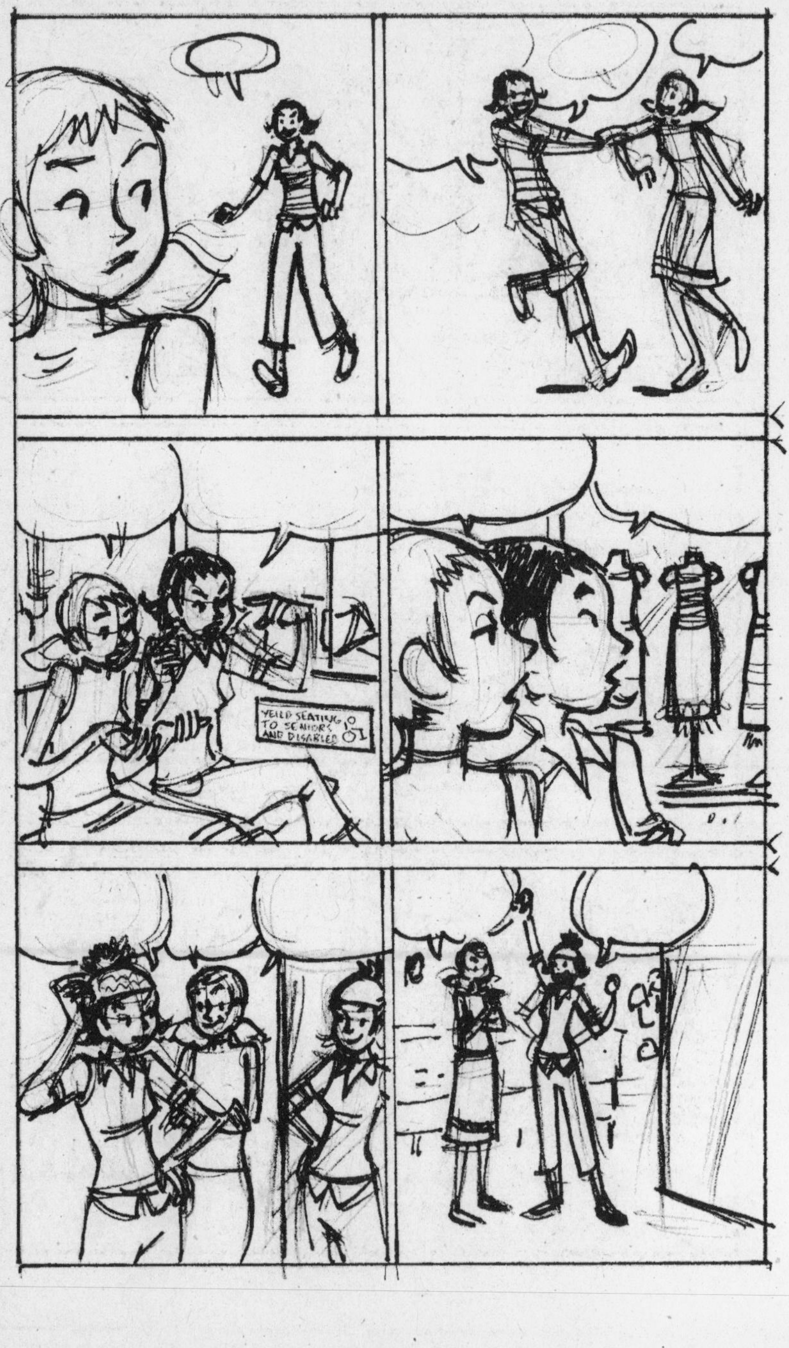
YEILD SEATING TO SENIORS AND DISABLED

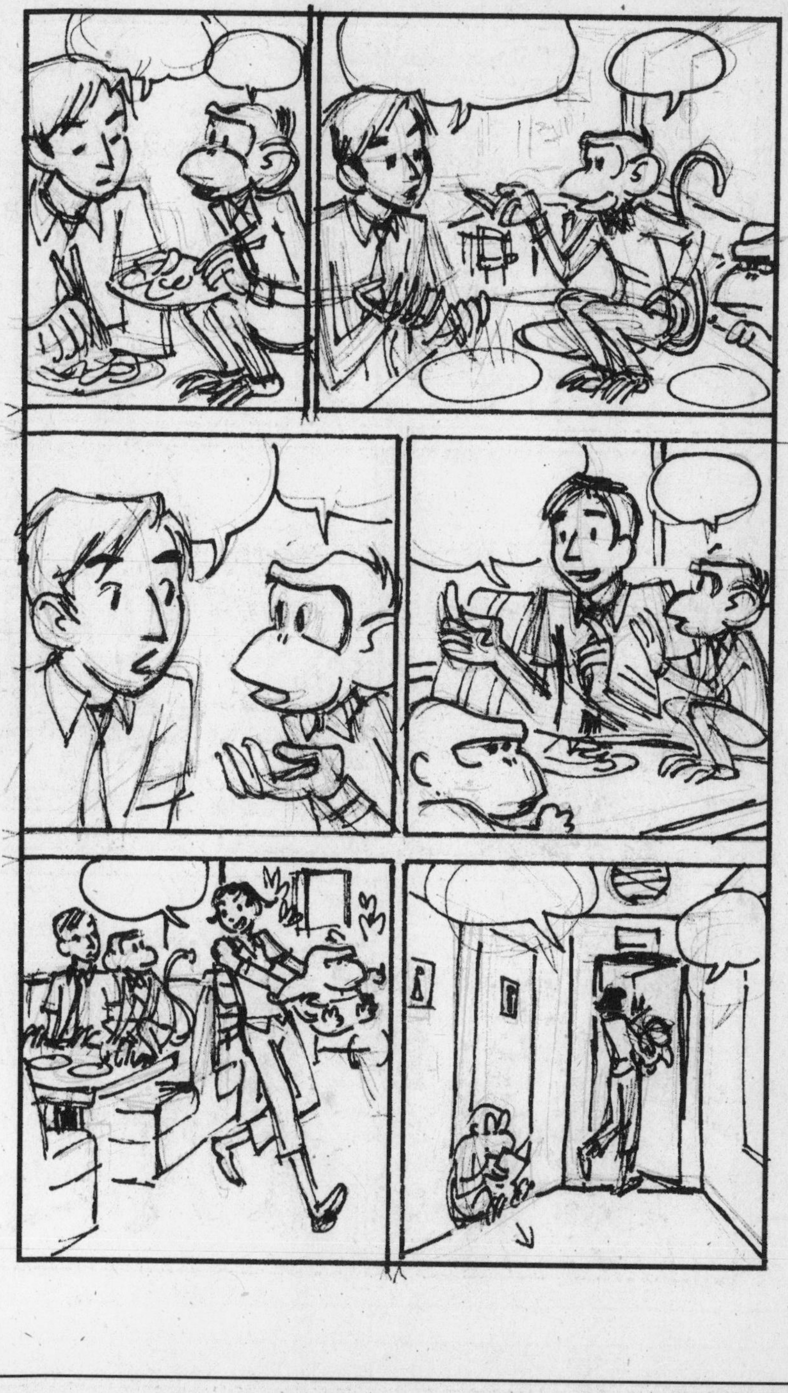

Also Available!

Alison Dare
DOUBLE-DOG DARE YA!
HEROES
VILLAINS
PARENTS

JASON AND THE
ARGOBOTS
BIRTHQUAKE

THE COLLECTED ALISON DARE™
by J. Torres & J. Bone
96 pages, black-and-white interiors
$8.95 US
ISBN 1-929998-20-1

JASON & THE ARGOBOTS, VOLUME 1: BIRTHQUAKE™
by J. Torres & Mike Norton
120 pages, black-and-white interiors
$11.95 US
ISBN 1-929998-55-4

MUTANT
TEXAS

TORRES / CHANTLER
Days Like This

MUTANT, TEXAS™
by Paul Dini & J. Bone
120 pages, black-and-white interiors
$11.95 US
ISBN 1-929998-53-8

DAYS LIKE THIS™
by J. Torres & Scott Chantler
88 pages, black-and-white interiors
$8.95 US
ISBN 1-929998-48-1

SIDEKICKS:
THE TRANSFER STUDENT
J. Torres / Takeshi Miyazawa

COURTNEY CRUMRIN AND THE NIGHT THINGS

SIDEKICKS: THE TRANSFER STUDENT™
by J. Torres & Takeshi Miyazawa
104 pages, black-and-white interiors
$8.95 US
ISBN 1-929998-40-6

COURTNEY CRUMRIN & THE NIGHT THINGS™
by Ted Naifeh
128 pages, black-and-white interiors
$11.95 US
ISBN 1-929998-60-0

HOPELESS SAVAGES
A GRAPHIC NOVEL BY
JEN VAN METER
CHRISTINE NORRIE
CHYNNA CLUGSTON-MAJOR

ONCE IN A
BLUE MOON

HOPELESS SAVAGES™
by Jen Van Meter, Christine Norrie, & Chynna Clugston
128 pages, black-and-white interiors
$11.95 US
ISBN 1-929998-75-9

ONCE IN A BLUE MOON™ Vol. 1
by Nunzio DeFilippis, Christina Weir, & Jennifer Quick
168 pages, black-and-white interiors
$11.95 US
ISBN 1-929998-83-X

Available at finer comics shops everywhere. For a comics store near you, call 1-888-COMIC-BOOK or visit www.the-master-list.com.

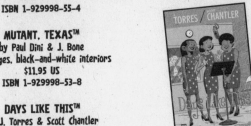